# The Corn Was Green

# The Corn Was Green

*The Inside Story of* Hee Haw

JOHN AYLESWORTH

McFarland & Company, Inc., Publishers
*Jefferson, North Carolina, and London*

LIBRARY OF CONGRESS CATALOGUING-IN-PUBLICATION DATA

Aylesworth, John.
The corn was green : the inside story of Hee Haw / John Aylesworth.
p.     cm.
Includes bibliographical references and index.

**ISBN 978-0-7864-3338-4**

softcover : 50# alkaline paper ∞

1. Hee haw (Television program)
I. Title.
PN1992.77.H39A95   2010      791.45'72—dc22      2009048931

British Library cataloguing data are available

Front cover: Scarecrow ©2010 Photodisc; sign ©2010 Shutterstock

Manufactured in the United States of America

*McFarland & Company, Inc., Publishers
Box 611, Jefferson, North Carolina 28640
www.mcfarlandpub.com*

To Mona Gould, my surrogate mother,
without whom I might never have discovered
my talent for and love of writing.
I have been given the privilege of spending my life
doing what I love largely because of her support,
encouragement, and unconditional love.
And to her son, John, my longest and dearest friend,
who helped me discover we could actually
spend our lives doing "a job laughing."

**John Aylesworth (left), Canadian poet-writer Mona Gould, and Canadian artist and musician John Gould just before Mona's death, early 1990's.**

# ACKNOWLEDGMENTS

To all my good friends who were with me during the birth and through the growth of *Hee Haw*, and were readily available to jog my memory when it needed jogging, I can only say thank you and a hearty *Hee Haw* "SA-LUTE!"

Bill Davis was a veritable Vesuvius of recall, providing both anecdotes and rare photos from those first three years at WLAC in Nashville. Also providing both recollections and photos were Jack Burns, George Yanok, Sam Lovullo, Francesca Peppiatt, and Gene McAvoy.

Some of the gaps were filled in by Marcia Minor, Barry Adelman, Ellen Brown, Sandy Liles, and my partner for over 40 years, Frank Peppiatt. To each of them a heartfelt thanks for the memories.

I owe a special debt of gratitude to Mike McKinney, Grady Nutt's former manager, for his diligent search for photos of the late Reverend Grady. Thanks also to Chuck McCann, who came to the rescue with photos from *Happy Days* when it seemed there were none.

Finally, very special thanks to Mike Dann of CBS, who made *Hee Haw* possible by advising Peppiatt and Aylesworth to create a show of their own. And, of course, to Perry Lafferty for helping to make it a reality.

Without my wife, Anita Rufus, with her diligent hectoring and strict editing, this book would never have happened.

# TABLE OF CONTENTS

# PREFACE

Over 20 years after going off the air, having produced almost 600 episodes, *Hee Haw* remains the longest running variety show of its type in television history. At the height of its popularity, it was seen in over 15 million homes every week, a faithful audience that included such luminaries as Boston Pops maestro Arthur Fiedler, newsman Walter Cronkite, entertainer Sammy Davis, Jr., and five United States presidents from Reagan to both Bushes.

Today, *Hee Haw* is an American classic. It has become a part of our language as a synonym for cornball country fun everywhere, from David Letterman's monologues to the *New York Times'* crossword puzzles.

In 2005, *Hee Haw* came roaring back as a series of best-selling Time-Life DVDs, and returned to the air briefly in a wildly-successful weekend marathon on the CMT cable channel.

Finally, here's the whole hilarious story as I experienced it, from the very beginning. The memories are mine, hopefully all accurate. Yet, with time, some things get embellished and some softened. Nevertheless, I've tried to put it all down as it happened.

I thoroughly enjoyed every minute—as they happened and as I recall them now. I hope you do too.

# PROLOGUE

The variety show was a staple of prime-time network television for over forty years. In the beginning, back in 1946, after decades of promises that it was "just around the corner," the miracle of television finally became a reality with an audience of pretty much nobody and a programming schedule of pretty much nothing.

Television sets had been displayed in appliance store windows with few takers and only occasional passers-by who gathered on sidewalks to watch. Why would anyone want a clunky box in the living room with a tiny, ten-inch glass screen displaying a snowy, black-and-white picture of a geometric test pattern or the occasional grainy cowboy movie?

Most homes were more than satisfied with their handsome console radios. They offered a wealth of great entertainment, from the comedy of Jack Benny and Fred Allen to the star-studded drama of *The Lux Radio Theater*, all in the vivid living color of the listener's imagination. Most television sets were merely a novelty over the bar at a local tavern or sitting in a storeroom gathering dust.

It was into this bleak wasteland that television's first "variety show" appeared on the fledgling NBC-TV network, on a Wednesday evening in the spring of 1946. Fittingly, it was called *The Hour Glass*, a rather primitive hour of singing and dancing, but a heck of a lot more entertaining than a test pattern. The response was encouraging. When it went off the air a few months later, *The Hour Glass* was considered a noble experiment worth another try at some later date, hopefully for a larger audience.

That audience arrived with the first televised World Series in 1947. It was viewed by an estimated 3.9 million people, most of them peering through store windows or elbow-bending in local bars.

With only two networks, NBC and a brave little pioneer called Dumont, there wasn't much incentive to actually own a TV set. It wasn't until 1948 that NBC decided to try another variety show, finally hitting the jackpot.

It was called *Texaco Star Theatre*. Naturally, you would assume that "Mr. Television," Milton Berle, was the host. You would be wrong. Hedging their bet, NBC put *Texaco Star Theatre* on the air June 8, 1948, trying out rotating hosts including entertainers and comedians like Harry Richman, Georgie Price, Henny Youngman, Jack Carter, Peter Donald, and Berle. "Uncle Miltie" was obviously the best, and thus he was made permanent host that September.

Suddenly, the barflies left their stools and joined the window-watchers marching into appliance stores to be the first on their block to own a television set. Within weeks, millions of Americans were laughing at Berle's inspired Tuesday-night buffoonery from their own living rooms. Neighbors gathered together, parents and children, to laugh out loud.

In the early 1950s, CBS and ABC joined the old Dumont network with competing variety shows hosted by comics of every stripe: Sid Caesar, Jackie Gleason, Red Buttons, Abbott & Costello, Eddie Cantor, Red Skelton, Jimmy Durante, and Martin & Lewis.

The only non-comical exception was a host with no talent at all: journalist and man-about-town Ed Sullivan. He debuted in June 1948, with his *Toast of the Town*, a video-vaudeville show with eclectic acts ranging from circus performers to opera singers. Sullivan was a smashing success.

As the 1950s wore on, the glut of comedians began to pall. With the notable exceptions of Gleason and Skelton, audiences were drawn to kinder, gentler variety show hosts. The homespun "Arthur Godfrey and His Friends" reigned throughout the decade. Personable singers like Dinah Shore and Perry Como were successfully promoted from 15-minute musical fillers to full-scale variety hours. Ed Sullivan inexplicably seemed likely to go on forever.

Variety used to be a family affair. The comedy was squeaky-clean, and the popular music of the day appealed to all ages. Since then, music has splintered into so many different forms that no single act could possibly appeal to such a trans-generational mass audience. It's hard to imagine Mom, Dad, and the kids all gathered in front of the TV set tonight to enjoy *The Snoop Dogg Good-Time Variety Hour*. Possible, but unlikely.

It was into that more stable era of variety that I moved from Toronto to New York in 1958, embarking on a fun-filled career writing for Andy Williams, Perry Como, Dinah Shore, Jackie Gleason, Steve Allen, Judy Garland, George Gobel, Carol Burnett, Jack Paar, Andy Williams, Jonathan Winters, Dean Martin, Frank Sinatra, Flip Wilson, the Smothers Brothers, Julie Andrews, Glen Campbell, Dolly Parton, and Sonny & Cher, among many others.

People often ask, "What does it mean that you 'wrote' a variety show?" After all, most of the songs are already written (unless there is original "special" material), the "patter" of host and guests between numbers is simply two friends chatting, and the "look" of the show is done by a creative staff.

What most people don't realize while watching a variety show is that absolutely everything said, sung, or done is "written." Unlike dramas and sitcoms, where dialogue is the primary concern, when writing for variety the dialogue is secondary.

Without the script, everyone involved with a variety show is totally paralyzed. Until there's a script that sets the concept, format, even which songs are to be sung, the scenic designer doesn't know what sets to build, the choreographer doesn't know what to choreograph, the musical director doesn't know what incidental music might be needed, the director doesn't know what to direct, and the star has no idea of what to say, do, or sing. Everything from the theme of the show, to the choice of songs, to the direction to the artistic crew of how the set should look and work, to every word of "patter" between two people who may never have met before—all you see from the opening to the sign-off is written in advance.

The variety show is all but gone now. Popular singers today make more money from one concert than the old stars made in an entire season. Most successful comedians now prefer the simpler format of sitcoms or uncensored cable specials. But the memory lingers on. Over the thirty years I worked in variety television, I had more fun and more laughs than I could ever possibly have imagined.

# INTRODUCTION:
## IN THE BEGINNING

*A long time ago, in a place far away (Canada), the seed was planted for two goofy guys to get together and in 1969 create a show called* Hee Haw....

I met Frank Peppiatt, my long-time writing partner, in the fall of 1950. I was 22, and going to work as a fledgling copywriter in the radio-television department at the MacLaren Advertising Agency in Toronto, Ontario, Canada. On my first day, I was ushered into the tiny office I was to share with Frank, a veteran of six months at the agency. He was to show me the ropes of churning out radio commercials. Being the same age and temperament, we hit it off immediately, soon becoming known as the office cut-ups, while turning out reams of advertising copy.

Our first act of true comic creation, a harbinger of things to come, was inspired by a boastful, loud-mouthed minor account executive named Ken. This tedious bore spent most of one Monday morning strutting around the department showing off his brand new hat.

"It's absolutely top of the line!" he crowed. "I got it at the Adam Hat Store across the street. Cost me plenty, too. I had my initials stamped in the sweatband so nobody could swipe it. How's it look?"

Everybody wearily agreed that was a fine looking hat, even though it was just an ordinary gray fedora with a red feather in the brim, and certainly no big deal in those pre–Kennedy days when everybody wore hats.

If he had just shut up about it after maybe an hour, Frank and I wouldn't have hatched our devilish plan. However, since he kept right on yakking, we decided action must be taken.

Luckily, his office was a glass cubicle not far from our office, so we could watch his every move. When he finally stopped preening and went to his desk, after hanging the hat on a rack in the corner, we waited patiently until he took a late morning washroom break. Then we rushed to thoroughly examine his stupid hat.

Later, on our lunch hour, we went across the street to the Adam Hat Store and, pooling our meager resources, bought a hat that was identical in every detail to Ken's coveted chapeau, complete with a red feather in the brim and his initials in the sweatband. However, there was one important difference. This hat was one full size larger.

That afternoon, while Ken was out of his office, we rushed in and switched hats. We could hardly wait for five o'clock, so we could see his expression when he put on the switched hat to go home.

Framed picture of John Aylesworth while at MacLaren Advertising Co., Limited, in Toronto, with shots of scenes from the late-night show *After Hours*, which Peppiatt and Aylesworth did at the start of their show-business careers in the early 1950s. Middle row and bottom left, Aylesworth (left) and Peppiatt; bottom right Jill Foster, Peppiatt and Aylesworth.

A couple of minutes before five, he got up from his desk, put a few things in his brief case and put on his hat. It was the perfect moment! Just as we'd hoped, it flopped down over his ears. The shocked look on his face was worth a million bucks, or at least the price of the duplicate hat. The former blowhard was reduced to confused jelly.

Lifting the hat from his ears, he took it off and examined it carefully, shaking his head in total bewilderment. The correct initials were in the sweatband so there was no doubt it must be his hat, but on a second try it still fell down over his ears. As we watched from our open office door, we barely managed to stifle our delighted snorts of glee.

Finally, a look of inspiration came over his face. Retrieving a few sheets of paper from his desk, he rolled them up and stuffed them inside the sweatband. When he put the hat back on, this makeshift solution at least kept it from falling over his ears and he headed to the elevators looking somewhat haunted.

When Ken came to work the next morning, wearing the altered fedora, he headed straight to his cubicle without a word, still looking a bit shaken.

"Nice hat!" I yelled to him through our open office door.

"Lookin' good, Ken," Frank chirped.

Ken mumbled some sort of acknowledgment and kept on chugging toward his cubicle, where he hung the hat on the rack. All that morning the former braggart sat at his desk fidgeting. We could hardly wait till he took his mid-morning washroom break. When he finally did, we rushed from our office, grabbed the hat, took the paper from the sweatband, stuffed it into the original hat and speedily replaced it on the rack.

At lunchtime, Ken got up from his desk and put on his hat, which now perched on top of his head and wobbled hilariously. He tried to pull it down but to no avail. Totally perplexed and deathly pale, he once again examined the cursed chapeau, and with shaking hands removed the paper and once again placed it on his muddled head. Of course it fit perfectly. He shook his head, heaved a sigh and walked off to lunch muttering.

That afternoon, Ken sat at his desk fidgeting and staring at the fedora as if he expected it to change shape before his very eyes. At the first opportunity, we again switched hats. By this time, we had let everybody in the department know what we were up to. When it was time to go home, all eyes were on Ken's cubicle when his hat once again fell down over his ears.

Totally unnerved and unaware of his delighted audience, this once obnoxious blowhard was now on the verge of insanity. With shaking hands, he took off the hat and gave it a thorough examination. Finally, with a sigh, he took more paper from his desk, rolled it up and stuffed it into the sweatband. When it finally fit to his satisfaction, he rapidly strode to the elevators avoiding eye contact all the way.

The next morning, Ken arrived later than usual, with haunted, red-rimmed eyes, and hatless. He made a beeline for his cubicle. The night before, Frank and I had decided he'd had enough punishment and we would let the poor fish off the hook, but he had beaten us to it. He must have burned the damn thing, because he remained hatless through the coldest winter in Toronto history. He was also a better person for the experience, and was never heard to brag about anything again.

The news of our escapade spread throughout the agency like wildfire. When added to accounts of various other antics we had hatched from time to time, we were encouraged to start injecting humor into our commercial copy. This was no mean trick with clients like household cleansers, credit jewelers, and Esso gasoline.

We came up with some pretty funny radio spots, although once we got a bit carried away with a one-minute spot for a cigarette company. Aside from being amusing, it carried all the catch phrases the client wanted. The account executive thought it was great, and the sponsor loved it. It would have gone on the air if we hadn't pointed out one important fact nobody had noticed: it never mentioned the name of the cigarette. Luckily, everybody involved could take a joke, but from then on all our copy was very carefully scrutinized.

There was also a fully-equipped recording studio in our department, which we put to use by taping comedy shows we would write and perform at night, splicing in laughs from Wayne and Shuster's radio shows to provide proper appreciation of our material. At the time, Wayne and Shuster were Canada's only comedians. Jim Carrey, Bill Murray and Mike Myers were as yet unborn. I had begun my career in radio while still in school, playing teenager voices on various shows, so the chance to play around like this and get paid at the same time was heady indeed.

Secure in our jobs and having a lot of fun, we didn't really think anything would come of our nighttime revelries until 1952, when television finally came to Canada. Even though we worked in the Radio-Television Department, the only television shows Toronto could watch came from Buffalo, N.Y, across Lake Ontario.

One of our colleagues in the department, Peter McFarlane, had taken a short course in television production south of the border, and was immediately hired as a producer by the Canadian Broadcasting Corporation. They planned to start TV production and go on the air in the fall of 1953. McFarlane's first assignment was to produce a weekly comedy show.

Unfortunately, Johnny Wayne and Frank Shuster refused to give up the security of their highly successful radio show for the still iffy future of television. The new network bosses told McFarlane he had to think of something, because they couldn't conceive of a schedule without comedy. It was then that our friend decided he would give the two zany cut-ups at the ad agency, also named John and Frank, a whack at it.

John Aylesworth (left) and Frank Peppiatt of the Canadian Broadcasting Corporation, Toronto, circa 1956.

An audition was to be filmed at six o'clock in the morning the next day. With the hubris of youth, we stayed up all night concocting comedy bits. Frank enlisted the aid of an actress friend, Jill Foster, to perform the female parts. Shortly after dawn, the three of us showed up at a CBC-TV studio ready to act silly for the cameras. That afternoon, McFarlane called to say his bosses had laughed a lot, and wanted us to do the first of a late-evening one-hour series, to be called *After Hours*, starting that Friday. This was the unlikely beginning of our career as Canada's first television comedy team.

With a meager budget and no

sets, we fumbled our way through the first season of writing and performing the weekly show while keeping our day jobs at the agency. This miraculously led to an additional two seasons with a much bigger budget, an orchestra, dancers, sets, an earlier time spot, a growing audience, and enough money to finally become ex-copy writers. We were also learning how to put together a comedy-variety show, which would soon lead to bigger and much better things south of the border.

At the end of our third season, the strain of writing and performing thirty-nine hour-long shows every year had taken its toll. Facing the fact that we were better writers than performers, we decided to concentrate solely on creating and writing variety shows. Unfortunately, the CBC had a policy of only one writer for each show, marking the end of Peppiatt and Aylesworth as a team until three years later when fate brought us together again in New York City.

We both had left Canada in 1958, having gained pretty good reputations in the United States as writers for various American guest stars on Canadian variety shows. My first job in New York was writing *Your Hit Parade* at CBS. I had been recommended by its director, Norman Jewison, another Canadian who had directed many of our shows on the CBC and would later win Oscars for directing such movies as *Heat of the Night* and *Moonstruck*.

Frank, on the other hand, had been brought to New York by Steve Lawrence to write a variety series for Steve and his wife Eydie Gormé. It was a summer replacement for *The Steve Allen Show*, which hired Frank to stay on as a writer that fall.

In the spring of 1959, CBS asked the entire *Your Hit Parade* team to create a summer variety series for Andy Williams. It was at that point that Jewison suggested Frank and I reunite as a writing team, which we happily agreed to do. The show was a big hit, leading to a Bing Crosby special that winter. Bing's guest star was Perry Como, who in turn hired us the write his *Kraft Music Hall* series at NBC starting that fall. We were off and running!

How does all this lead to *Hee Haw*? Read on.

# 1

# THANK YOU, JIMMY DEAN

*"It just ain't right," groaned a miserable Jimmy Dean in the fall of 1963, stand-ing in an immaculate tuxedo on the set of his first ABC network variety show in New York City. "I'm just a plain old country boy and they dress me up in this cat-haired outfit and stick me with an opera singer and a city comic for guest stars. Why can't we just do a plain old country show? This ain't gonna please anybody."*

Jimmy Dean's plaintive plea was made to his two head writers, Frank Peppiatt and me. We had just completed three happy years writing *The Perry Como Show* with the leg-endary Goodman Ace. After the third season, Perry decided to retire from television and we accepted an offer to write *The Jimmy Dean Show*.

As Canadians, we still said "eh" a lot and were generally referred to as "hockey pucks" by our fellow New York writers. Perry Como had been a joy to work with. He was a star who could easily fit into any situation. But Jimmy Dean was pure country. He was a raw-boned young Texan in the early 1960s, back in his pre-sausage days, and he'd had some success with a hit record called "Big Bad John" and a popular local TV show in Wash-ington, D.C.

In 1963, Bob Banner, who had produced two hit series starring Dinah Shore and Garry Moore, and happened to be a fellow Texan, decided it was time for Jimmy to headline a network variety show. Banner sold the idea to ABC.

In our first meeting with Banner, a soft-spoken Southern gentleman with a will of iron, he outlined his vision of what the show ought to be. Since Jimmy was a country boy, the Banner blueprint dictated that we should surround him with sophistication. He had already booked opera soprano Anna Moffo and cult comedian Dick Shawn for the first show, insisting on something for everybody, from opera fans to hip New Yorkers. For the children, Bob had ordered a robot to be built as a kiddie-friendly mechanical sidekick for the star. When we asked how Jimmy—a country boy—felt about that, Banner seemed sur-prised by such a question.

"I never ask a star what they think about anything," he said. "I expect them to do what they're told."

Assuming this lordly philosophy also extended to writers, we wisely buttoned our lips.

In our first staff meeting with the star, Jimmy was appalled at who his guest stars would be. "Why can't we just have some of the great county people I'm used to working with?" Jimmy asked ruefully. "Folks like Buck Owens or Roger Miller or Minnie Pearl?"

"Nobody's ever heard of those people," said Banner.

"Well, who the hell ever heard of this Anna Moffo?"

"Jimmy, this is New York. You'll have a whole new audience on a major network. All we're trying to do is give you some class."

Jimmy snorted angrily and stomped out the office. He was a very unhappy star.

Banner just chuckled. "He'll snap out of it. What we still need is something for the kiddies, something cuddly and cute that might cheer Jimmy up. See what you fellas can come up with."

Whatever we found to entertain America's moppets, we felt sure, would be a heck of a lot better than Banner's robot sidekick, which turned out to be an eight-foot monstrosity with all kinds of buzzers and flashing lights. Bob's plan was to put a midget inside the robot to move it around and have an off-camera actor supply the voice. When they tested it at a pre-school, it scared the hell out of the little kids and the midget almost died from lack of oxygen. Happily, it was promptly hauled off to the junkyard—sans midget.

We happened to mention our quest for a kiddie-pleaser to an agent-friend, Bernie Brillstein, who asked, "How about a Muppet?" Few people, including us, had ever heard of a Muppet in 1963, so Brillstein arranged a meeting with his client, Jim Henson, in a loft in Greenwich Village packed with all kinds of strange-looking wooly creatures.

Henson was a gaunt, bearded young guy with long hair, a tattered wardrobe, and a gentle nature. With the help of his wife and a couple of devoted assistants, he constructed weird, wooly-headed creatures with which he performed for children's groups, TV commercials, and the occasional shot on *The Ed Sullivan Show*. Kermit and Miss Piggy were yet to be born, and the early Muppets mostly did pantomimes to popular records in which they either ate each other or blew each other up.

When we explained that we needed a funny, kiddie-friendly character that might serve as Jimmy Dean's sidekick, Henson showed us his latest creation, Rowlf, the shaggy dog that would later become known as the piano player on the now classic *The Muppet Show*. When Henson slipped his hand into the furry puppet, it immediately came to life.

"Hi, guys!" said Rowlf, in Henson's gruff dog voice. "I'm a big fan of Jimmy Dean, and it'll be an honor to be his best friend. Besides, Henson needs the money. Ha, ha."

**Jimmy Dean and his sidekick Rowlf, 1963.**

With his ping-pong ball eyes and shaggy coat, Rowlf was both funny and lovable. We happily shook his paw and made a tentative deal with Henson on the spot.

When we brought them to the office the following morning, Banner was delighted. It seems that Jimmy was still steamed about the direction the show was taking.

"A good old hound dog is just what Jimmy needs," Banner said. He suggested that we hide Henson behind the couch in Jimmy's office with Rowlf peeking over it and resting his head on his paws.

"What a fine surprise this is gonna be!" Banner crowed. "Jimmy's coming in this afternoon about three."

Henson happily agreed and at two-thirty he took up a cramped position behind the couch with Rowlf peeking over the top. At about three, Jimmy Dean made his entrance. He cut an imposing figure, at least six-foot-four of good-ol'-boy Texas arrogance, and in a pretty foul mood.

It seemed at least an hour passed as Jimmy unloaded his grievances on his producer and (naturally) blameless writers, until Banner finally suggested we move the discussion into Jimmy's office where a hopefully happy surprise awaited. It must have been pretty cramped behind that couch, and we hoped Henson would still be up to having Rowlf greet his new master.

When Jimmy strode into his office, Rowlf was as perky as ever, his paws resting on the back of the couch and his ping-pong eyes seeming to light up at the sight the rangy Texan. Rowlf barked a joyful greeting.

"What the hell is that?" asked an incredulous Jimmy.

"I'm a dog. My name is Rowlf. I'd like to be YOUR dog, if you'll have me."

"I already got a dog!" Jimmy growled as he turned to Banner. "Where'd this ugly lookin' critter come from?"

"We thought Rowlf would be a fun sidekick for you on the show. Kids'll love him."

We all stood frozen, waiting for Jimmy to either smile or pull out a gun and shoot the poor animal. It was a long wait, as our star stood gazing at Rowlf with the eyes of a cobra waiting to strike.

Finally, he burst out laughing, walked over to the Muppet and whacked him on the head so hard one of Rowlf's ping-pong eyes popped out and flew clear across the room.

"Well, if this ain't the stupidest lookin' hound dawg I ever did see. He oughta be a lot of fun."

"You bet, Jimmy," barked Rowlf. "I'll be a smash. Everybody loves a man with a dog, and I'll be the best friend you ever had. Don't worry about the eye. I got plenty more back in my kennel."

"Well, you fellas have finally come up with something I like, and it's about damn time," Jimmy said, smiling happily. "And Bob, anytime I walk in this office I want that funny old hound to always be where he is right now. That's an order!"

When Jimmy left that day, Banner hammered out an agreement with Henson's agent. Henson would get a weekly fee for Rowlf's appearances on the show, plus an hourly stipend for his time spent crouched behind the star's couch.

"Just one more thing," Banner said to Henson. "You may be wondering why I didn't introduce you to Jimmy. I didn't want to spoil the illusion. So far, Rowlf's the only thing that's made him happy about this show. Keep up the good work, and just don't ever stand up while Jimmy's around."

And so it came to pass that Rowlf the dog was a big hit on *The Jimmy Dean Show*, while Henson spent an average of about twenty hours a week crouched behind that couch as Rowlf and keeping Jimmy amused. The two Jims never did meet each other as far as I knew.

Jimmy eventually got to book a few country artists, but the network kept cutting the budget due to low ratings. After three seasons, the show finally went off the air. Since the tension was so unbearable in the beginning, Frank and I escaped after the first five weeks, accepting an offer to write *The Judy Garland Show* in Los Angeles.

Happily, when Jim Henson was able to escape from behind that couch he went on to fame and fortune with *The Muppet Show*, *Sesame Street*, and all those great Muppet movies.

As for Peppiatt and Aylesworth, we learned two valuable lessons from that experience: If we were ever going to do a country-variety show, it would be packed full of country stars, and we would damn sure book a hound dawg!

# 2

# HOW *HEE HAW* WAS HATCHED

*"Just got a letter from Mamma down in Mount Idy," said Cliff Arquette as old Charlie Weaver on* The Jonathan Winters Show *in 1968. "She says here that Grandma Ogg is still tryin' to get Grandpa to shave off his beard. It's gettin' so long, last week he was runnin' for a streetcar and he ran right up his beard and kicked all his teeth out."*

After Peppiatt and Aylesworth left *The Jimmy Dean Show*, our careers spanned series and specials for such stars as Frank Sinatra, Groucho Marx, Jack Benny, Steve Allen, Herb Alpert, and, of course, Judy Garland. The closest we came to country was a special with Dinah Shore, whose only rural connection was a Southern accent. In between, we even wrote *Hullabaloo*, the first major network rock 'n' roll series, for NBC.

Finally, after six years of writing variety shows, we got a call from our old friend Perry Lafferty. He had been the producer of *Your Hit Parade* and *The Andy Williams Summer Show* that had reunited Peppiatt and Aylesworth as a writing team. Lafferty had recently become vice-president in charge of CBS programming for the West Coast. He told us that the time had come for us to become producers, and offered us *The Jonathan Winters Show*, with the condition that we wouldn't do any writing. That was fine by us, because the money was good and nobody could write for a zany, free-wheeling comic like Jonathan anyway.

Jonathan was a classic manic-depressive. In his drinking days, he was more manic than depressive and could keep everybody laughing for hours on end in a bar. However, in 1960, he totally flipped out in San Francisco and famously climbed the mast of a sailing ship, from which he refused to come down. This led to a stay in a private mental hospital, following which his drinking days were over.

When we went to work with him on his new show, a bone-dry Jonathan was much more depressive than manic. He was a pretty morose individual most of the time, until we found the key to opening up his fertile comic mind at will. All we had to do was tell him to be a five-year-old kid, a French gigolo, or an English tea pot and he would instantly come alive with a brilliant routine. As a result, we made one of the main ingredients of the show a segment during which members of the audience would ask him to become various people or objects.

One of the characters Jonathan was best known for was Maudie Frickert, a sweet old lady with a tart tongue. Consequently, we opened every show with Maudie, wearing a white wig and a gingham dress, sitting in a rocker and commenting on the events of the day. The audience loved Maudie and she got tons of fan mail, with the result that Jonathan started hating her because he thought Maudie was more popular than he was.

15

"I can't stand that old lady," he once moaned. "Do we have to keep using her on the show?"

Our only answer to that, of course, was, "Jonathan, if we get rid of Maudie, we'd have to get rid of you."

"I never thought of it quite that way. I guess I'll just have to put up with the old bat," he responded.

Since Jonathan was essentially a monologist, it was hard to fit him into comedy sketches with other actors. He was used to standing in one spot, being all the different characters, and providing his own sound effects as he painted hilarious vignettes all by himself. Even though we had singers and dancers and musical guest stars, it was difficult to fill a full hour every week with Jonathan standing alone doing funny characters. Although we had hired several good writers, there was virtually nothing for them to do.

We finally decided to get some good comedy sketch artists with whom we could do a bunch of blackouts as a regular feature of the show. We reached out to the best comic actors we knew, Paul Lynde and Alice Ghostley.

Jonathan also suggested a very funny man he had enjoyed working with on the old *Jack Paar Show*. His name was Cliff Arquette, and he had created a rural character named Charley Weaver, who became known for his quick wit and his homespun letters from Mama Weaver back home in Mount Idy. Arquette was a terrific ad-libber, so we added a weekly spot on an old front porch with Charley Weaver and Jonathan's bucolic character, Elwood Suggins, which always ended with Charley's letter from Mama.

By the thirteenth week, the show had really come together. Alas, the Nielsen ratings were another story. CBS was the "Tiffany Network" with most of the Top Twenty shows, while Jonathan rarely made it into the Top Forty.

It was no surprise when Mike Dann, president of the network, flew in from New York in December for meetings with Perry Lafferty to discuss the CBS programming schedule for the fall season. *The Jonathan Winters Show* would not be part of it. The show would finish the remainder of its twenty-six-week run in April and that would be the end of it. Dann, a very nice man and a good friend, delivered the news to us personally.

"It's not that it isn't a good show, fellas," he said. "We're very happy with what you've done with it. The problem is that Jonathan is

John Aylesworth trying to avoid headaches with Jonathan Winters. In the background is the first director of *The Jonathan Winters Show*, Bjorn Winthur (August 1968).

*Top:* The cast, crew, and production team of CBS's *The Jonathan Winters Show*, 1968. John Aylesworth at far left, Jonathan Winters standing center. *Bottom:* Frank Peppiatt and John Aylesworth flanking Jonathan Winters, 1968.

**Cliff Arquette as Charlie Weaver (left) and Jonathan Winters as Elwood Suggins, *The Jonathan Winters Show*, 1968.**

just too special for a mass audience. Now, I'm going to give you a bit of advice. You guys are terrific writers and now you've shown you can be good producers. Instead of working for other people all the time, why don't you create a show of your own? If you can come up with a good idea, I'd be happy to give it a shot. I'll be in town for the next two weeks. Think about it."

It was a hell of an invitation, but first we had to break the news to Jonathan. We took him to dinner that night and told him the bad news.

He was pretty broken up about it at first, but finally took it reasonably well after we led him into some funny bits as a tardy cuckoo clock and an elf who had just been fired by Santa.

The next day, during rehearsals for that week's show, Frank and I were distracted thinking of what kind of new show we could present to CBS. At one point, we were watching Jonathan and Charley Weaver exchanging funny country banter when we looked at each other and exclaimed in unison: "COUNTRY VARIETY!"

Back in our office, we looked at the latest Nielsen ratings. Practically the entire Top Ten were CBS country-oriented sitcoms, leading off with *The Andy Griffith Show*, *Gomer Pyle*, *The Beverly Hillbillies*, *Green Acres*, and *Petticoat Junction*. Then, in a real movie moment, we glanced over at the coffee table and saw a copy of a magazine with a full-page photo of Loretta Lynn on the cover and the headline "COUNTRY MUSIC HOT!" in big red letters.

Talk about omens! There had never been a completely country variety show, and since rural comedy was a major mainstay at CBS, we figured country humor plus musical numbers by that genre's biggest stars ought to be a sure thing.

We called our manager, who was then Bernie Brillstein, and told him what we had been thinking. *Laugh-In* was a big hit that year on NBC, and he suggested we come up with country version of that show. We agreed with the basic premise and started thinking of a funny title. "Yee-Haw" was an expression used by a lot of rural characters when they were elated, such as when Slim Pickins rode that nuclear bomb to oblivion in *Dr. Strangelove*, but it just didn't seem right as a title. What if we used a comical animated cartoon donkey braying "Hee Haw"? That sounded just about right, so now we had a title and a logo.

Next, we dreamed up a mythical place called "Cornfield County." It would be inhabited by all kinds of country characters: a comical barber, a dippy doctor, a funny general storekeeper; and it would have a huge cornfield with various townspeople popping up and down telling outrageous corny jokes. There was also a monthly cartoon in *Esquire* magazine featuring a moonshiner's shack with hillbillies lying on the porch doing "lazy" jokes, so we decided to throw that into the mix as well. The *Esquire* cartoon also had a hound dawg in it, so how could it miss?

In order to write a presentation for the show, we were hampered by the fact that as two citified Canadians we knew absolutely nothing about country music. We had once had Buck Owens on Jonathan's show as a guest, because he had sold almost as many records as the Beatles. Another guest had been Roy Clark, an amazing instrumentalist from Oklahoma who was also a very funny man. We figured that together they could be perfect hosts, like a rural version of Rowan and Martin.

We then scoured *Billboard*, the weekly show-biz magazine, which tabulated the best-selling musical albums and singles in Top Hundred lists of every genre. Buck Owens and Loretta Lynn were right at the top of the county music listings, along with George Jones, Conway Twitty, Charley Pride, and Johnny Cash. We were convinced that a combination of these musical stars and plenty of good country comedy ought to guarantee a hit show. Now all we had to do was convince CBS.

We wrote a short presentation, and arranged to meet Bernie Brillstein for breakfast the next morning in the Polo Lounge at the Beverly Hills Hotel to show him what we had done. We figured when he heard the title we had come up with, he would probably say we were nuts.

# 3

# A POWER BREAKFAST

---

*"You're nuts!" bellowed Bernie Brillstein. He was seated at his regular booth in the Polo Lounge at the Beverly Hills Hotel with a couple of dopey-looking Canadian clients wearing tweed jackets. "Who'd want to watch a show called Hee Haw?"*

---

Bernie calmed down after we explained the possibilities of a goofy cartoon donkey in a place called Cornfield County. We explained that we had expanded on the idea of a country *Laugh-In*, adding full musical numbers by major country stars, a lot of outdoor film vignettes, a bunch of animated farm animals along with the donkey—like dancing pigs and hound dawgs—and all the country comedy. Bernie finally agreed, and said he would set up a meeting at CBS so we could pitch the show.

At that point, in another movie moment, both Mike Dann and Perry Lafferty walked in for breakfast and took a booth.

"Why wait?" said Bernie. "You both know Mike and Perry. They're the guys who make all the decisions. Go pitch it now."

We did, and ten minutes later we had a development deal as a possible summer replacement show. They even liked *Hee Haw* as a title.

"It's certainly got potential," said Mike. "If we can find a spot for it, we'll give it a try."

So far, so good. But by March 1969, the outlook was pretty dreary for our little brainchild. The network was still intrigued by *Hee Haw* as a summer replacement, but there were no available time slots. Back then, network shows didn't automatically go into repeats in the spring. Each variety show had the right to produce its own summer replacement, with the regular star's own production company generally controlling that time spot. On CBS that year, all the returning shows had opted to replace themselves.

In the meantime, we still had a few more shows to tape with Jonathan Winters. We had told both Jonathan and Cliff Arquette about *Hee Haw*. They both agreed it was a fine idea and said they would be glad to come to Nashville to appear as Elwood Suggins and Charlie Weaver on some of the shows, if we could get it on the air.

Once a month since we had arrived in Los Angeles, we had a standing lunch with Perry Lafferty in his executive dining room at CBS Television City. That March was no exception. When we arrived, Lafferty was all smiles.

"I've got good news for you fellas. Doris Day has finally decided to do television. It'll be a sitcom on CBS and we'd like you to produce it."

"Great! But what about *Hee Haw*?"

"Frankly, I'd suggest you forget about that," said Lafferty. "There's still no opening for it, and this would be a great opportunity for you."

He set up a meeting for us with Miss Day for later in the week. Our only option at that point seemed to be either going back to New York to write variety shows or take on the world of sitcoms with a big movie star. The latter seemed the wisest choice, so we showed up at Miss Day's huge movie-star house at the appointed time on a Friday afternoon.

We had a very pleasant meeting. Miss Day was just as blonde and beautiful as she had always been in the movies. However, rather than discussing her new show, she rattled on quite bitterly about her "skunk of an ex-husband," Marty Melcher, who had recently died after embezzling $20 million of her money, thereby forcing her to do television to make ends meet.

Since we had had a similar experience a few years earlier with Judy Garland and her "skunk of an ex-husband," Sid Luft, we took our leave of the beautiful movie star and decided to opt for a miracle that might rescue *Hee Haw*.

Failing that, we figured we could always go back to good old New York City and find somebody else to write for. Call us crazy or merely foolish—both of which were two of our most appealing traits back then—but somehow Lady Luck had been very good to us over the years.

Her Ladyship didn't let us down. She indeed came up with a miracle!

# 4

# THE MIRACLE

*"CBS CANCELS* SMOTHERS BROTHERS SHOW*"—Los Angeles Times, April 4, 1969*

Everyone was shocked. *The Smothers Brothers Comedy Hour* had been one of the network's most successful shows. It had made its debut on a Sunday night at 9 P.M. in February 1967, opposite the top-rated *Bonanza*. It immediately attracted a younger, hipper audience with its irreverent digs at the war in Vietnam, organized religion, and the presidency. This led to public battles over censorship, culminating in cancellation due to the Smothers' failure to submit a review tape of their latest show to the network in a timely manner. From today's perspective it all seems pretty silly, but back then it was serious business.

In any case, the Smothers' cancellation automatically revoked their right to produce a summer replacement, and *Hee Haw* was standing in the wings with its squeaky-clean homespun corn. It would make its debut at eight o'clock one Sunday night in June.

We immediately hired two of our favorite writers, Jack Burns and George Yanok. Our first meeting, however, was mostly a staring match since none of us had a clue about country comedy—unless you counted childhood viewings of Ma and Pa Kettle movies. In desperation, we put in a call to an old friend, Gordie Tapp, in Toronto, where he played Cousin Clem on a Canadian show called *Country Hoedown*. We wanted to find out where he got all his comedy material.

Gordie put us on to his country comedy connection, a local Nashville writer-singer-comedian named Archie Campbell. Archie knew absolutely everything about country comedy, and we knew we needed him desperately.

The next day, we flew Gordie and Archie from Toronto and Nashville to Los Angeles. Gordie Tapp was a walking joke book whose only conversation was a constant stream of gags spoken in every imaginable dialect. He was a hearty and handsome young fellow who became a regular performer on *Hee Haw* from the very first show.

Archie Campbell was a charming older man with kindly features topped by a jet-black toupee. Before his arrival in Los Angeles, Archie had sent us a very funny LP that contained a routine about hockey, which we thought was hilarious (even though we had no idea the term "hockey" in the South referred to human excrement). The album also included Archie's specialty, called Spoonerisms, including stories like "Pee Little Thrigs," "Rindercella," and "Beeping Sleauty."

Best of all, Archie included a song that would be a big part of every show for all of *Hee Haw*'s 25 years. It was, of course, the immortal "Pffft, You Were Gone." Old Archie was an absolute godsend as a writer and as a performer. We couldn't have done the show without him.

During the next two months, we all pitched in and wrote enough comedy material for the 12 one-hour shows CBS had ordered for the summer. This was accomplished in our *Jonathan Winters Show* offices after Jonathan had left. George Yanok still has his desk blotter with a drawing of a marlin inscribed: "J. Winters ... out of work '69." We must have written at least 8,000 pages of comedy bits. Archie was an inexhaustible source of seemingly brand-new jokes. "I got a blue million of 'em!" he claimed.

John Aylesworth at his Yongestreet Productions office, circa 1970.

We also began looking for a suitable animator who could make our *Hee Haw* donkey come alive. In a stroke of good fortune, we found exactly what we had been looking for in a man named Herb Klynn, whose Format Productions supplied the freshest animated material we had ever seen on network television. It was Klynn who brought our dancing pigs to life, along with our braying logo and sundry other barnyard animals.

In the meantime, we had formed a company with Nick Vanoff, who had been our producer while writing *The Perry Como Show* in New York from 1960 to 1963. Nick was then producing *The Hollywood Palace*, with his partner Bill Harbach. The four of us would be equal partners in the *Palace* and use our new company to develop future series, none of us really believing *Hee Haw* could possibly survive past its first summer.

We called our company Yongestreet Productions, after the main street of Toronto, our hometown. Vanoff was from Buffalo, N.Y., and had relatives in Toronto. Harbach, a somewhat pixilated New Yorker, went along with it because it sounded youthful and he wasn't much of a speller.

All this was accomplished while taping the final Jonathan Winters shows. I must say, looking back on it, that was a damn good show. Our talented head writer, Ron Friedman, had kept up the quality of the comedy black-outs. Bill Davis, the best director in the business, was making the musical numbers look fantastic with the help of Gene McAvoy's brilliant scenic designs. Sam Lovullo, the associate producer CBS had assigned to watch the store, was doing just that.

Frank and I fulfilled our most important chore as producers by valiantly trying to keep Jonathan in a reasonably happy mood until the last show was taped. We were aided in this endeavor by the fact that Jonathan was a bit tight with a dollar, and we had arranged for him to keep all the suits and costumes that he wore on the show.

When we could finally turn our full attention to *Hee Haw*, once Jonathan's show went into repeats, Archie Campbell convinced us that the only place to tape the show would be Nashville, Tennessee. It was the home of the Grand Ole Opry, and all the country musical and comedy talent lived there. It took a while to convince the network that a country

# Letters

## Hee Haw History

■ I enjoyed the article on *Hee Haw* [Finnigan's File, by Joseph Finnigan, February 1989], and I would be remiss if I didn't add to the history of the show.

When the show was first being developed, Frank Peppiatt and John Aylesworth of Yongestreet Productions asked me to help develop an animated opening. Since there was no script at the time, we at Format Productions created a main title featuring the *Hee Haw* donkey together with a series of animated characters and gags and sound effects that could be matted with the live-action sequences or work independently as bridges.

This resulted in a cast of animated pigs, ducks, donkeys, skunks, dogs, chickens, et cetera, that became the linkage for the show format. By the time we finished the *Hee Haw* tenth anniversary special, we had created a dancing donkey and an animated library that was considered worth cataloging and was fed into a computer along with the live-action sequences.

To this day the show continues to be computer-structured, combining the stock animation with the various new acts. In fact it is Sam Lovullo who should receive credit for using the computer for the first time to structure a TV show in this fashion.

In closing, I thought you would perhaps enjoy seeing some of the first rough sketches for the show.

*Herb Klynn*
*Format Productions*
*Tarzana, California*

© FORMAT PRODUCTIONS, INC.

## Foreign Correspondence

■ When I first bought *Emmy*, I did it just out of curiosity, but I've found it so interesting that I decided to subscribe. I thank you for your marvelous magazine and hope to get it as soon as possible. Too bad that here in Portugal we can see only a small number of American programs and series. Fortunately, the large majority of them are excellent—thank God for that!

*Joseph N. Valent*
*Evora, Portugal*

## Behind *Behind the Music*

■ [Regarding New Tech, February 1989] (1) we did not shoot the entire film [*Liberace: Behind the Music*] on soundstages. Nearly 50 percent of the picture was shot on various locations around Montreal and four locations in Los Angeles and Valencia, California. Contrary to your article, we did spend time scouting locations and transporting entire crews and equipment between scenes—not between shots, as you wrote. That is rarely done except in expensive commercials.

(2) I regularly use two cameras and so do many other directors; on some occasions, we use more than two.

(3) I never film "simultaneously from two different angles" because that would necessitate flat lighting. I shoot with the two cameras side by side, i.e., the same angle.

(4) Parkie Singh did not edit *Liberace: Behind the Music*.

(5) The film was never "turned over to Kushner-Locke for . . . audio, mixing, and titles." (I suppose you mean 'audio-mixing'?) The mixing, spotting, and titles were done by producer Murray Shostak [of Canadian International Studios] and myself, though the titles were remade by the executive producers.

(6) The stock footage with time code on it was supplied by the Kushner-Locke Company, and I—not "the Canadians"—tried unsuccessfully to cover up the code. In the end, we didn't "recut" it. We rejected it as unusable and Kushner-Locke came up with something entirely different.

*David Greene*
*David Greene Productions*
*Santa Monica, California*

**Letter published in *Emmy* magazine, June 1989, from Herb Klynn, Format Productions, discussing the approach and evolution of animation for *Hee Haw*.**

**(Left to right) Bill Davis, George Yanok, and Frank Peppiatt on the first *Hee Haw* film shoot in Los Angeles, 1969.**

show should be shot in the country, but when they finally agreed there was one condition: we would have to do the show at their Nashville CBS affiliate, WLAC.

We happily agreed and set out on a survey trip to see if that was going to be possible. Since Frank didn't like to fly, I left the next morning on a flight to Nashville along with Bill Davis, Gene McAvoy, and Sam Lovullo. When we arrived at WLAC, we found a pretty average local TV station with two tiny studios. One of them was devoted to their local newscasts, while the other was used to shoot commercials and a couple of small syndicated shows.

At first glance, it just didn't seem big enough to accommodate the kind of show we had in mind, but we soon discovered there was no alternative. The Ryman Auditorium, which housed the Grand Ole Opry, had a nice big stage but it was already booked for a

new show starring Johnny Cash that was to be our rival that summer on another network.

Somehow, we had to make things work on that matchbook stage at WLAC. Luckily, the technicians there were top notch, as was all the completely up-to-date equipment. As Bill Davis recently noted, "We were amazed that this little CBS affiliate in the bowels of the country had so much!"

At that point, Lady Luck threw another miracle our way. Someone had recently developed "time code" editing, making it possible to keep track of whatever was shot on the video tape so that we could easily locate each scene by a computer code number and transfer everything to a master tape in whatever order we chose. Up until that time, video tape had to be edited by cutting it with a razor blade, an extremely risky business with often disastrous results.

*Above and opposite page:* **Preliminary sketches by Herb Klynn, Format Productions, for *Hee Haw*'s animated characters, drawn in the early spring of 1969: series of six drawings that show the "hipness" that belied the corny image of *Hee Haw*; dressed pigs in a chorus line; animals "boo"-ing bad jokes; series of four drawings showing the progression of a skunk disapproving of a corny joke, with notes and direction.**

The new system had been developed by the Electronic Engineering Company of California, who named it "EECO," their initials. No matter what they called it, we will be

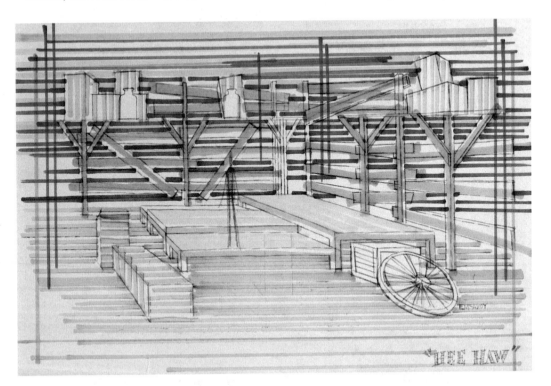

**Gene McAvoy's original final sketch for *Hee Haw*'s main barn set for the show's original summer series, 1969.**

**Bill Davis (left) and Sam Lovullo, clearly surprised by a live chicken on the KORN set, 1969.**

eternally grateful to those guys for making *Hee Haw* possible. Since we had an order for twelve shows, we would shoot enough material to fill that many hours, take all those miles of video tape back home, and put each show together in the comfort of an editing bay in Los Angeles.

We decided that Archie would be the barber, doing comedy routines and his favorite "Spoonerisms" with Roy in the barbershop chair; Gordie would be the Proprietor of the General Store; Archie and Roy would play shiftless Moonshiners in front of a shack with a hound dawg; we would have Buck picking his red, white, and blue guitar and Roy picking his banjo highlighting a bunch of two-man jokes in a spot called "Pickin' and Grinnin'"; Gordie would be the Old Philosopher on a front porch, dressed as a Mark Twain–type character wearing a wide brimmed straw hat, spouting gibberish such as "The only difference between a smart man and a dumb man is that the smart man is smarter than the dumb man," after which his hat would be knocked off with a rubber chicken.

These would be our main set pieces, as well as non-stop jokes in an enormous cornfield featuring Archie and Gordie along with other members of the cast (whoever they might be, hopefully to be found when we got to Nashville).

We decided that since the Cornfield was our biggest piece of scenery and would take up the whole studio, we would shoot it last. We would start by taping all the musical numbers in either a large abstract barn set to be created by Gene McAvoy, or on a big old-fashioned porch, and then bring in the various small sets to tape the comedy spots.

Arrangements were made to put us all up at the local Holiday Inn for the rest of the season, and we celebrated that night by having about a thousand drinks and cutting such crazed didos as shoving a hooker into the straight-as-an-arrow Sam Lovullo's room and holding the door closed as he fought with the strength of 10 tigers to get it open. He finally won the battle and took off down the hall like a blue streak. We gave the hooker a bonus for a game try, and I sometimes wonder if Sam still has nightmares about that insane night.

The next day, nursing monumental hangovers, we made a meek apology to Lovullo and bid a fond farewell to McAvoy, who would have to stay in Nashville and start getting the sets built while the rest of us got to work back in L.A. Lord knows we had plenty left to do before the whole bunch of us descended on Music City, USA, to actually start shooting *Hee Haw*. We had accomplished a good survey trip, but the best, funniest, downright weirdest was yet to come.

# 5

# NASHVILLE BOUND

*The Super Chief is flashing through the night on its way to Chicago in the spring of 1969. Four well-dressed young men are seated at a table in the bar car, drunk off their asses, playing high-stakes poker with an Irish priest.*
*"Last call, Father," says a reverent bar steward. "It's getting late."*
*"Bugger off!" bellows the crocked cleric. "I'm $50,000 into church funds!"*

On a misty morning in early April 1969, four seemingly ordinary men gathered at Union Station in Los Angeles about to embark on an extraordinary mission to Nashville, Tennessee. Due to his fear of flying, Frank Peppiatt had talked me and our fellow writers, Jack Burns and George Yanok, into making our historic journey by train. Frank convinced us it would be a real lark, since we would be traveling on the famous *Super Chief* to Chicago where we would stay overnight before boarding the not-so-famous *Dixie Flyer* to our final destination.

The four of us stood outside the station awaiting the arrival of the highly eccentric writer-actor Pat McCormick, an imposing figure standing six-foot-four and carrying considerable girth since his days as a trim champion hurdler at Harvard University. Pat had plans to attend the Kentucky Derby, and would head for Churchill Downs after our arrival in Nashville.

We had written a number of shows with McCormick back in New York, where he was determined to become a comic legend by dropping his pants at every opportunity. At one point, he made it known that he would ceremoniously drop his trousers at high noon every day on the grassy divider in the middle of Park Avenue at 54th Street. True to his word, at the stroke of noon each day, down would fall his trousers as Pat stood beaming while puffing his ever present cigar, to the amusement—and quite often gasps—of passing pedestrians.

McCormick even got a few mentions in the New York press, which once emboldened him to seal his legendary status by flying to London with the intent of dropping his pants in Westminster Abbey. Jack Burns accompanied him just for laughs, and gleefully related the result of this dubious venture on their return.

Striding into the Abbey on a Sunday afternoon, puffing on an extra large "Churchill" cigar, Pat had pushed his way through a throng of tourists at Poet's Corner and proceeded to drop his pants.

A uniformed guard, who had watched the occurrence, immediately walked over to Pat with an ominous glare.

"Sir," the guard said calmly. "I must inform you there is no smoking in Westminster Abbey." The perfect squelch.

**Party time at home with old friends: comedian George Burns (standing, left) conducts John Aylesworth (seated, left), singer Mel Torme (seated on floor, center), actor Jim Backus (seated, first from right), comic-writer Pat McCormick (back right), among other notables at one of Backus and Aylesworth's legendary New Year's Eve parties. McCormick generally entered late in the festivities dressed as the New Year's Baby.**

To be topped by a security guard was more than McCormick could take. To my knowledge, he never dropped his pants in public again. He did, however, gain a modicum of fame in the movies when he partnered with tiny Paul Williams in several *Smokey and the Bandit* movies, and had recently contributed his comical screen presence for the benefit of *Hee Haw* when we shot a bunch of film vignettes in the San Fernando Valley that we planned to insert into the show.

The most memorable of these involved Pat and the equally hefty Lulu Roman, a gem of a discovery passed on to us by Buck Owens' manager. In a pastoral setting, Pat and Lulu rushed toward each other amorously in slow motion, accompanied by romantic music which built to a climax as these two extremely large people crashed into each other and fell sprawling to the ground.

Obviously, one never knew quite what to expect from McCormick. His arrival at Union Station that morning was no exception, as a black sedan pulled up, driven by his wife wearing a nun's habit. McCormick was in the back seat, and when his wifely nun got out and reverently opened the door for him, he emerged dressed as a very large and imposing priest.

As McCormick was extracting his luggage from the trunk of the car, a number of awed redcaps rushed to his aid, seeking a blessing from Father Patrick, which they all happily received in lieu of tips.

Upon our boarding the train, the blessings went on for hours as various porters and passengers sought absolution, which McCormick was glad to give until the whole thing started to pall. It was reminiscent of the time Jay Burton, a fellow writer on the *Perry Como Show*, had come to play in one of Perry's staff golf tournaments wearing a tuxedo. It was amusing for the first three holes, but the rest was a real drag.

The train itself was somewhat disappointing. The *Super Chief* was no longer all that super. Amtrak hadn't taken over the railways as yet, but the service and amenities were already less than luxurious. After stowing our luggage in sleeping compartments that could give mice claustrophobia, we went to the club car to relax and watch the countryside roll by.

Alas, the once-magnificent Art Deco club car, which had long ago been the scene of glamorous movie stars dressed to the nines and sipping high-balls, was now shabby and unkempt. As for the porters, beaming uniformed attendants from whom one had once happily received any amenity simply by flipping them a shiny quarter, we were now at the mercy of surly attendants who appeared to consider every request an imposition.

Luckily, having Father Patrick with us brought a modicum of respect to our party as he continued to bestow blessings on porters and passengers alike.

Our other star attraction was Jack Burns, who had gained fame as a comedian with his partner Avery Schreiber. The team of Burns and Schreiber had been wildly successful, until Jack decided to give up performing and concentrate on a writing career. Unfortunately, nobody could quite place him without his chubby, mustachioed partner by his side, causing him to be generally referred to by our fellow passengers as "that guy on television in the back of the taxicab."

When the gong sounded to announce that lunch was being served, yet another disappointment awaited. The *Super Chief* dining car, which had once rivaled the finest eateries in the land, was now little more than a rolling beanery. At least the tablecloths were still white and the silverware had yet to become plastic, but the menu was more Denny's than Chasen's. We all griped except Frank, who had taken countless cross-country train trips over many years due to his aversion to flying. He just looked melancholy, no doubt lost in remembrance of things long past.

Upon our return to the club car, someone produced a deck of cards and suggested we while away the afternoon with a friendly game of poker. We convincingly feigned delight when Father Patrick agreed to join us in our game of chance and then even accepted the offer of a cocktail. We immediately ordered doubles of everything and started dealing the Bicycles.

The hours flew by. I doubt that we even stopped for dinner. My memory of the occasion is simply a blur of cards being dealt and the ingestion of much strong drink. Suddenly, it was past midnight and the weary barman informed us he was closing up and did we want a last round. By this time, Father Patrick's clerical collar had sprung from his neck and his priestly demeanor had turned to desperation as he lost hand after hand.

"Bugger off!" he roared. "I'm $50,000 into church funds!"

The barman, quite naturally shocked, shrugged his shoulders and proceeded to start closing up the bar.

"Hold it!" said George Yanok, quite sensibly. "Perhaps you'd better just bring us each a bottle. It's going to be a long morning."

"I don't know if I'm allowed to do that," the barman replied. "Regulations, you know."

"JUST DO IT!" growled Father Patrick, in a strong Irish brogue. "OR I'LL CONDEMN YOUR IMMORTAL SOUL TO THE FIRES OF HELL!!"

The barman thought this over, meekly complied with our request, and quickly left the club car without looking back.

I don't know when we went to bed. My last memory is of Jack

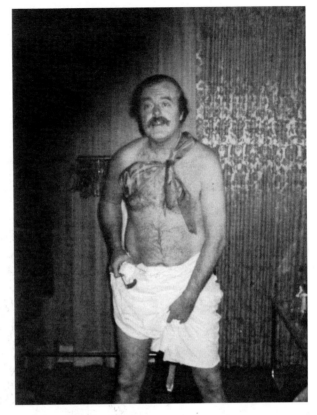

**Pat McCormick as the 1975 New Year's Baby.**

Burns kneeling outside Father Patrick's compartment seeking absolution for, among other things, felonious mopery and exposing himself in front of an elephant. It was a lengthy confession, and I dozed off as Jack was being forgiven for fondling a mannequin in Macy's window.

The following day around noon, we all staggered from our compartments with enormous hangovers and headed to the club car for "hairs of the dog" in order to feel even vaguely human again. McCormick had ditched the priest outfit and was a civilian again, much to the mystification of our fellow travelers. From the looks of him, McCormick was in dire need of a blessing himself, but he settled for a Bloody Mary.

Following a greasy lunch in the rolling diner, we spent a fairly foggy afternoon trying to ingest enough hair of the dog to recreate a good-sized Saint Bernard until at last, early that evening, the train finally pulled into Chicago. Feeling little pain by that time, we looked forward to a fun evening in that toddling town, which I suppose we had. I don't remember. Through the mist of memory only two vignettes remain.

One involved a visit to the College Inn, where singer Mel Torme was appearing as the star attraction. We totally disrupted his show, with McCormick's huge frame dancing on a table top, and the rest of us shouting out one-liners. Luckily, Mel was an old pal of ours from *The Judy Garland Show*, and he took our antics with somewhat forced good humor.

It was during intermission that Mel expressed shocked dismay when we told him what had brought us to Chicago and the nature of our mission in Nashville. Mel was a total jazz fanatic who detested any music that didn't reside in the Great American Songbook. Years earlier, he had gently chided us for writing a *Coke Time* special starring Pat Boone and Frankie Avalon. Our venture toward country was just too much for him to bear.

"You're going to do WHAT?" he cried in total amazement. "I may never speak to you guys again!"

I also remember that McCormick had been talking throughout the trip about a big party he planned to attend in Chicago that would be hosted by the legendary comic Shecky Green. When the rest of us decided to call it a night, the last words I recall him saying were: "Wait a minute, guys, what if the Shecky thing doesn't work out?" I don't know if it did or not, because McCormick failed to show up the following morning when we boarded the *Dixie Flyer*.

Once again, we were nursing gigantic hangovers which were unrelieved due to state liquor laws that made the run to Nashville bone-dry. This state of affairs heightened our anxiety over what lay ahead in Music City. It didn't help that the *Dixie Flyer* was a misnomer. The damn thing barely crept to our destination.

To pass the time in our wretched state, we started thinking up comedy "wild lines" to be delivered by various solo cast members as transitions, the most memorable of which were "The circus was invented by some clown in Detroit," and "The longest snake in the world wears a hat." They didn't have to make sense as long as they got a laugh.

None too soon, the train pulled into Nashville under cover of night at about 9 P.M. We were all close to collapse, since the jolting of the ancient cars had made sleep impossible. It was in this wretched state that we were hauled in hay wagons pulled by donkeys through the deserted streets of Nashville to the Holiday Inn, the brainstorm of an obviously demented local public relations guy. Peppiatt was quoted in *Time* as saying, "We thought there would be throngs to meet us, but we ended up waving to each other."

To make matters worse, we were met in the lobby of the motel by a steely-eyed veteran columnist for the *Nashville Banner* who informed us that we wouldn't be too welcome in his town.

"A show with a name like *Hee Haw*," he announced gloomily, "is gonna set country music back twenty years!"

With our frolicking and binging on the train a thing of the past, there was now serious work to be done. We had just two short weeks of preparation before taping would begin. It wouldn't be easy.

# STRANGERS IN A STRANGE LAND

---

*"Welcome to Nashville, boys," said Tom Baker, president of WLAC-TV.*
*"It's the Athens of the South."*

---

Nashville had gained its appellation "the Athens of the South" because of its full-sized replica of the Parthenon, which stood near the downtown area in Centennial Park. It had been built in 1897 to celebrate Tennessee's first 100 years during which—one can only assume—they must have thought they were Greek. The people certainly talked funny, but if they didn't we wouldn't have had a show.

Way back in 1969, Nashville was a sleepy mid-size hamlet immortalized that same year by Bob Dylan's "Nashville Skyline." Despite the fact that it was the state capital of Tennessee, it appeared to have not quite decided to join the twentieth century.

Our train had arrived at Union Station, an enormous gothic mid–Victorian edifice of gray stone. The state capitol building was an imposing nineteenth century structure with an elaborate dome, high on a hill in the center of town. Most of the surrounding buildings were of a similar vintage, and were it not for a few fairly recent mini-skyscrapers—and the fact that cars had replaced horses—to our contemporary California eyes Nashville looked to still be in the era of Andrew Jackson, the 7th president of the United States.

In fact, Old Hickory's plantation still stood just outside of town. It was called The Hermitage, and appeared not to have changed one bit since Old Hickory himself was in residence.

Yet another huge plantation on the outskirts, dating back to 1805, was called Belle Meade. This quaint Southern souvenir had lent its name to the surrounding neighborhood where all the rich folk lived in their antebellum mansions. We were told that driving through Belle Meade of an evening, you could "still hear the darkies humming." Apparently, the people of Belle Meade were still as antebellum as their mansions.

Yet the most intriguing historic site of all was smack in the middle of town, the Ryman Auditorium. This large, stately tabernacle had been built in 1892 as a gospel church, named after a roistering riverboat captain who financed its construction after an unexpected religious conversion. In 1943, the building itself was converted into the home of the world famous Grand Ole Opry, the "Mother Church of Country Music." It was here that such pioneers as Hank Williams, Bill Monroe, and Patsy Cline shaped the future of an American art form we intended to broadcast throughout the land.

The Opry, from its inception, had been broadcast on the radio by WSM with a clear channel, 50,000-watt signal throughout the South. That signal was so powerful that for miles around anything metal could serve as a radio. Minnie Pearl once recalled, "We was

**Peppiatt and Aylesworth—"outstanding in their field"—Nashville, 1969.**

all so poor where I grew up in the Ozark Mountains, none of us could afford a radio. We'd all go down to a nearby farm on a Saturday and listen to the Opry on this big old wire fence around the barn. My uncle Nabob had some steel bridgework in his mouth, and he claimed he could hear it from as far away as Florida."

I'll never forget the overwhelming feeling of awe that came over me as I stood in the wings of the Ryman for the very first time in 1969. I marveled at the sea of faces gazing up at the stage, as countless adoring fans sat in the original 1892 church pews awaiting the appearance of their country music idols. For most, it would be their first and perhaps only opportunity to see such beloved performers as Roy Acuff or Tammy Wynette in the flesh. These people were the genuine article, plain country folk who had come from far and wide, having saved for months and sometimes years to afford the trip to actually see with their own eyes what they had only heard on their radios.

The men were mostly clad in overalls, while many of the plainly-dressed women breast-fed their young right there in the audience. They had come as if to a rural Mecca to witness rural royalty, and they would cherish this enchanted evening as long as they lived. Never had I felt more like a stranger in a strange land.

Stranger still, on a lighter note, was the sight of a huge billboard on our way to the studio that first morning. It showed a young lad about to ingest a large brown object called a Goo Goo Bar. The boy was obviously ecstatic about the prospect and exclaimed in a cartoon bubble, "I LOVE GOO GOO!" Apparently, Goo Goos were one of Nashville's favorite confections. I could only imagine that the president of the candy company must have been a three-week-old baby.

\* \* \*

With the frolicking and binging on the train a thing of the past, there was now serious work to be done. We had two weeks of preparation before actual taping would begin. The sets were being built, the scripts were being mimeographed, and almost a quarter-million cue cards were being printed.

There would be no time for rehearsals or learning lines on this show. Our plan was to shoot all the music first, which would require no rehearsal since Buck had his own band, "The Buckaroos." Our studio musicians knew most of Roy's routines, and the guest stars would all bring their own bands. Buck introduced us to a fresh, young musical duo—the Hager Twins—and Jim and Jon became regulars.

When we got to the comedy, we figured everybody could just read off the cue cards. We would tape everything. The mistakes and the goof-ups would be part of the show, skillfully edited to make a large part of the hour one big blooper. With a little luck, we could be out of there in five weeks with ten miles of videotape containing, hopefully, enough material to stitch together a dozen hour-long shows. The only thing we still needed was a few more good country comics. Plus, not forgetting Jimmy Dean's Rowlf and our vow of six long years ago, we had to get ourselves a hound dawg.

# 7

# Bring in the Clowns

*"Comedy's a fickle mistress, boys. I was at the Opry the night the Duke of Pad-
ucah lost his funny."* —Archie Campbell

Archie Campbell led us to the cream of the country comedy crop: Minnie Pearl, Grandpa Jones, and David "Stringbean" Akeman. With the additional performing talents of Archie and Gordie Tapp, we were in pretty good shape. Still, we knew we'd need more, so we decided to hold open auditions for rural novelty acts.

The results were less than heartening. From trained chickens to musical pigs, our search produced acts that were bizarre, sometimes cruel, and otherwise unusable. We saw so many blacked-out teeth, it was like a dental phantasmagoria, topped by the rustic hilarity of removing entire sets of false choppers to contort faces into frightening shapes that still haunt my dreams to this day.

The only two acts to make the cut were a man named Nobel Bear, who could simulate the sounds of practically anything—from buzz saws to diesel trains—and two pixilated locals named Riddle and Phelps, who made a weird kind of rhythm known in the country as "Eefin' and Hambone," created by rapid knee-slapping mixed with a rapid intake of breath that sounded like musical hiccupping.

The Duke of Paducah's audition was particularly sad considering his past success. Born in 1901, Benjamin Francis "Whitey" Ford was a leading country comedian from the late 1930s to the mid–1950s. Unfortunately, we couldn't use him.

We did, however, find an excellent hound dawg. Alas, he couldn't talk, but he was a fine looking bloodhound. Although his talents were mostly eating and sleeping, we nevertheless named him "Kingfish, the Wonder Dog."

Our partner, Nick Vanoff, had sent two of his most trusted aides from *Hollywood Palace* to help us pull off this new venture: Rita Scott, an excellent production assistant we had known from the Perry Como days, and a sharp-eyed money man named Al Simon to help keep our meager budget in check. The deal we had made with CBS Business Affairs called for a scant $75,000 per show, but with our taping schedule we figured we could amortize everything over the full 12 shows and hopefully still come out a bit ahead.

Rita Scott's main job was to keep track of how much comedy we would need for the 12 shows, and we still had a way to go. Weekly television is a hungry animal that must be constantly fed.

During one of our non-stop writing sessions, someone came up with the idea of a country radio station, carrying all the news from Cornfield County. Frank and I immediately thought of Don Harron, a very funny Canadian actor-writer who played a comical

**Jimmy Riddle (left) and Jackie Phelps (first from right), the "Eefin' and Hambone" duo, with producer Sam Lovullo (first from left) and director Bill Davis (right).**

old farmer named Charlie Farqueson, ostensibly from rural Ontario. He had a lot of hilarious material that would fit perfectly into a rural newscast. We figured that a farmer is a farmer no matter where he's from, so we called Harron and he said he would be delighted to come up with at least two funny spots per show. Naturally, we called the radio station KORN.

Archie Campbell, a randy old coot if there ever was one, brought up a valid point during one of our many meetings: Where were the pretty girls? Aside from the matronly Minnie Pearl and the comical Lulu Roman, Cornfield County didn't have one pretty young resident. In the words of writer George Yanok, "Man does not live on jokes alone. There must also be ladies."

We immediately hired a comely "Daisy Mae," a blonde beauty named Jeannine Riley who had been a regular on the CBS sitcom *Petticoat Junction*. We also hired a budding young actress from Los Angeles, Jennifer Bishop, a brunette contrast to Jeannine.

Since we couldn't afford to import any more talent, we decided to plumb the supply of local belles and hold a "Miss *Hee Haw* Contest." We advertised the event in both local papers, but apparently the cream of Nashville's beauties would rather die then apply for such a thing. The candidates who did show up were sadly lacking in either pulchritude or personality. It was one of those rare contests that nobody won.

**Sam Lovullo (left) and Bill Davis (first from left) with the owners of Kingfish the Wonder Dog, 1969.**

*Top:* Grandpa Jones and Junior Samples in the foreground of the "Moonshiners" set with Kingfish the Wonder Dog and (left to right) Jennifer Bishop, Jeannine Riley and Archie Campbell on the porch. *Bottom: Hee Haw* was a "family" affair from the beginning. Here is Garrett, director Bill Davis' son, with Kingfish the Wonder Dog, 1969.

On our return to WLAC, we came in the back way where the sets were being constructed, grabbed a cute little blonde named Cathy Baker out of the paint shop, and still in her spattered overalls we officially appointed her "Miss *Hee Haw*." Cathy retained that title until the last show was taped 25 years later with a final "That's all!" Sometimes, you just luck out.

As the time to begin taping was about to arrive, Gene McAvoy's crew of hard-working carpenters and painters were nearing completion of our colorful sets, despite the fact that his occasionally drunkenly-insane but brilliant head painter, who called himself Vern Gagne (after the famously ferocious wrestler), had to be chained to his post in order to complete his work. McAvoy's assistant was nice young man named Bill Camden who later married Cathy Baker. *Hee Haw* was fast becoming a family affair.

We had already met the president of WLAC, a courtly Southern gentleman named Tom Baker, who apparently considered us to be California carpetbaggers and had greeted us with all the warmth of a cobra. His young assistants, however, were extremely helpful, particularly WLAC vice-president Roy Smith. They even seemed to accept us as harmless human beings who just wanted to do a show, a rare attitude for us to encounter in Nashville.

On the first day of taping, the musicians took their places and started tuning up. Walking into the studio that day and hearing that music was one of the most unforgettable thrills of my life. The die had been cast. *Hee Haw* was on its way!

* * *

During that first summer taping, Buck Owens and his Buckaroos were the major contributors to the regular musical segments on the show, backing Buck's numbers, Roy's songs, and all our incidental segue music—the bridges that moved us from one setting to another.

We had already met with Buck in L.A., and explained that we wanted most of the cast numbers to be bright and upbeat to go along with the spirit of the show. He understood immediately, and delivered in spades. Our opening number with the full cast was a rocking version of "Johnny B. Goode," and Buck's numbers were mostly his up-tempo hits like "Act Naturally" and "Who's Gonna Mow Your Grass."

Buck's manager, Jack McFadden, was on good terms with everybody in the country music business, so we gave him the title of talent coordinator. He and our associate producer, Sam Lovullo, handled the guest-star bookings. Frank and I, along with our trusty writers, concentrated on the comedy, which we considered the main ingredient in a show called *Hee Haw*.

The first of our musical guests was the most difficult. Our plan was to devote the first two weeks to music, with each guest star taping four numbers to be edited into various shows. Unfortunately, Jerry Lee Lewis was the first to arrive in the studio like a great ball of fire, along with his teenage cousin Myra, a mousy little thing rumored to be his third wife. He loudly insisted on doing eight numbers because he was twice as good as anybody else who would be on the show. He wanted a special piano so Myra could dance on it while he reduced it to kindling with his huge hands pounding on the keys.

We agreed to everything, figuring we would tape six songs and only use four of them anyway. By the time Jerry Lee left, the studio was a shambles and we could only hope all our guest stars wouldn't be like that. As it turned out, all the others that first two weeks of taping were pussycats by comparison.

Loretta Lynn, our lucky inspiration from *Newsweek*, was both lovely and accommodating. Charley Pride, the only black country singer in the business—and one of the best—was a joy to work with. Charley and Loretta were the two guest stars on our very first show.

Tammy Wynette was a sweetheart. George Jones, Faron Young, and Ferlin Husky came and went without complaint, leaving us with some great music. Merle Haggard bridled at performing in a barn setting with all that hay, figuring it would soil his image as an "outlaw" country star, so the resourceful Gene McAvoy and his crew quickly cobbled together a living room with a blazing fireplace. It may not have been "outlaw," but at least it didn't have hay. Haggard delivered.

We had brought along a musical director from Los Angeles, Bob Alberti. He was a very talented arranger-conductor we had worked with a few times, but when the taping began in Nashville he was at a total loss.

"These people don't even read music," he groaned. "I have no idea what the hell they're doing. They just yell out a bunch of numbers, and suddenly they have a complete arrangement. I just don't get it."

I still don't completely understand it myself. Apparently each number represents a chord, and when you put them all together it comes out just fine. The leader yells out, "5, 9, 3, 7 and 2," the band starts playing, the singer sings the song, and somehow it all works.

*Hee Haw*'s first director, Bill Davis (left), with Gordie Tapp, on the *Hee Haw* set (with what appears to be something interesting happening in the background), summer, 1969.

**John Aylesworth demonstrates the fine art of knocking a hat off with a rubber chicken with Sam Lovullo in the Cornfield, 1969.**

The two weeks of musical numbers, including those of Buck Owens and Roy Clark, went by in a flash.

We tried out one of our animation bits during one of Roy's comedy songs. During the number, a chorus line of dancing pigs would pass back and forth through the frame. Roy's double-takes were perfect.

Things were running like clockwork, and at this point I must say that none of it would have been possible without the excellent WLAC stage crew and brilliant technical people: Joe Hostettler in the control room, Larry Sullivan on audio, and Reid Skinner, our wizard in the tape room. What a great surprise to find such eager, proficient people operating in a tiny local station in the bowels of the country.

We also had our amazing director, Bill Davis. Not only was his direction faultless and professional, but his calm demeanor and general good humor won the admiration of both cast and crew. They happily did everything he asked of them, including extremely truncated lunch hours at a nearby cafeteria, aptly named Speedies.

As an added attraction during the musical segments, Roy Clark had recently recorded a song called "Yesterday, When I Was Young," and it turned out to be a smash hit just as we began taping. Talk about good omens.

* * *

The taping of the comedy segments began the following Monday, and for the first week things went along as smoothly as had the musical numbers. The talent was getting along nicely. Of course, they didn't have much choice, due to the size of the station. There was just one dressing room for the women and one for the men. Of course, they all mingled together in the tiny cafeteria, with coffee and sandwiches available at all hours from dispensing machines. All egos were checked outside the front door—there was no room for them inside—and the whole gang felt like one big happy family.

We started the comedy segments with Archie Campbell's routines in the barber shop set at one corner of the studio, and Gordie Tapp in the general store in the other corner. We writers laughed heartily at all the routines, joined by the crew who found the material genuinely funny. This was a big help to make the laughter sound natural when we added laugh tracks back in L.A. Listening to the shows today, you would swear we had a huge audience.

Among the most memorable of all the comedy sequences we taped that first summer were the thirty Old Philosopher spots with Gordie Tapp. For each of them, Gordie would walk through a door onto our porch set dressed in a white frock coat and a wide brimmed straw hat. He would then spout some truly ridiculous piece of mock philosophy, as Frank Peppiatt waited eagerly off-camera to knock Gordie's hat off with a rubber chicken. Frank took great pride in the variety and ferocity of each hit, sometimes causing the hat to spin through the air as many as three times after each whack. At one point, the beak of the chicken almost knocked one of Gordie's eyes out, but he didn't complain. Like all of us that summer, he would do anything for a laugh.

We decided to tape the Cornfield segments last, partly because it was our biggest set and the full-studio backdrop was still being painted. The other reason was that we wanted the entire cast to appear in the Cornfield, and we were still hoping to find at least one more country comic as genuine as those people sitting in the pews at the Opry.

We just couldn't imagine who it might be.

# 8

# A STAR IS BORN

One morning, Frank and I were having breakfast at the Holiday Inn coffee shop when a local agent came to our table with an extremely large man in tow. The man was wearing bib overalls and carrying a cane, walking with a pronounced limp. The agent introduced his client as Junior Samples, who had just driven in from Cumming, Georgia, to see if he could get on our show.

Junior certainly looked comical enough, with his big beaming face and mischief in his eyes. However, when he sat down and started speaking, his Georgia accent was so thick and he talked so fast that we couldn't understand a word he was saying. The agent, acting as interpreter, explained that Junior would have come a lot sooner except for the fact that his son got his leg caught under a tractor, which Junior had lifted up to set him free.

Following this display of amazing strength, he dropped the tractor on his knee causing him to be unable to walk for several days. We were invited to touch Junior's injured knee to see how hot it was. Truth is, it felt like a smelting furnace. We figured that any man who could lift a tractor, let alone drive hundreds of miles with an injury like that and still walk, certainly deserved an audition.

After breakfast, we took Junior to the studio and asked Director Bill Davis to put him on camera. We picked one of the one-liners from the cue cards and asked him to read it for us so we could see how he looked on the tube. We rushed back to the control room to watch the result. We had given him one of our longer jokes, which he stumbled through— slowly reading the card as best he could with only a third-grade education and ending up with most endearing smile I've ever seen on television. Our instincts about him that day were right, and when the shows went on the air, Junior Samples was *Hee Haw*'s biggest comedy sensation.

Luckily, Davis had caught the audition on tape, and it became Junior's first appearance on the very first show. In case you missed it, the joke was: "To get into show business, you just put a bunch of marbles in your mouth and start talking. The first thing you know, a marble'll come out, and by the time you lose all your marbles you're a star."

In Junior's case it was his third-grade reading ability slowing him down so everybody could understand him that made him a star. Of course, that big beaming face and bashful manner certainly didn't hurt. In the weeks to come, we had great fun putting difficult words on the cue cards for him to wrestle with. The results were always hilarious.

That first day with Junior in the studio, we knew we had a keeper. We booked a room for him at the Holiday Inn and told him he would be a regular on the show. I don't think he quite understood what that meant. At the end of the day's shooting, Bill Davis announced on the intercom that it was a wrap and everybody could go home. The next morning, when the cast assembled in the studio, Junior was missing.

We called the hotel and were told that he never checked in. We finally tracked him down at his home in Cumming, Georgia, and told him he was needed in the studio.

"I wish I'd known that," he replied. "The man said we could all go home, so that's what I did. This here is my home."

It seemed obvious that Junior had no concept of what we were doing. We explained that this was a network television series, that he would be a part of it, and that he would have to stay in Nashville for the next few weeks. He still seemed a bit confused.

"Are you gonna pay me for it?" he asked.

When we told him what he would be paid, Junior was stunned.

"That's a heck of a lot more than I'd make moonshinin'," he said. "I'll be there as quick as I can get my boots on." He arrived that afternoon all ready to go, still not realizing that not only fortune but fame lay ahead for Alvin "Junior" Samples.

\* \* \*

We kept checking with Rita Scott to see how much material we were amassing. Unfortunately, the musical numbers had taken a lot less time than we had planned, so we needed a lot more comedy.

Frank and I were sharing "The Dolly L. Wilson Suite" at the Holiday Inn. It consisted of two bedrooms and a large living room which we used as an office to accommodate all us writers as we churned out page after page of new material. A large, framed portrait of a placid elderly woman, who we assumed to be Dolly L. Wilson, hung prominently on one wall staring at us as we frantically churned out new segments. Needless to say, Ms. Wilson soon acquired a goatee and a moustache courtesy of a big black grease pencil supplied by our two bright young cue card guys, Tom Lutz and Stan Ascough, who were soon to join our writing staff. We never did find out who Dolly was, but as the days wore on we came to detest the old crone whose placid smile we now considered a nasty smirk.

During these frenzied sessions, we writers came up with a lot of new segments including Archie Campbell's "Doctor" spot with its animated skeleton, and the board fence that would whack anyone who did a really stupid "Whatta ya get when you cross a kangaroo with an elephant?" kind of joke.

Jack Burns became our hero one morning when he came in with 24 episodes of a goofy *Hee Haw* soap opera that he had devised and written through the previous night. It was called "The Culhanes of Cornfield County." It starred Junior, Grandpa, Gordie, and Lulu as the lunatic Culhanes, and featured such unlikely events as rubber tire storms. These vignettes were my own personal favorites that first season.

On the first show, we fade in on the Culhanes seated side by side on a couch in an old Victorian living room, all staring straight ahead with no expressions whatsoever. They each have old-fashioned dial telephones in their laps.

In a voice-over, the announcer tells us that as we look in on them today, the Culhanes are making their annual telephone call.

Cousin Gordie says: "Hello. Is Grandpa there?"

"Yep. I'm here," says Grandpa.

"Is Lulu there?"

"I'm here. I'm on the extension. Is Junior there?"

**"The Culhanes of Cornfield County"**—(left to right) Gordie Tapp ("Cousin Clem"), Junior Samples ("Junior"), Grandpa Jones ("Grandpa"), and Lulu Roman ("Lulu"), 1969.

"I'm here. Keep talkin'. It's your nickel," says Junior.

"How are you all?" Gordie wants to know.

"Fine ... fine," says everyone else.

Then Grandpa says, "Well, I'm gonna hang up now. But I'll see you all in Baltimore on the 13th."

"Are you gonna be in Baltimore on the 13th?" says Gordie.

"No, but I'll be in Washington with a huge telescope."

The announcer says, "Tune in next time, when we'll hear Cousin Lulu say..."

"There's an alligator in my washing machine."

To which Cousin Junior replies: "Is my alligator dry yet?"

It may have been a bit hip for the show but—to his everlasting credit—Junior was the only one of the four to immediately get the joke.

Grandpa Jones further eased our load by offering to tell the cast one of his funny stories each week, as well as country-style menus introduced by the cast yelling, "HEY, GRANDPA! WHAT'S FOR SUPPER?" Whatever Grandpa said was always a keeper. As writer George Yanok puts it, "Grandpa was a classic example of a comic who says things funny, as opposed to comics who merely say funny things."

**A behind-the-scenes look at how The Culhanes was taped when John Aylesworth visited the set.**

We still hadn't quite figured out what to do with Stringbean, Grandpa's best friend. He was a tall, skinny, mournful-looking man, who wore a costume with its belt around the knees to accentuate his beanpole appearance. He certainly looked funny, so we decided to make him a scarecrow in the Cornfield making wry remarks about the corny jokes. It worked out just fine.

* * *

It wasn't all work and no play for our group of harried writers. We enjoyed many pleasant evenings of laughter and relaxation in the Holiday Inn cocktail lounge, sullied only by the occasional presence of the production staff from the *Johnny Cash Show*, which was currently taping its summer series at the Ryman Auditorium. They were experiencing a lot of problems in the old building, such as cameras falling through the Ryman's ancient floor, and took out their frustrations by taunting us as "hillbilly bait" and "corn huskers."

"We're a classy show," declared their producer. "When we go on the air this summer, we'll bury you guys!"

Unfortunately, most of our cast and crew agreed. They considered the *Johnny Cash Show* to be an important event and tried to catch every taping. They really had no idea what we planned to make out of all the silly foolishness going on in the tiny studio at WLAC.

Shortly before we were scheduled to shoot the Cornfield, CBS vice-president Perry Lafferty called from Los Angeles to say he planned to visit us in Nashville. Apparently,

Tom Baker, president of WLAC, had called to complain that one member of our group, "a gentleman of the Hebraic persuasion," was meddling with their financial department. He was obviously referring to Al Simon, whose job was to protect us financially.

When we asked Al what was going on, he explained that we were being double- and sometimes triple-billed for almost every item. We were being robbed blind! Al knew we had our hands full, so he had gone directly to Tom Baker to complain which had led to Baker calling the CBS vice-president to silence this impudent hawkshaw.

Perry was looking forward to the trip, not only to calm down the larcenous Mr. Baker but to see how the show was going. Since Lafferty was always delightful company, we looked forward to his arrival.

When we informed Baker of Lafferty's impending visit, and that he was a *very* good friend of ours, the billings miraculously dropped to their proper level, and it was announced that Mr. Baker was planning a gala celebration for the visiting dignitary—a sumptuous party to be held in the penthouse ballroom of a downtown private club. There would be ice sculptures of our trademark donkey along with exotic dishes hitherto unheard of in Tennessee.

We went to Reid Skinner in the tape room to arrange our own surprise for Lafferty in the form of a short presentation reel of what the show would look like when it was edited. Reid was ready and willing, despite the limited editing facilities at his command, and together we came up with an impressive 10-minute demo.

Not only did the demo move with the speed of a bullet, it looked absolutely astounding with the great sets of Gene McAvoy, brilliantly lit by Leard Davis, and under the artful direction of Bill Davis. We also used some of our animated bits, plus a few of the pieces we had filmed in L.A., including McCormick and Lulu's romantic classic; one of our segues using Burma Shave style signs; and even yours truly jumping out of an outhouse dressed as Superman.

When we gave the cast a preview of the edited demo, they finally understood what we were doing. They all cheered, and suddenly the Cash show wasn't the biggest thing in town.

Nothing could stop us now, we thought, but storm clouds were looming on the horizon.

# 9

# THE BIG PARTY

---

*"Can I help you, sir?" asked the waiter, standing at an elegant buffet table
with his carving knife poised over an eight-pound filet mignon.*
*"Naw, that'll do just fine," Junior replied, sinking his fork into the meat and
hefting the entire slab onto his plate.*

---

Perry Lafferty, vice-president and head of West Coast programming for CBS, arrived in Nashville early on a Friday morning. He had been an important part of my life since 1958, when I first met him in New York. I have never known anyone quite as witty and wise.

Lafferty had worked his way through the ranks at CBS beginning in the 1930s. Born in Davenport, Iowa—but made in Manhattan—he had come to New York as a talented young musician. Soon he'd become a successful arranger-conductor for many of the networks' top radio shows. When television arrived, Lafferty put down his baton and became the director of countless live television dramas before finally becoming a producer of musical-variety shows.

In 1958, director Norman Jewison and I were imported from Toronto to New York by CBS. Norman, the first to be hired by the Tiffany Network, had been Canada's top TV director, and his first assignment in New York was to direct *Your Hit Parade*. Since I had written the Canadian version of that show for three years, Norman suggested I join him on the show. CBS agreed, and we both were blessed with the good fortune of having Perry Lafferty as the show's producer.

Lafferty was patient, kind, and always helpful in the ways of a giant network. From my point of view, I was most impressed by his appreciation of writers, especially in the pressure-cooker of a weekly live television show. His words should be engraved in stone as the mantra for all writers who have deadlines: "DO YOU WANT IT GOOD OR DO YOU WANT IT WEDNESDAY?"

In a way, Lafferty was responsible for *Hee Haw* the day he made it possible to reunite the team of Peppiatt and Aylesworth in 1959. That spring, *Your Hit Parade* had proven such a success that CBS wanted to keep our entire production team together for a one-hour summer variety series starring Andy Williams.

Since Norman Jewison had directed many of our shows in Toronto as Canada's first television comedy team in the early 1950s, which we wrote as well as performed, he suggested we team up again as writers for Andy's new show. If Lafferty had said no, we wouldn't have been picking him up at the airport in Nashville that day. Happily, he had agreed, Andy's show was a big hit, and the rest is history.

We decided to give Lafferty a brief tour of Nashville before heading for the studio.

With his musical background, he was excited to be in "Music City, USA," even after we informed him that—after insurance and Bible publishing—the music business placed a poor third. We started our tour with "Music Row," a fairly short street lined with plain three-story brick buildings which housed all the record companies.

The story goes that a man named Owen Bradley had a house on that street in the early fifties, with an adjacent Quonset hut which he turned into Nashville's first recording studio. Many of country's greatest hits were recorded in that studio, which became widely known as "Owen Bradley's Barn." Over the next few years, Bradley is often credited with creating the famous "Nashville Sound."

Legend has it that the acoustics were so perfect in that little hut that when the big recording companies started to spring up along the street, Columbia Records decided to construct their building around Owen Bradley's Barn, taking care to keep it exactly as it was when all those great records were cut.

It was said they even went so far as not emptying the ash trays of butts that might have been smoked by Hank Williams, or disturbing half-full coffee cups that could have touched the lips of Patsy Cline. It was thought remotely possible that disturbing anything in that hut could diminish those great acoustics. I never did find out if any of that was true, but it sure made a hell of a yarn.

After swinging by the state capitol and the Parthenon, we stopped at the mother church of country music, the Ryman Auditorium. Lafferty was mightily impressed by the grand old building, having listened to the Opry in his youth when WSM's powerful signal reached all the way to Davenport, Iowa.

Finally, after having lunch at a place called Irelands, renowned for its delicious "Steak 'n Biscuits," and giving Lafferty a chuckle by driving past the Goo Goo billboard, we arrived at WLAC.

We had given everybody the afternoon off to get ready for the big party that night, so the first floor was pretty much deserted. When he saw the studio, Lafferty was predictably amazed that we could actually shoot a big variety show in a space that small. We then amazed him further by taking him to the tape room and showing him our sample reel.

"Fellas," he said, "I think you've got a hit. Nobody's ever seen anything quite like this. Congratulations!"

Having made our day with his effusive reaction, we then took him upstairs to the executive offices where we introduced him to Tom Baker and his aides. They did everything but genuflect in the presence of a genuine vice-president from CBS in Hollywood. We soon slipped away, assuming that Lafferty would enjoy a pleasant afternoon of Southern groveling, and headed back to the Holiday Inn for a pleasant nap before dressing up for the huge fete WLAC had planned for their distinguished guest.

* * *

The party began at 7:30 that evening. It was indeed an elegant setting to honor Lafferty's visit. There wasn't a haystack in sight, and the glistening ice sculptures of our *Hee Haw* donkey were the only evidence of the humble country show that was the sole purpose of the CBS V.P. coming to Nashville. To his credit, Tom Baker had invited all the stage crew and technicians along with the cast. Everyone was dressed to the nines, and even Junior was wearing his best pair of overalls. Evidently, he only owned two, and these were the ones he reserved for Sundays and special events.

White-gloved waiters were everywhere, ready to carve choice cuts of filet mignon from behind steaming tables laden with silver receptacles containing the finest dishes ever seen below the Mason-Dixon Line. This was indeed to be an august occasion, but this was still April and our hard-working cast and crew were ready to raise some hell.

The evening began splendidly before the booze began to flow. I had told Tom Baker the day before that Lafferty's favorite tipple was Cutty Sark Scotch, and now there was so much of it prominently displayed at the open bar that the only thing missing was a bag-piper. Since most of the guests drank bourbon, Lafferty was in for a hell of a night. And since the bourbon was just as plentiful as the Scotch, everybody was ready for a real hoot. Besides, for most of the guests it was a real novelty to be swigging high-class hooch of choice out of cut-glass crystal tumblers.

The biggest surprise of the evening was the news that Archie Campbell was bringing his wife. Everyone knew that Archie was married, but no one had ever actually seen Mrs. Campbell. Since Archie had a roving eye and was usually seen squiring adoring young cuties, it was a pretty good bet that Mrs. Campbell rarely saw Archie. Old Arch must have been close to 60, so we all assumed that his wife would be a matronly woman who spent her lonely evenings knitting booties for their grandchildren.

When Mr. and Mrs. Campbell finally made their grand entrance at about eight o'clock, a hush fell over the room. Everyone was astounded to discover that Archie's wife was a statuesque young beauty who easily could have been his daughter.

Of course, it was all a hoax—Archie had planned it with Jack Burns as the target. Burns, as much a ladies' man as Archie, had dubbed himself "the King of Hearts," and Archie had enlisted his beautiful ersatz bride as bait to lure Burns into a trap. The fake Mrs. Campbell had been instructed to flirt with "the King of Hearts," which would then lead to an intimate tryst later that evening. Archie would then burst in on them as the enraged husband and challenge Burns to a duel. We were all in on the gag, and couldn't wait to see what happened.

Meanwhile, since Buck Owens was the only member of the whole *Hee Haw* gang who didn't drink and wasn't likely to stay through the night, he was the first to be intro-duced to the guest of honor. This was followed—according to protocol—by his co-star Roy Clark, who *did* drink and was likely to be among the last to leave. After Roy Clark, the next cast member to be introduced was Junior Samples. Perry was anxious to meet our comic discovery after seeing the demo tape.

"Junior," said Tom Baker. "I'd like you to meet our vice-president."

Mightily impressed by a man in such a lofty position, Junior gripped Lafferty's hand and said, "I'm proud to meet you, Mr. Agnew!"

By the time everybody had been introduced to Lafferty, and a lot of the food and drink had been consumed, everybody was really starting to loosen up. Out came the guitars and banjoes, and the old City Club really started to rock.

By midnight, several members of our cast and crew had passed out. McAvoy's head painter, the crazy little guy who looked like Barney Fife yet insisted on calling himself Vern Gagne after the famous wrestler, sustained a broken nose for drunkenly insulting Tom Baker. The ice sculptures were lying melting on the floor, about 18 cases of booze had been consumed, Lafferty was reeling around speaking with a twang, and what was left of the entrees served as ammunition for a monumental food fight.

In other words, a wonderful time was had by all.

Fortunately, everybody would have the weekend to rest up. First thing on Monday, we would start taping our very first Cornfield for two full days. It was our biggest set, and Lord knew how that was going to turn out. We'd just keep our fingers crossed.

* * *

Oh, by the way, I suppose you're wondering how Archie Campbell's practical joke turned out. Well, it was such a great party that nobody claims to remember a damn thing about it. However, I'll end this chapter with a different sort of surprise.

During that summer of 1969, the switchboard operator at WLAC was Oprah Winfrey!

# 10

# THE CORNFIELD

*"I do believe that's the worst joke I ever heard."—Stringbean*

On the Monday morning following the big party, we walked into the studio and saw the Cornfield on stage for the very first time. It looked just the way we'd hoped it would. McAvoy and his crew had done a magnificent job.

Our cue card guys, Tom and Stan, had been up all night to finish printing all the jokes. There must have been at least a thousand of them for the twelve shows, and the big white cards were stacked all over the studio.

A very nice young lady named Sandy Liles had come to the show with Cathy Baker to work in the paint shop, but Sandy was soon promoted to probably the toughest job on the show: keeping track of everything that was taped and cataloguing each individual piece by computer code number.

Computer editing was still in the Stone Age back then, so Liles had to write down code numbers for every song, comedy sketch, one-liner, blooper, and outtake so we would have some hope of putting it all together when we got back to Los Angeles. The Cornfield would be a nightmare to keep track of—we intended to just keep the tape rolling and catch absolutely every mistake or foul-up in our never-ending search for comedy gold.

We still hadn't quite figured out what to do with Stringbean on the show. He sure looked funny, and he could deliver a comedy line with the best of them, but so far we hadn't found the right spot for him. The Cornfield would be his chance to shine. Every cornfield has a scarecrow, and Stringbean's lanky stature and his mournful look made him ideal for the role. Somebody suggested we put a puppet crow on his shoulder. McAvoy provided the crow, with a moveable beak, so all we needed now was a good, harsh "Caw" to start the Cornfield segment and accent the jokes.

Just about everybody in the studio had a crack at it, but nothing sounded just right. Even Nobel Bear, who could sound like anything from a diesel train to a baying wolf, couldn't cut it.

Finally, Bill Davis came roaring out of the control room, walked to the mike boom, and instantly gave us the perfect "Caw." We all cheered and applauded. Davis took an elaborate bow and his "Caw" was part of the show for the next 25 years. He and I often exchange e-mails these days, and when I asked him for his favorite *Hee Haw* memory, this incredibly talented director simply replied, "The thing I'm most proud of is to have been the voice of that angry crow on Stringbean's shoulder in the cornfield!"

When the full cast arrived, they were impressed with the set and raring to go. Everyone was bright and cheerful, looking forward to a day that ought to be lots of fun. Bill

Davis explained the concept. The members of the cast were to crouch down behind the cornstalks and wait for their cues to pop up and deliver a joke, either individually or in pairs, then duck back down again.

Everything went perfectly that first Cornfield day. The jokes were all funny and everyone was having a ball. The highlight was Junior Samples trying to say the word "trigonometry" in a two-man joke with Roy Clark. Since it was the punch line to the joke, poor Junior tried his best to get it right, but every time Roy gave him the straight line, Junior just couldn't say that word properly. We just kept the cameras rolling and couldn't have been happier because a 30-second joke spun into a five minute classic routine, with Roy breaking up about 20 times as Junior battled valiantly to say "trigonometry" in the punch line.

Except for a brief lunch break at good old Speedies, we just kept going at a rapid pace all day with every one of our jolly jesters in a wonderful mood, popping up and down among the stalks and delivering at least 100 really funny kernels of corn.

My personal favorite, which to this day I consider the perfect *Hee Haw* joke, was when Grandpa Jones was asked, "Pa, did I hear you hold your pigs up to the tree so they can eat apples off the branches one at a time? Don't you think that's an awful waste of time?" To which Grandpa reasonably replied, "Well ... what's time to a pig?"

At the end of the day, everything had gone better than we could ever have hoped. If things went as well the next and final Cornfield day, we would be in hog heaven. Then, we could call it a wrap and head back to L.A. with all the tapes and start editing.

Alas, this was not to be.

# 11

# THE CORNFIELD—PART TWO

---

*"I ain't felt this sore since I fell off Bailey's barn."—Junior Samples*

---

As the second day of taping in the Cornfield began, it appeared it would not be the joyous occasion we had experienced on the first. We hadn't taken into account the various ages, shapes and physical capabilities possessed by our band of country comics. When a person is not used to crouching down and hopping up repeatedly for an eight-hour day, such activity tends to take a toll on one's back and leg muscles, especially if you're grossly overweight like Junior or your name is Grandpa.

As our cast hobbled into the studio after the previous day of Cornfield calisthenics, their groans and moans were heartbreaking. It was obvious there would be no more crouching behind the stalks this day.

Happily, our ever-enterprising stage manager, Jimmy Norton, came up with a brilliant solution.

"Stools!" he cried. "We need a whole bunch of low stools!"

Our cast suddenly brightened. It was as if Jimmy had invented the wheel, although one would have wished he'd invented it a day earlier. As the stools were produced by the dozens, our crippled cast was mightily relieved that there would be no more hunkering down below the corn stalks. They could all sit and relax until their cue to pop up, or at least rise as quickly as their aching joints would allow, and deliver their lines.

Meanwhile, back at the Holiday Inn, a "billing" war that had been going on for some time continued unabated, with Sam Lovullo as referee. Roy Clark's manager, Jim Halsey, insisted that his client's last name come first at the top of the show because alphabetically C came before Buck's O. Owens' representative, Jack McFadden, argued that Buck should have top billing since he was the bigger star. Halsey countered that Roy was funnier, to which McFadden retorted that Buck sold more records. Halsey shot back that records don't get laughs and this was, after all, a show called *Hee Haw*.

They went on like this for days on end, until it was finally agreed that Buck would have top billing on the first show, and from then on we would reverse the order on each alternate episode.

Luckily I was the announcer, and when the first show aired, even though Buck came first, I stretched out Roy's name for extra emphasis: "Welcome to *Hee Haw*, starring Buck Owens and Roooooooy Clark." All parties agreed that it sounded just right, and that's the way it remained for the next 25 years.

As it so often happens in show business, both Buck and Roy were apparently blissfully unaware of their managers' manipulations. They were simply doing their duty in the

Cornfield on our final day of shooting, with no other thought than to finally go home and rest their weary bones.

A few of the musical guests had opted to stay over for some of the comedy. One of these was Sheb Wooley, who had already taped a few numbers for us from several of his successful novelty albums. Sheb was a versatile performer, working as an actor in a long trail of Western movies topped by *High Noon*. He then turned to music and recorded "Purple People Eater," one of the biggest hits of 1958, before returning to acting as a regular on the television series *Rawhide*. For the past few years, he'd had great success with a series of albums as a comedy drunk named Ben Colder, doing parodies of current hit songs.

During a break on that last Cornfield day, Sheb came ambling over to us—after all those Westerns, he was a hell of an ambler—and told us he had written some theme music for *Hee Haw*. Since we hadn't even thought of an instrumental theme, we asked him to play it for us. He whipped out a tape player and switched it on.

The music sounded perfect to open the show as our animated donkey burst through the corn, rolling his eyes and braying. The lyric was nothing more than "Hee-hee-hee-haw-haw" with a blistering banjo background, but it seemed to fit perfectly. We immediately agreed to use it, and Sheb looked mighty pleased as he ambled off to register it with BMI so he could be paid every time it appeared on the show. That could amount to a pretty sizeable hunk of change when you consider it kicked off 26 shows a year for about 35 years.

We soon learned the rascal had sold us a 40-year-old song written by Jimmie Rodgers, called "Blue Yodel #8," later known to everyone south of the Mason/Dixon line as "Mule Skinner Blues." Old Sheb had pulled a fast one on us city slickers, but what the heck. Jimmie Rodgers had long since departed this world, so since it was Sheb who brought it to us, *Hee Haw* got itself a dandy theme. We're very thankful.

At five o'clock sharp that afternoon, the final Cornfield joke was taped. We all cheered, hugged and hoped we could get together again soon if the show was a hit.

We knew we couldn't afford a wrap party that could possibly top the event at the City Club, so we settled on picking up all the tabs at the Holiday Inn bar that night. It turned out to be a heck of an evening, with lots of laughs, slobbering pledges of undying friendship, no end of lively "pickin' and grinnin'," and a bar bill that would have bought a brand new Winnebago.

* * *

The following morning, we started packing up for the trip home from WLAC to CBS Television City. We had to transport at least 10 country miles of two-inch video tape on dozens of reels the size of wagon wheels. Sandy Liles' meticulous notes, without which we would have been totally lost, were under lock and key in a metal attaché case which we seriously considered handcuffing to the wrist of Sam Lovullo.

Somehow, we got it all loaded onto a plane. In 1969, there were no metal detectors or Homeland Security guards. If there were, with all our exotic tapes and equipment, we never would have gotten out of Nashville.

And so, on a late May afternoon, as our plane rose slowly into the west, we all crossed our fingers and toes in the hope that this whole crazy trip had not been in vain.

# PUTTING IT ALL TOGETHER

---

*"Observing one of those early Hee Haw editing sessions was like watching snails mate."—Perry Lafferty*

---

Our precious cargo of video tapes arrived safely in Los Angeles, along with all the voluminous accompanying electronic coding files without which there would be no show. Those thick computer read-outs contained the details and timing of every sketch, one-liner, cornfield joke, and piece of music that had been recorded during those wild and crazy weeks in Nashville. Each piece had been graded by either Frank or me from A+ to D based—if not on quality, then certainly on "funny." We all agreed that the first show would consist entirely of A+ material.

Bill Davis, *Hee Haw*'s indispensable director, took it upon himself to do the rundown for show #1, principally because he had been present for every moment of the shooting, including each fragment of incidental musical intros and play-offs. He certainly had a lot to work with.

Represented in that daunting pile of video tapes were approximately:

100 one-liners,
at least 40 General Store sketches,
12 Barber Shop routines,
24 episodes of "The Culhanes of Cornfield County,"
25 KORN radio spots,
24 Grandpa Jones stories,
24 "Pickin' and Grinnin'" sequences with Buck and Roy and the cast,
30 "Doc" Campbell gags,
40 board fence jokes,
all kinds of animated cartoon animals like the dancing pigs,
30 Old Philosopher segments,
40 Moonshiners,
50 sound effects from Nobel Bear,
26 filmed Outhouse sight gags,
about 30 Schoolhouse jokes,
32 "Pffft You Were Gone" choruses with Archie and Gordie,
about 30 "Eefin'" quickies with Riddle and Phelps,
sundry sight gags and guest intros shot outdoors on film,
26 Grandpa's menus ("YUM, YUM!"),
24 opening songs with the entire cast,
24 songs by the Hager Twins,
several individual numbers by other cast members,
at least 30 songs by our guest stars,
and over 200 Cornfield jokes.

For that first run-down, Davis would look up a specific A+ item in the electronic files, assign it to the opening show, mark it used, and go on to the next item. This was the system he would use for the remaining episodes, and it boded well for the rest of the series that few of the pieces had rated less that a B+.

With less than two weeks to go until our first air date of June 15, Davis descended into the bowels of CBS Television City with a completed run-down to begin editing. Not only was *Hee Haw* a brand new show, but it marked the beginning of a bold new editing experience.

Luckily, the editor assigned to our show was not only excellent but willing to try anything. His name was Marco Zappia, one of the few people connected to *Hee Haw* to actually win an Emmy for his work on our show. Marc was familiar with the new EECO system, which was a big plus, since it had never been used before on an entire series. It would be a TV first!

The first thing Marc did was thread up a blank master reel which, if all went well, would become our first show, on one machine. Then he placed the reel of tape containing our first item on the machine next to it and started spinning through it until the computer stopped it at the requested code number—which should have been the opening animation, and which indeed it was. We were thrilled—the coding system actually worked!

A cheer went up from our little group, which included the assistant director, Dick Harwood, and a charming young production assistant named Ellen Brown, who now had charge of Sandy Liles' meticulous notes. Marc just smiled patiently like the pro he was and said quietly, "I knew it'd work." Everyone was excited. We were making television history! We were the Wright Brothers of the Idiot Box! (We TV people tend to get a bit carried away, in case you hadn't noticed.)

Once the opening donkey logo animation was successfully transferred to the master tape from the animation reel, it was then rewound to free the machine for another reel of tape containing all the opening songs with the full cast. That was spun through to the code number indicated in the rundown to be then transferred to the master. It was "Johnny B. Goode," our very first musical number on our very first show, featuring Buck Owens and the whole *Hee Haw* gang.

This was arduous, time-consuming work. It often took just as long to spin through one of the dozens of reels to arrive at a five-minute song by a guest star, or an eight-minute Barber Shop routine, as it did to locate a three-second one-liner.

Frank and I dropped in from time to time to see how things were going, but at that point there wasn't much we could contribute. Perry Lafferty was also an occasional visitor, always with an encouraging word followed by a stifled yawn. Watching tape being edited was hardly a spectator sport. At that point, Lafferty was not only our biggest fan, he was our only fan.

It took a full week to assemble that first show. It's a tribute to the unstinting devotion of Bill Davis, Ellen Brown, and Dick Harwood—not to mention the skill of Marc Zappia—that it didn't take a full month. The system was primitive, to be sure, but if we had been consigned to still making splices with razor blades it couldn't have been done at all.

\* \* \*

There was another new kid on the block that spring. A few machines away in the CBS editing room, a new half-hour sitcom was being prepared for a summer tryout. While we were busily making history, it was that other little show that was getting all the buzz. Since it was done in front of a live audience, it didn't even take much editing.

When they gave us a sneak preview of a rough edit one night, we understood immediately what all the excitement was about. The show was *All in the Family*.

\* \* \*

Now that our first *Hee Haw* was assembled, there was one more important step to be taken before we could present it to the network for broadcast. We would have to go into an audio studio to add additional musical play-ons, play-offs, sound effects, the voice-over announcer, and finally a laugh track to mix with the reactions of our crew in the studio so *Hee Haw* would sound as if it were taped in front of a large audience at the Grand Ole Opry itself. This process was referred to in the business as "sweetening," a procedure that would enhance comedy shows suffering little or no studio audience response.

This final enhancement could handily be achieved by bringing in the much demeaned "laugh machine." Developed by an audio engineer named Charley Douglass in the 1950s as a solution for filmed comedy shows lacking sufficient mirth, his laugh machine was a compact black box that stood two feet in height and had a keyboard resembling that of a typewriter. Each key represented a particular audience response, ranging from a titter to a hearty belly laugh, elicited from audiences of various sizes.

It has been said that Charley obtained these tracks chiefly from audience reactions to sight gags, unencumbered by the spoken word, from such likely sources as *I Love Lucy*, *The Jackie Gleason Show*, and the mother-lode of speechless comedy recorded by Charley at live performances by world-famous mime Marcel Marceau.

But laughter wasn't the sole commodity on Charley's machine. Several keys were devoted to that which all performers strive ... APPLAUSE ... ranging from smatterings to stirring ovations. As time went on, several other reactions were added to Charley's repertoire, such as expectant "Ooohs," sympathetic "Awws," and even a groan or two.

To this day, the laugh machine remains a standard element in the production of comedy shows, and even though many of the tracks have been up-dated and no doubt digitized, several of the originals survive. This leads to the ghostly thought that audiences from the early fifties, now long dead, are still guffawing at the sitcoms of today.

As is often the case, Charley was not the best operator of his own invention. Having worked with him several times before, I found him to be an extremely pleasant man, but when he sat down at the keyboard Charley was extremely heavy fingered. This may have made him Bob Hope's favorite "sweetener," due to Hope's demand that every joke be a real gut-buster, but if you wanted your show to sound as if a real audience was reacting to it, one of Charley's employees was the man to get. His name was John Pratt, and he played the laugh machine as delicately as Yo-Yo Ma does the cello.

Pratt brought that first *Hee Haw* show to vibrant life—as he did practically every one of our shows thereafter—by making it sound as if a large audience in a big studio was having a genuinely good time. In fact, Pratt seemed to be doing just that as he watched the show with a big smile and worked his magic accordingly.

In the early 1980s, Pratt left Los Angeles to fulfill his own personal dream. For years, he had been putting money away to buy and operate a sheep farm in Tasmania. Go figure. He was a happy, gentle man and we all wished him well. I would imagine that somewhere in Tasmania there are some very happy sheep.

We delivered the completed tape of our first show to the network almost a full week before its scheduled airdate. Lafferty immediately shipped it off to New York, where it received mixed reactions. There were some grumblings about "that awful backwoods woman singing about a 'squaw being on the warpath'" and that strange old man with the banjo declaring it was the instrument for him.

We quickly explained that the backwoods woman happened to be the Queen of Country Music, and one should never insult royalty. As for Grandpa, it was nasty to criticize the elderly. Such nit-picking was unimportant, fortunately, since our friend Mike Dann, head of programming, loved the show.

* * *

Two days before that first show hit the air, Nick Vanoff called an emergency meeting of all four partners in Yongestreet Productions. He had a troubling announcement to make. *The Hollywood Palace* had been cancelled by the ABC network. Naturally we were stunned.

*The Palace* had been on the air for six successful years and was generally accepted as one of the classiest variety shows on television. Emanating from the refurbished and re-named El Capitan Theater in Hollywood, this star-studded one-hour variety show featured a different guest host each week, including multiple appearances by such show-business luminaries as Fred Astaire, Bing Crosby, Milton Berle, and Jimmy Durante.

The star would introduce an entertaining mix of vaudeville acts and star attractions such as Frank Sinatra, Judy Garland, or The Rolling Stones. Each and every Saturday night, America looked forward to *The Hollywood Palace*, its glittering array of stars, its exciting vaudeville turns, its comedy and musical entertainment, plus—of course—its beautiful "Billboard Girls," one of whom later became famous as Raquel Welch.

It was a crushing blow. Yongestreet had started out with one sophisticated network variety show on the air, and another possible—though hardly as urbane—entry about to begin its summer tryout. We suddenly found ourselves with just one hope for survival. Our fledgling company may have lost its "class," but at least we still had our "ass."

# 13

# *HEE HAW* HITS THE AIR

*"The most irrelevant, stupid and ghastly program in recent history."*—Cecil Smith, Los Angeles Times, *June 1969*

On Sunday, June 15, 1969, at 9 P.M., in the hour formerly occupied by *The Smothers Brothers Comedy Hour, Hee Haw* made its debut on the CBS television network. I threw an opening-night party at my home in Beverly Hills, inviting all my friends in the business to celebrate what Frank and I had created.

At the appointed hour, fortified with liberal amounts of strong drink, my guests could hardly believe what they were seeing. Peppiatt and Aylesworth, urbane authors of wit and whimsy for many of television's most sophisticated variety hours, had finally sold out!

As our once admiring coterie gaped in shocked disbelief at our braying donkey, our chorus line of pigs prancing across the TV screen, and all those bucolic bumpkins uttering rustic wheezes from a cornfield, it became apparent that we were to become pariahs among our peers forevermore.

The following day, television critics all over the country were ruthless in their condemnation of our odious offering. Indeed, they were shocked that such a worthless enterprise could be allowed to befoul the nation's airwaves. After all, it's a critic's duty to protect the public from the kind of mindless programming that defined the "vast wasteland" of television entertainment.

These public defenders certainly did their duty with a vengeance after viewing our show. Here, a few critiques following the debut of our harmless little hour of heartland humor and song:

*"...an outhouse* Laugh-In."—Cleveland Amory, *TV Guide*
*"...possibly the worst show I've ever seen."*—Ann Hodges, *The Houston Chronicle*
*"...the most vile program on television."*—a Nashville viewer.

The words most utilized by television critics around the country were "tripe," "vile," "degrading," and just plain "awful." Most agreed that "CBS ought to be ashamed."

Apparently we had hurt the feelings of an entire nation. Actually, two nations. Even Canada got its licks in. The *Toronto Star*, back in our hometown, printed the nastiest condemnation of all: "Anyone who would watch 'Hee Haw' doesn't deserve to own a television set."

But were we downhearted? You're damned right we were! CBS had given us a golden opportunity to create a show of our own, and we had obviously blown it. We had delivered the biggest TV turkey of all time, and brought shame upon both our mentors at the network and upon ourselves.

Perry Lafferty tried to cheer us up by reminding us that other shows had been panned by the critics, but went on to be successful. "*Gilligan's Island* had terrible reviews, but the public loved it," he told us. "Just wait for the ratings to come out."

This was scant comfort. Never having been a fan of *Gilligan's Island*, I hoped we might be a cut above that equally reviled show. But it was certainly true that if the Nielsen ratings showed that 30 million people were willing to watch grass grow for an hour, it would be a hit. *Gilligan* had stayed on the air for three years due to good ratings—proving, then as now, that critics have very little effect on television audiences.

People will always watch what they want to watch, and in 1969 a show had a much better chance of being sampled. There were only three networks and no cable. We would just have to cross out fingers and hope for the best.

It didn't help our gloomy outlook when CBS announced that the official replacement for *The Smothers Brothers Comedy Hour* in September would be a new variety show hosted by Leslie Uggams, a sprightly young singer whose past TV exposure included a few seasons as a regular on *Sing Along with Mitch*, another successful show abhorred by the critics.

*Sing Along* was a weekly hour-long show featuring a chorus of middle-aged men booming out hoary chestnuts, led by a goateed record producer named Mitch Miller. The viewing audience could read the lyrics at the bottom of the screen and presumably sing along to such "golden oldies" as "Shine On Harvest Moon," a dubious delight leavened only by Miss Uggams' occasional contemporary solo. At least *Gilligan* had jokes.

The fact that terrible shows could become hits didn't alleviate our despair one bit. We considered *Hee Haw* an excellent show that truly deserved to be a hit for what it was. The cast was terrific, the jokes were funny, the music was first-rate, the production values were great, the colorful sets jumped right off the screen due to superlative lighting and technical prowess, the pacing was snappy and the editing was superb. If I do say so myself. If you look at a DVD of the old show at its best, it hasn't aged one bit. It was a technical marvel!

As the days dragged by, we found ourselves becoming increasingly paranoid. Even though Jonathan Winters and Cliff Arquette graciously called to say they enjoyed the show, and wished they could have made it to Nashville to be a part of it, we had the feeling that people were avoiding us in the halls of CBS Television City. They had every reason to. Our fate was sealed. We were doomed, and *Hee Haw* was destined for obscurity on the scrapheap of forgotten television flops. It was all so totally unfair! (Sob!)

At week's end, the ratings finally came out.

# 14

# SURPRISE! WE'RE A HIT!

*"Pure entertainment for America's tired brain."—Neil Hickey,* TV Guide

It was a miracle.

*Hee Haw* was the number one show in the country with an average of 27.3 million viewers! Frank and I had been vindicated. Suddenly, our phones were ringing off the hook, mostly from colleagues who had been ignoring us all week.

Nick Vanoff and Bill Harbach, our partners in Yongestreet Productions, were over-joyed. Due to the untimely demise of *The Hollywood Palace*, and the early critical recep-tion accorded to *Hee Haw*, we thought we had been doomed to be forever showless. Now, with our heads held high, we were back in business with a bona fide hit on the air.

Even some critics were relenting. Neil Hickey of *TV Guide* wrote, "'Hee Haw' is a rapid rural romp of retrogressive rejoinders distilled into idea-free, pure entertainment for America's tired brain." While not exactly a rave, it was certainly a step up from all the pre-vious vitriol.

And *Time* said, "In a TV summer season stolen by Armstrong and Aldren ... [l]ike so much of TV, *Hee Haw* is a show that nobody likes—except the viewers."

That same week, we became official members of the CBS family when we received a very special invitation. The legendary William S. Paley, founder and chairman of the Columbia Broadcasting System, had arranged a big West Coast reception to introduce Bob Wood, who had just been named the new president of the network. Wood was an affable fellow with a shiny dome who greeted his West Coast contingent with warmth and a keen interest in their various projects.

When Lafferty finally introduced us as the fellows responsible for *Hee Haw*, Mr. Wood looked suddenly stricken as his face turned an alarming shade of vermillion. The new president of CBS, it became apparent, hated *Hee Haw* and everything even remotely rural with every fiber of his being. As he was about to embark on a full-blown rant, I inter-jected: "Gee, Mr. Wood, it's only a summer show."

"Thank God for that!" he snapped. We immediately made a quick retreat, not want-ing to spoil the guest of honor's entire evening. I couldn't help but wonder what invective he had reserved for the producers of *The Beverly Hillbillies*. Then again, that show had been a huge hit since 1962, so he probably forced himself to be as nice as pie.

A few minutes later, we were introduced to Mr. Paley, a genial man with snow-white hair and a bearing befitting a true industry legend. He greeted us warmly, and we experi-enced a measure of the poise and aplomb of that great man when he merely winced at the mention of *Hee Haw*.

After congratulating us on the ratings success of our first episode, he wished us well. One could only wonder if the creator of the once high-toned "Tiffany Network," with its current line-up of hillbilly sitcoms, might consider *Hee Haw* to be the last straw. Did the spirits of Ed Murrow and Alistair Cooke haunt his dreams, crying "Shame!"?

Mike Dann, who had flown in from New York with Mr. Paley, caught us just as we were leaving. "Don't get too excited about this week's ratings, fellas," he said. "Wait till next week. That's the key. If you do well next week, then you can start celebrating."

CBS ran promotion spots showing some of the show's most outrageous moments, saying: "The critics are unanimous about *Hee Haw*—but watch anyway."

The following week, when the second ratings book came out, we were still number one! Mike Dann announced from New York that we were the biggest summer hit in the history of broadcasting. When the third week's ratings appeared, Dann was quoted in *Daily Variety* as saying, "We're stuck with a hit. Too bad we can't keep it on the air come September."

Perry Lafferty, however, told us that Dann wanted to keep us in reserve as a mid-season replacement. I could only imagine what Bob Wood might think about that, but you can't argue with success.

* * *

Meanwhile, back at Yongestreet Productions, with dwindling bank accounts due to the miniscule summer budget allotted to *Hee Haw*, Frank and I pressed our two new partners to come up with something to do. Nick Vanoff had heard that Herb Alpert and his partner Jerry Moss (the A and M of A&M Records) wanted to do a television special with The Tijuana Brass based on their latest album, *The Brass Are Comin'*. Since Frank and I had written Alpert's first TV special a couple of years earlier and were well acquainted with Herb and Jerry, we were overjoyed when Vanoff made a deal for Yongestreet to do the special.

The album cover for *The Brass Are Comin'* depicted Herb and the members of the Brass in cowboy outfits standing on an old Western street. In those days, country music was always referred to as Country-Western, accounting for the fact that so many country singers wore cowboy hats. Now, we would have the chance to add some Western to the Country of *Hee Haw*.

In his liner notes for *The Brass Are Comin'*, Herb wrote, "When I was a kid I wanted to be a cowboy and ride into town with my own gang. When I got older I wanted to be a trumpet player and ride into town with my own gang." In the opening sequence of the show, Herb got his wish as he led the members of the Brass, all on horseback, into a Western town in a scene that ended with a wild barroom brawl, featuring just about every stuntman in Hollywood.

Herb had a wonderful time playing cowboy. Dressed entirely in black, with a six-shooter in his holster, he ceased being his usual cheerful self and convincingly became a hard-eyed, monosyllabic gunslinger throughout the entire shoot. It was as if he had turned into a very good-looking, trumpet-playing Billy the Kid.

The special was a great success, and we had utilized the key members of our *Hee Haw* production staff, including Sam Lovullo, Ellen Brown, and our favorite director, Bill Davis. All the critics raved about the show, ensuring that this would be only the first of many quality productions to come from the Yongestreet partners in the years to come.

The Alpert special had been a pleasant and lucrative diversion in that summer of 1969, and *Hee Haw* stayed at the top of the ratings right through to the end of September and the debut of *The Leslie Uggams Show*.

To top everything off, Frank and I were made "Men of the Year" at the Academy of Country Music Awards show in Los Angeles. Glen Campbell and Charley Pride made the presentation. We were now officially a couple of "good old country boys," even though our country was actually Canada.

That summer of 1969 felt like perhaps the best year ever in the careers of Peppiatt and Aylesworth. We were recognized in our new positions as important "country folk"— shucks, no less than the Academy of Country Music had validated us.

We could hardly wait to see what would happen next.

# 15

# HERE WE GO AGAIN

*"Keep your fingers crossed, fellas. I think you're a shoo-in for mid-season."—*
*Mike Dann, senior V.P. of programming for CBS*

*The Leslie Uggams Show* debuted at 9:00 P.M., September 28, Sunday, booting *Hee Haw* into limbo. It was a pleasant variety hour, with lots of singing and dancing and weekly guest stars. What set it apart from most shows of its kind was a continuing comedy sketch called "Sugar Hill," dealing with the lives of a middle-class black family in a large city. It was produced by an old Canadian colleague of ours, Saul Ilson.

The critics were generally kind to the new show, and it looked as if it might be a hit. This did not bode well for the future of *Hee Haw*, so in a fit of childish pique Frank and I sought out Ilson's brand new Rolls Royce in the CBS parking lot and slapped one of our *Hee Haw*–donkey bumper stickers on its rear end.

Ilson was furious and immediately suspected that we were the culprits. He called us the next morning in a rage, informing us that a Rolls Royce was no place for such a cheap trick, and our tawdry sticker may even have damaged its expensive paint job. Our hysterical laughter and lack of remorse only made him more irate, demanding restitution and threatening to sue.

It didn't help when we reminded Ilson of our humble past in Toronto when we all drove second-hand Chevys, and that to own a Rolls Royce you should be royalty or at least wear a monocle. He finally just growled, hung up, and that was the last we heard about it. Looking back, I suppose it was a pretty dumb thing to do, but I still chuckle when I think about it.

The first few weeks of the Uggams show was a bit of a disappointment in the ratings. Despite the quality of the show, it just didn't catch the public's fancy. By mid–October, CBS called and told us to get ready to be back on the air by the end of December with 17 new shows to carry through till June. We negotiated a much better deal for the new episodes, so at least we would make a few bucks this time around. Once again we assembled our writing staff for another marathon session.

Archie and Gordie flew in from Nashville and Toronto, while Jack Burns and George Yanok simply had to drive in from Malibu. We also added our very bright cue card guys from the summer show, Tom Lutz and Stan Ascough, as permanent members of our writing staff. They lived in Los Angeles as well, and we needed all the help we could get.

We all got together at our office early on a Monday morning to start work. Gordie, as always, was a virtual joke machine. Archie, however, who had assured us that he had "a

68

blue million" sure-fire bits, was a little slow coming up with his usual stream of new material. When we asked him why, he simply said: "Hell, fellas. How was I to know we'd be doing more shows?" Being the sly old bird that he was, however, Archie soon reassured us that he had files at home brimming with hilarious jokes that were so old nobody would remember them.

"Remember, boys," he counseled us, "an old joke is brand new if you've never heard it before."

Reluctantly, we let Archie leave to cull through his ancient files. He vowed to produce reams of great material, including 17 top-notch Barber Shop spots, as he rushed out the door to catch an early afternoon flight back to Nashville. The rest of us were left to concentrate on filling all those hours of comedy in the least possible time.

"You fellas didn't actually think everything Archie wrote for the first 12 shows was new, did you?" Gordie said, with a knowing smirk.

"You mean it wasn't?"

"Hell, no. Like he said, an old joke is a new joke if you haven't heard it before."

"Then why did he want to go back to Nashville?"

"Business. He owns a theatre in Gatlinburg where he puts on shows every weekend. He makes a fortune. It's about three hours from Nashville, but it's a heck of a lot farther from L.A."

We were naturally surprised, but in the long run it really didn't matter as long as the jokes were funny. Even if Abe Lincoln had once laughed at a *Hee Haw* joke, that was okay with us.

"Is your stuff new?" we asked Gordie.

"What's the difference? How would you know?" he replied.

We laughed, of course, but it was true. Frank and I, throughout our careers, had always written original material. Our specialty was comedy sketches, not one-liners. We had heard about joke files, but had never actually used one.

Archie and Gordie had a point. Television is a hungry medium, so you do whatever it takes to keep it fed. If the audience doesn't complain, why should we? After all, we had 17 hours of comedy to fill. But old habits are hard to break, so we set about thinking up brand-new comedy segments for the various members of our cast.

All kinds of ideas started flowing as everyone pitched in. By the end of the day, we had settled on a fey country poet named Claude Strawberry for Roy Clark to play; Junior Samples as a hilarious used-car salesman with a lot full of Edsels; our own version of *The Gong Show* with cast members doing awful acts while being pelted with rotten tomatoes and being booed off the stage; The Empty Arms Hotel with Roy as the desk clerk handling goofy complaints from the guests; and more comedy outdoor film shoots—we all agreed there should be more of those.

We knew we could count on Jack Burns to supply plenty of new episodes for "The Culhanes of Cornfield County," and someone had the idea of a classical theatre spot featuring Junior as Hamlet. Jokes and one-liners can be old as the hills, but this original comedy was the stuff that made *Hee Haw* really special.

We wrote as much as we could in the next couple of weeks, but remembering our marathon sessions in the spring of 1969, while ensconced in the Dolly L. Wilson suite, we decided to head down to Nashville. Eschewing the *Super Chief* for lack of time, Peppiatt put his fear of flying in abeyance and we all took a plane. It wasn't as much fun, but it was a heck of a lot faster.

Upon arrival we went straight to WLAC, which was a hive of activity getting ready

**Director Bill Davis reads the palm of Don Harron as Charley Farqueson (left) in "Doc" Campbell's office on the *Hee Haw* stage, 1969.**

for the impending shoot. Sam Lovullo immediately informed us that he had made a deal for our cast and production people to stay at the Ramada Inn, which was a lot closer to the station than our old digs at the Holiday Inn.

This meant that we'd have to forego the Dolly L. Wilson suite and do our writing in a small office across from the tape room at WLAC. Although it was a bit cramped, and we would miss adding facial hair to Ms. Wilson's portrait, this would be somewhat of an advantage. We would be a lot closer to the studio and the various performers into whose mouths we'd be placing whimsical words.

Our first visitor was Grandpa Jones.

"Good to see you again, Pa," I said. "How are you today?"

"Outrageous!" he replied.

That was always Grandpa's reply when asked how he was. I'm sure the reply would have been the same if he had a raging fever. Nonetheless, he seemed troubled and went

*Opposite, top:* **A fun moment in the WLAC studio in 1970. Left to right: Jack Burns, Frank Peppiatt, John Aylesworth, Bernie Brillstein, Jim Hager, John Hager, Bill Davis.** *Opposite, bottom:* **In the WLAC studio with Jack Burns, Frank Peppiatt, and sound-effects wizard Nobel Bear.**

on to explain that he had no idea the show would go beyond the first 12 episodes, and that he was "plumb out of funny stories to tell."

He then suggested that if we could find some of the tales Bob Burns used to tell on the old Bing Crosby show, back in the 1930s, he'd be much obliged. Bob Burns was a rural comedian best known for his invention of a musical instrument he called a "bazooka," a name later famously adopted by the armed forces for a piece of artillery in World War II. It was becoming increasingly apparent that folksy comedy was indeed ageless, perhaps accounting for the fact that Mark Twain and Will Rogers are quoted a lot more often than Leno or Letterman.

We told Grandpa we would see what we could do, and called Bernie Brillstein in Los Angeles to see if he could have somebody look into finding the folksy monologues of Bob Burns. When Bernie asked why we were delving into ancient history, we replied that much of the future material on this show apparently lay in the past.

This was made even more evident a couple of weeks later when Don Harron, who supplied his own material for his KORN newscasts as Charlie Farqueson, told us he had been finding some of his best items from dusty tomes at the university library, containing wit and wisdom as far back as the 17th century. Wouldn't our critics be abashed, I thought, to know that *Hee Haw* had quips dating back to the japes of Ye Olde London's Dr. Johnson in 1764?

Happily, something brand new did come our way that November 1970. Young and shapely former *Petticoat Junction* cast member Gunilla Hutton had been added to our cast, joining Jeannine Riley to provide additional beauty to *Hee Haw*'s flock of bucolic bumpkins.

We had been writing a bunch of new Doctor sketches for Archie the day Gunilla walked into the studio. George Yanok took one look at the statuesque Miss Hutton and exclaimed, "At last! We've found our Nurse Goodbody!" It was the appellation Gunilla would retain for many years to come.

There were other pleasant surprises that November. Minnie Pearl, who had made only one guest appearance on the first show of our summer series, agreed to become a regular member of the cast.

An additional bonus came when I bumped into Stringbean, all 6'5" of him, in the hallway outside our writer's room.

"Bossman," he said, "I sure do appreciate being on this show. I like bein' the scarecrow in the cornfield well enough, but I was wonderin' if I could do a little more than that. There's a routine I do called "Letter from Home" that gets some good laughs, and I'd like to do some of 'em on the *Hee Haw*."

With 17 hours to fill, this was music to a writer's ears. When he demonstrated his routine for us that day, it was manna from heaven. Unlike his best friend, Grandpa Jones, String said he had dozens of letters just as funny as that one.

Stringbean would always begin by announcing to members of the cast gathered around him that he just got a letter from home, and had it right next to his heart. When he didn't find it there he would search every pocket, repeating "Heart, heart, heart" until finally finding it in his back pocket. This always got a big laugh, followed by at least eight good jokes that would make Charley Weaver green with envy. These spots became a highlight of every show.

As for Grandpa, Brillstein finally called to say that someone had actually located the guy who wrote Bob Burns' material. He was in his late nineties and more than willing to make a deal. He was given a token payment and the stories were on their way to us by air express. When we turned them over to Grandpa, he was thrilled.

**In the hallway outside the writer's room, (from left) John Aylesworth, Jack Burns, manager Bernie Brillstein (waving), a visiting Nashville agent, and George Yanok, circa 1970.**

Unfortunately, the very next day, the thrill was gone. Grandpa came to us with a sour look on his face, holding the Bob Burns stories in his hand as if they were rotten fish.

"This stuff stinks!" he groaned. "I always thought Bob Burns was funnier."

"Maybe it was the bazooka," I said.

"I was wondering if you could get hold of a few Herb Shriner stories."

Herb Shriner was a rural comedian during the forties who played the harmonica and is probably best remembered now as Will Shriner's father.

"We'll see what we can do, Pa."

As it turned out, Sam Lovullo had already made a deal with Pat Buttram, Gene Autry's comical sidekick for many years, to provide us with the kind of folksy material Pa was looking for. We were all relieved to hear it. If the Shriner thing didn't work out, Grandpa would probably have us beating the bushes for some *really* obscure hayseed humorist like Josh Billings, who was a real howl back in 1858 with memorable lines like, "It's the squeaky wheel that gets the grease."

While all this was going on, our musical guest stars were taping their numbers in the studio. We had brought back most of the superstars from the summer series, such as Tammy Wynette, George Jones, and Loretta Lynn, plus a few new faces, including Linda Ronstadt and Hank Williams, Jr.

Pretty soon, the whole cast would be arriving from all over the country for the opening numbers and "Pickin' and Grinnin'," after which we would dive into the comedy spots. Everybody had been invited back except Nobel Bear, who had run out of sound effects, and Jennifer Bishop, who was busy acting in a movie.

One other attractive addition, in addition to Gunilla Hutton, was the statuesque Lisa Todd, who we cast as Junior's sexy paramour, "Sunshine Cornsilk." Lisa was not only beautiful, but she took to constantly "chanting" for the success of the show. We were all for that. We figured we needed all the help we could get.

Grandpa and Stringbean lived in Nashville, which accounted for their many visits, as well as Minnie Pearl, who in real life was a society lady named Mrs. Sarah Cannon who lived in a Belle Meade mansion with her husband, Henry.

Minnie dropped in one day to suggest a weekly Schoolhouse sketch, in which she would play teacher to our gaggle of comic characters dressed as kids. The idea was as old as Vaudeville, but we welcomed Minnie's contribution with open arms. She was a charming lady and I'll always remember her kindly—in designer dresses as Mrs. Cannon, or just plain Minnie Pearl with a $1.98 price tag on her hat.

Putting all the material together for this second trip was a whole lot easier than the previous summer. Being familiar with all the members of the cast and their various comic abilities was a big help, as were their various contributions of jokes and routines. When we started taping the comedy, we weren't as concerned about filling the time. The time just seemed to fill itself.

Aside from all the hilarious goof-ups and bloopers, we did a lot of experimenting with nutty, off-the-wall ideas. My all-time favorite was the time we had Grandpa Jones recite the entire lyric of Cole Porter's "Night and Day," with no musical accompaniment, in a tight close-up and with a completely straight face. To me, it was one of the funniest three minutes ever seen on television. What's more important, a thing like that could only happen on a show like *Hee Haw*.

Meanwhile, our new digs at the Ramada Inn were not only closer to the studio but offered more comfortable accommodations. There was a very pleasant cocktail lounge, called the Governor's Nook, which was heartily enjoyed by all the members of our troupe save Buck Owens, who didn't drink.

Unfortunately, the Ramada also housed the staff of *The Johnny Cash Show*, the producer of which had earlier promised to "bury" us. He was himself being buried by low ratings and waning public interest, despite the considerable drawing power of the magnetic "Man in Black."

The Cash show was still being taped in the conventional manner of a weekly musical show at the Ryman Auditorium, home of the Grand Ole Opry, and thus plagued by the hazards of working in a very old building. The cameras were continually falling through the aging floors, and sundry other production delays were driving the producer to a state of near insanity. His taunts were even nastier than the summer before.

One member of Cash's staff, a funny little guy named Bernard Glow, made the mistake of stopping at our table one night for a pleasant chat. He was evidently fired the next day for "fraternizing with the enemy." Naturally, we hired him immediately, with no earthly idea of what to do with him.

Back at WLAC, we finished the Cornfield segments in record time. Archie's jokes, despite their vintage, were funnier than ever. We then prepared to pack up our many miles of videotape for shipment to Los Angeles, where we would immediately start editing for our first air date in December. We would be up against stiffer competition than in the summer, so all we could do was hope for the best.

When we said goodbye to our cast and crew that November, it was pretty emotional. We had grown very fond of our *Hee Haw* family, and had no idea if we would ever see them again.

# 16

## *HEE HAW* RIDES AGAIN

*"Critics, get out your pans!* Hee Haw*'s coming back."*—CBS promo, December 1969

When all the new tapes were loaded into Marc Zappia's edit bay at CBS Television City, he sized up the huge stack of two-inch tapes on their wagon wheel reels and gave a weary sigh.

"You guys have got to be kidding!" he moaned.

We explained that we had to tape a lot more material for 17 shows than for the 12-week summer run. He just shook his head, saying it looked as if we had enough stuff for twice that many shows and unless we had more tape machines, the process would be a lot slower than the previous spring.

Once again, it was Perry Lafferty to the rescue. He made a call to the head of technical operations, and that afternoon two more machines were rolled into our edit bay. Bill Davis had once again made an excellent run-down for the first of the new shows, with Tammy Wynette and Merle Haggard as guest stars. Frank and I left Davis and Zappia to their work and went back to our Yongestreet office to fret about what the future might hold.

Nick Vanoff brightened our day with the news that CBS was planning a special starring Don Knotts and that Don wanted our company to produce it. Naturally, we were thrilled. It would give us a chance to write the kind of urban sketch comedy we had built our reputations on over the years in Canada and New York. Knotts was a terrific comedian, a very nice man, and we knew he would be a pleasure to write for. Besides, keeping busy would ease our worries over *Hee Haw*'s fate on its return against stiffer competition.

By the first week of December, the first show in the new series had been completely edited, "sweetened," and ready to go on the air. It was by far the best show we had done so far—full of good music, great production values, and the craziest, goofiest comedy yet. What's more, it moved like a speeding bullet.

On Sunday, December 17, 1969, *Hee Haw* reappeared on CBS in our new time slot on Wednesdays. The critics were no less appalled at this state of affairs. In fact, most of them pretty much ignored our second coming.

The viewers, on the other hand, were ecstatic. The fan mail began flowing in even greater volume than during the summer series. When the ratings came out, we were once again smack-dab in the Top Ten. Obviously, we were on top of the world. Nothing could stop us now. *Hee Haw* was a certified hit for all seasons! Our stock was never higher with CBS, particularly after the *Don Knotts Special* went on the air and won rave reviews, not to mention a great Nielsen rating.

A few months later, on the basis of his successful special, a rival network offered Knotts a weekly variety show. With his movie career beginning to slow, he leapt at the chance and immediately signed a deal with NBC for a 26-week series starting that September. When Knotts asked us to write and produce his new show, we fully expected *Hee Haw* would be picked up by CBS for its first full season in the fall, and respectfully declined.

Meanwhile, when CBS heard about Knotts' new commitment to NBC, they immediately called our manager, Bernie Brillstein, to make an offer of $150,000 to keep me and Frank exclusive to CBS. Brillstein happily accepted this generous offer on our behalf, and then called us laughing hysterically. Apparently, if CBS had looked at our contract, we were *already* exclusive to CBS. But what the heck? The network was a lot richer than we were, so we gratefully took the money.

While all this was going on, we had given our new employee from *The Johnny Cash Show*, Bernard Glow, a small office at our Yongestreet headquarters on Canon Drive in Beverly Hills, still with no earthly idea of what to do with him.

Glow was a strange, gnome-like little fellow, with several nervous tics and a habit of constantly swatting the side of his neck. Bill Davis suggested Glow might be trying to rid his neck of an imaginary vampire bat, which we all decided was a definite possibility.

Glow was in possession of a thick, illustrated book containing colorful pictures of every conceivable pharmaceutical pill, with accompanying descriptions of their effect on the human mind and body. He was more than willing to share the information gleaned from this heavy tome, but nobody paid much attention since our recreational indulgences of choice at that time came from a bottle, not a pillbox.

Since no one seemed to know what his job with the Cash group might have been, and with Glow himself being somewhat hazy on the subject when asked, we simply honored our commitment and left him in peace to pursue his chemical studies.

As the weeks and months flew by, *Hee Haw* held steady in the ratings and was judged a bona fide hit. As spring approached, Perry Lafferty informed us that we would be allowed to produce our own summer replacement.

This was good news indeed, and boded well for a full season of *Hee Haw* beginning in the fall. We immediately got together with Jack Burns and George Yanok to create a new show that would be poles apart from anything rural.

Peppiatt, Burns, and I had all grown up during the days of big bands and old radio. Since we remembered them fondly, and with the war in Vietnam still droning on at an ever more depressing rate, we decided it would be a good idea to do an upbeat series about the good old days of the '30s and '40s. We had brought joy to the hitherto ignored country music fans in the heartland. Now, we would attempt to do the same for similarly underserved middle-aged urban viewers. We would call it *Happy Days*.

The network loved the idea. CBS president Bob Wood's hatred of *Hee Haw* was leavened by his admiration for the concept of *Happy Days*. Commercially, it was extremely salable.

Back in 1970, aging viewers weren't reviled as they are today. Advertisers had not yet determined that the only audience worth reaching must be between the ages of 18 and 35, based on the notion that anyone older would not be as receptive to new products as the younger demographic.

The glaring error in this theory, of course, is simply that old products continually cease to exist. Otherwise, as a senior citizen myself, I would still be driving a Packard, brushing my teeth with Ipana, and writing this book on a Royal portable.

**Comedian Louis Nye on the set of *Happy Days*, 1970.**

In addition, the network executives in those days were mostly mature adults with many years of broadcasting experience. Today, networks seem loath to employ anyone over 30. I mention this only to put the likelihood of selling a show like *Happy Days* to a national network in the proper context.

We immediately started making plans for the series. We would shoot it in pieces on coded tape, just as we did with *Hee Haw*, the difference being that *Happy Days* would be produced in a large studio at CBS Television City.

During the next few weeks, we assembled a terrific cast of regulars. These included the round and jovial Chuck McCann, who was not only known for his spoofs of old comic strip characters—like Little Orphan Annie and Dick Tracy—but did a spot-on impersonation of Oliver Hardy, and would re-create classic comedy bits with Stan Laurel look-alike Jim McGeorge; Julie McWhirter, a cute little blonde impressionist, who would provide Shirley Temple dance routines; a singing quintet, à la The Pied Pipers, assembled for us by Henry Mancini's wife Ginny, featuring herself and Alan Copeland, a former member of Glenn Miller's "Modernaires"; top conductor-arrangers Jack Elliott and Allyn Ferguson, who would be our "Twin Maestros" leading a big band of L.A.'s best musicians; and beloved comedian Louis Nye, famous for his routines on the old *Steve Allen Show*, as our old-time radio announcer.

***Opposite, top:*** **Writer George Yanok (left) and John Aylesworth preparing to record the pilot of *Happy Days*, on LP, 1970. *Opposite, bottom:* Producers-writers Frank Peppiatt (left) and John Aylesworth (first from right) with writer George Yanok (right) and arranger-conductor Jack Elliott, recording the LP pilot for *Happy Days*, 1970.**

Our list of guest stars quickly fell in line. Edgar Bergen agreed to bring Charlie McCarthy out of his suitcase one more time to recreate bits from their Chase & Sanborn radio show; Bob and Ray would do weekly satires of 1940s soap operas, such as *Ma Perkins* and *Our Gal Sunday*; Duke Ellington, Harry James, Buddy Rich, and many other big band leaders would join our musicians as they played their greatest hits; and we would utilize everybody in spoofs of 1930s dance marathons, period comedy blackouts, and snappy tap numbers by the Wisa D'Orso dancers.

*Happy Days* was a veritable orgy of nostalgia. Before we started production, we rented a recording studio and made an audio demo of the show to get the network excited. It was probably the first and maybe the last time a TV pilot had ever been recorded on an LP.

It worked! CBS was so impressed they made hundreds of copies and sent them out to all their affiliated stations. The reaction was tremendous. Everybody loved it, predicting that *Happy Days* would be a much bigger hit than *Hee Haw*, which remained rock solid in the Top Ten through its entire run on the network. Could lightning strike twice? We certainly hoped so. The taping of all 12 shows went so smoothly, we could hardly believe our good fortune.

In the spring of 1970, the annual CBS affiliate meeting was to be capped by a gala dinner party in the Grand Ballroom of the Century Plaza Hotel. When we previewed the first episode of *Happy Days* for the CBS brass, they were totally enthralled and asked us to produce the entertainment portion of the gala with our entire cast and orchestra.

It was quite an honor. Never before had the CBS affiliate gathering concluded with a stage production devoted to just one show, and a summer replacement show to boot. Edgar Bergen, as well as Bob and Ray, readily agreed to appear in the show, which we rehearsed for a full week.

When the big night arrived, hundreds of CBS affiliate representatives were happily wining and dining after an arduous week of meetings at Television City. As the curtains of the large stage parted, the band was playing Glenn Miller's "Moonlight Serenade," and I heard a delighted sigh from the large, middle-aged audience. Right from the get-go, we had them in the palm of our hand.

The show went smoothly, with plenty of laughter and applause scattered throughout. Following a spirited dance number, the curtains closed to the repeated strains of "Moonlight Serenade." The audience immediately rose to its feet and gave us a five-minute standing ovation. Bob Wood gave us his hearty congratulations and, according to Perry Lafferty, it was the only time in the history of affiliate dinners that such a reception had been accorded the entertainment portion of the evening. For Frank and me, it was perhaps the most unforgettable night of our lives.

*Happy Days* debuted on the CBS network from 8 to 9 P.M. on June 25, 1970. It did not replace *Hee Haw* on Sunday evening for the summer, having been slotted in what was considered a more advantageous spot on Thursday nights. It got respectful but tepid reviews, and the Nielsen ratings were quite disappointing, to say the least. During its 12-week run, it sank like a stone. On August 27, *Happy Days* went off the air as if it had never happened.

How can a show the president of a network hates be a hit, and a show he loves be a bomb? As writer William Goldman observed in "Adventures of a Screen Writer," "NOBODY KNOWS ANYTHING!"

# 17

# HERE WE GO AGAIN, AGAIN!

---

*"We might as well knock off all the effete snobbery and accept* Hee Haw *as a fact of life, like Brussels sprouts or the measles."—Neil Hickey,* TV Guide *cover story, March 7, 1970*

---

In 1970, after 16 successful years on the CBS network, *The Red Skelton Show* was cancelled. Although it was still popular, it had become too expensive to be cost-effective and the search was on to find a suitable replacement. Several pilots had been made and were waiting in the wings, but when the time came to firm up the fall schedule, it was decided that only one show was deemed suitable to fill the Skelton time slot. That show was *Hee Haw*.

Naturally, we were thrilled! This would be our first full season, and if our ratings held up we would be on the air for 26 glorious weeks. We could hardly believe our good fortune, and assumed Mike Dann had prevailed over Bob Wood.

It wasn't until a year later that I learned, from Les Brown's indispensable book *The Business Behind the Box*, that it was actually Bob Wood who made the decision. After all, we were a hit show, relatively inexpensive, and business is business. Or maybe it was just penance for Wood's misjudgment of *Happy Days*. In any case, it was Bob Wood who made it possible for a show he detested to survive.

Mike Dann called to congratulate us, still championing our show. He had yet to figure out what made his new boss tick, and shortly after that we lost a good friend at the network when Dann resigned from CBS to become vice-president of the Children's Television Workshop, producers of *Sesame Street*. I guess he figured Oscar the Grouch would be easier to get along with than the volatile Bob Wood.

We immediately got together with Sam Lovullo and Bill Davis to make plans for the new season. *Happy Days* was still on the air but all the shows had been edited, so we decided to get our troops together and head to Nashville in late August to shoot our first 13 *Hee Haw* shows. We would return in early fall for the next 13. We had no idea at the time that this would become our regular taping schedule for the next 20 years.

Before we left, Perry Lafferty invited us to lunch in his private dining room to meet Mike Dann's replacement as programming chief, a pleasant young man named Fred Silverman. He made no secret of his distaste for *Hee Haw*, although respectful of its success, and tried to talk us into booking some big-name urban guest stars.

After telling him the Jimmy Dean story and pointing out that even an appearance by Bob Hope hadn't done much for *The Johnny Cash Show*, he backed off and finally agreed with us that—like it or not—a show like *Hee Haw* simply was what it was. It just had to be accepted on its own terms.

We arranged to have all the writers meet us in Nashville to amass enough new material for the first 13 shows of our first full season, since that arrangement had worked so well for the previous shoot. Once again, Lovullo had made a deal for a different hotel to house our cast and production staff. This time, it would be a brand new hotel, having been built since our last visit. It was called King of the Road, after Roger Miller's hit song, by arrangement with Roger himself (who was evidently an investor in the enterprise).

The King of the Road certainly belied its hobo-inspired name. It was a towering, stark, ultra-modern edifice that would certainly never offer the "rooms for let ... fifty cents" of Roger's lyric. The entire top floor was a penthouse nightclub, completely sheathed in glass. In all, it was hardly the sort of hotel one would expect to find in Nashville back in 1970, especially considering the fact that upon our arrival the featured act in the nightclub was Jewish comedian Jackie Mason! It was like booking the Blue Collar Comedy Tour into the Algonquin in New York.

The rooms were spacious enough, though a bit sterile, with one particularly annoying feature. In most hotels, the telephone is on a night table beside the bed. At the King of the Road the phone was far across the room on a desk. Not only was this a nuisance when placing or answering wake-up calls, it was also a big pain when making goodnight calls to one's family back in Los Angeles. I was naturally curious as to what genius had come up with this maddening innovation. I had known Roger Miller for years, and shortly after our arrival I bumped into him in the downstairs bar one evening and asked about it.

"I was wondering that very same thing," Roger said. "What they told me was that people sitting on the side of the bed making phone calls tend to cause the mattresses to wear out in a couple of years, so they put the phone on the desk across the room."

After we had a couple of drinks, Roger added, "Hell, with that kind of thinking, the place probably won't stay open long enough to make much of a dent in the mattresses."

He was right—it was soon to become a Days Inn. As for Roger, one of the funniest and most innovative artists in the country field, he needed a hotel like a hole in the head.

Whatever the shortcomings of our new digs, it made a hell of a fun playground

**John Aylesworth and Roy Clark (trying to remember what we did last night), 1970.**

for us hardworking writers after our long days of sating *Hee Haw*'s insatiable appetite for comedy. We pretty much avoided the penthouse nightclub, favoring the cozy downstairs bar where most of the cast and production staff would congregate.

At our first writer's meeting for the new season, Archie Campbell brought along a bright young Nashvillian named Bud Wingard, who was hoping to write for *Hee Haw*. When he told us some of his ideas, we hired him on the spot. Bud's future contributions to the show were funny musical segments that became

**Roy Clark, Gunilla Hutton, Lulu Roman, and director Bill Davis with the cue cards that made**
*Hee Haw* **possible, 1971. (Apologies to the cue card holder for forgetting his name.)**

favorite weekly spots, among which were the "Gloom, Despair and Agony on Me" number for the male comics on the show, and the "Gossipy" segment for our pretty female cast members. Bud was always a very cheerful, upbeat kind of guy with a good comedy mind, and we welcomed him with open arms.

After a couple of weeks, our musical guest stars began taping their numbers in the studio. Since this was our first full season, we had booked some extra special acts. Roy Rogers and Dale Evans had always brought big ratings to whatever show we had them on as guests in the past, and they were happy to join us on *Hee Haw*.

Ray Charles was another special guest, a completely unexpected feature on a show like *Hee Haw*, until you considered the fact that Ray's country albums back in the early 1960s were huge hits. His version of Hank Williams' "I Can't Stop Lovin' You" hit number one on the singles charts and remains a classic of its kind these many years later. Ray just loved working with Nashville musicians, and the feeling was mutual. It was a glorious day in the studio when Ray did enough material with our band for at least four guest appearances that season.

Roger Miller made his first appearance on the show during that shoot, as well as the "Old Storyteller" Tom T. Hall. Most of our other guest stars—like Loretta Lynn, George Jones, Charley Pride, and Tammy Wynette—had done the show so often they were practically regulars. *Hee Haw* was the only show on a national network to allow their millions of loyal country fans to see them on television.

Pretty soon, the out-of-town members of our cast started drifting in. Junior Samples was among the first to arrive, wearing a slouch hat, dark glasses and an enormous overcoat covering his accustomed overalls. Junior had achieved TV stardom, and was beginning to be surrounded by adoring fans wherever he went, asking for autographs and thus

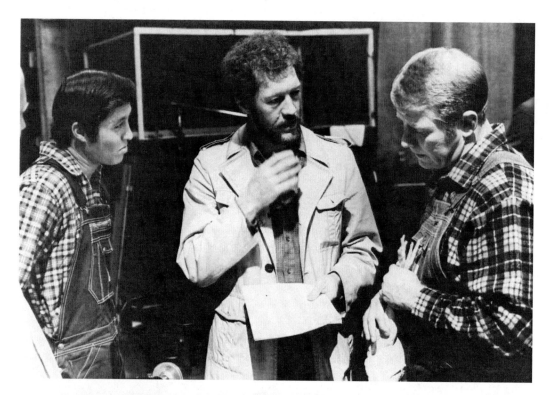

*Top:* Yankees Bobby Murcer and Mickey Mantle on the *Hee Haw* set with director Bill Davis, 1971. *Bottom:* Singer Ray Charles in his first appearance on *Hee Haw*, with the Nashville Edition singers and associate director, Dick Harwood (at right), 1970.

forcing him to wear a disguise that fooled absolutely no one. He even had a rubber stamp made of his signature since he had recently developed writer's cramp when surrounded by a large throng of admirers.

When it came time to start taping the comedy segments, the rest of the cast began streaming into WLAC. They were joined by the sole representative from CBS to attend every taping since the beginning. His name was Chuck Schnabel, from the network's Standards and Practices department. He was a pleasant fellow who, as might be expected in his line of work, was pale as a ghost and had a shock of matching

**Junior Samples with Amanda Blake of *Gunsmoke* on *Hee Haw*, 1971.**

snow-white hair to match. Most of the people from Standards and Practices back then looked as if they had never been outdoors.

It was Schnabel's job to make sure that no curse words such as "damn" or "hell" were uttered, which seemed highly unlikely on a show in which "dang," "heck," and the occasional "tarnation" were about as far as our characters were likely to go.

Chuck's other concern, since such shapely beauties as Gunilla Hutton and Lisa Todd were part of the cast, was to make sure that the display of cleavage and shapely limbs was kept to an absolute minimum. In the world of Chuck Schnabel, female breasts and legs should exist only on poultry. All this may seem quaint looking back from the 21st century, but in 1970 it was serious business.

* * *

Sam Lovullo came to our office one day with a little old guy we had never seen before and introduced him to us as Bix Reichner, a very successful ASCAP composer. Assuming he must have a funny song to sell us, we asked him what that might be.

"You're already using it," he said. "I wrote 'Pffft, You Were Gone.'"

Archie later admitted that he had known it wasn't his song, and explained that he took only took credit for it because he didn't know where to find Bix. Unfortunately for Archie, Bix had found *him*.

Considering that the song had been used at least twice on every show since the beginning, a large amount of past royalties had to be paid to the rightful party out of Archie's pocket. Archie ruefully took this in stride and offered his sincere apologies to Mr. Reichner, a long-time ASCAP member with many past novelty hits, such as "Papa Loves Mambo" to his credit.

From that day on, Bix came to Nashville for every taping and wrote countless comical verses for his "Pffft, You Were Gone" over the years. As for Archie, he was a chastened man and never again took credit for material that wasn't his (barring the occasional

**Producer Sam Lovullo (left) and director Bill Davis with the adorable Barbi Benton, 1970.**

wheeze from the immortal Joe Miller, an 18th century English actor and humorist, whose bon mots were first collected in *Joe Miller's Jests* in 1739).

\* \* \*

The addition of Bud Wingard made our writing load a great deal lighter, leaving our evenings completely open for fun and games. The fun part was mostly in the downstairs bar socializing with the cast and crew. The games included a form of poker in one of the upstairs rooms. The players were mainly just us writers, with the occasional visitor sitting in.

Few of the non-regulars ever returned for the simple reason that after a few drinks it appeared that someone began to cheat. Knowing this, we regulars just threw in our hands when it was his deal so that all he got were the antes. However, if he was losing late in the evening, the alleged cheater would often declare the winning hand and throw it in the pile without showing his cards. If someone complained, he'd act indignant and start rummaging through the pile, saying, "They're in here somewhere." To this day, Peppiatt denies it was him.

One time our manager, Bernie Brillstein, came to Nashville on a visit and sat in on

**Peppiatt and Aylesworth's manager, Bernie Brillstein (left), on a rare visit to the *Hee Haw* set at WLAC, Nashville, 1970.**

one of our games. When it was over, as Jack Burns and I were walking him to the elevator, Brillstein asked, "Do you realize one of those guys is cheating?"

"Sure," I replied. "He does it almost every night."

"Then why do you play with him?"

Burns laughed and said, "Hey, it's the only game in town.

\* \* \*

We still hadn't figured out what to do with Bernard Glow, our strange little inheri-
tance from *The Johnny Cash Show*. Since he was certainly fun to have around, we made
him our recreation director. In addition to poker, we decided to seek a different kind of
diversion that would combine both fun and a game. That would be Bernie Glow's job. He
jittered, gave it some thought, pulled himself up to his full 5'2", batted an imaginary gnat
from his neck, and declared, "I've got the perfect game! It's almost time to go back to
L.A., so I'll save it for the next trip. You're gonna love it. It's called 'The Murder Game.'"

It certainly sounded intriguing, but we had to ask if anybody would actually get killed.

"Not necessarily," he replied.

Though the fun part might be questionable, the game part sounded pretty interesting,
and Bernie Glow was assured of another trip to Nashville. We could hardly wait for him
to show his true worth.

\* \* \*

All the comedy spots for the initial 13 shows of our first full season went off without
a hitch, and every one of our guest stars shone more brightly than ever before. It was the
easiest shoot yet. Everything was running like a well-oiled machine. We had the giddy
feeling that this could go on forever, the "good Lord willin' and the crick don't rise"—not
to mention the unpredictable whims of Bob Wood, lord and master of CBS.

# 18

# Junior Goes Hollywood

*"All that lumber and no knots."—Junior Samples in Los Angeles after seeing his first palm tree*

To kick off our first full season of *Hee Haw*, the CBS publicity department went all out to promote the show. Suddenly, the market was flooded with *Hee Haw* comic books, joke books, comedy LPs, lunch boxes, and all kinds of novelty merchandise, most of which featured the show's favorite star by far, Junior Samples.

The most frequent question asked about him by his fans—and a skeptical press—was "Is Junior for real?" Watching him on the show, it was admittedly pretty hard to believe, but the answer was simply an emphatic "Yes!" Not even Laurence Olivier could have put on an act like that.

Junior's entire wardrobe apparently consisted of a few T-shirts, a pair of boots, and two sets of overalls. The boots were a fairly recent acquisition, since he had pretty much gone barefoot until he was well into his thirties. Although he could have been a fearsome sight with his massive torso and ham-hock arms, with that round cherubic face and the twinkling eyes and winsome smile, when you put the whole package together he was just pretty darn adorable.

Junior got fan mail by the bushel which I am not sure ever got answered. It would be quite a chore to write thousands of letters when all you had was a third-grade education. Neither, I'm sure, would most college graduates have handled it if they reached the kind of fame and fortune that had come to Alvin Junior Samples, the difference being that Junior would have sincerely wanted to respond if he could.

When *Hee Haw* came back on the air in September 1970, it was as popular as ever, more than equaling the Top Ten ratings of its predecessor, *The Red Skelton Show*, at 8:30 on Tuesday nights. No matter what night we were scheduled, we always came out a winner. At that point, the publicity department decided to bring our most popular character to Los Angeles for TV and newspaper interviews. When they made the arrangements, Junior was thrilled.

Except for Nashville, Junior had evidently never been far from Cumming, Georgia. We called him at home and suggested he ditch the overcoat and slouch hat and just be himself when he came to L.A. He readily agreed, and asked if it would be all right to bring his autograph stamp. We told him he would really need it for this trip, because plenty of people would want his signature.

Junior was picked up at the airport by a stretch limousine. He took a long look at it and said, in amazement, "Cars sure do grow big out here."

On the way to the Beverly Hills Hotel, Junior was awestruck by all the palm trees lining Sunset Boulevard.

"I've never seen trees like that," he commented. "What are they?"

"They're palm trees, Junior," the CBS promotion man replied.

"I wish we had trees like that back home," Junior mused. "All that lumber and no knots."

Every comment he made was dutifully written down by the CBS man for later release to the press. Everything he said was pure Junior. He couldn't have been better if he had been scripted and rehearsed.

When the limo arrived at the hotel, Junior was ushered to one of the VIP bungalows.

"This is the first hotel I ever seen that had houses instead of rooms," he said in wonder.

The morning after Junior's arrival, Frank and I went to visit him with Perry Lafferty prior to a press conference that had been set up for that afternoon. He was overjoyed to see some familiar faces, and told us he was having the time of his life. His only regret was not having his wife with him to enjoy it all. We told him we would try to arrange for her to be with him on his next trip.

Junior's wife was a worn little woman named Grace, who had obviously lived a hard life in rural Georgia but was totally devoted to her husband as he was to her. They seemed to have a good life in Cumming with their several children, one of whom—a teenage boy—had evidently once fallen off the roof of a barn, landed on his head, and hadn't been quite right ever since.

When the press arrived, Junior told his story: raised in the backwoods of Georgia, quit school after the third grade and became, at various times, a sawmill worker, a stock car racer, a carpenter, and a highly successful moonshiner. (It was said, no doubt apocryphal, that he owned his own still at the age of 11.) A lot of this was news to me, except for the moonshiner part. I had tried Junior's "white lightnin'" one time, and believe me, that stuff could curl your cuticles!

Junior's first brush with show business had come when a relative of his had gone to Florida, caught a giant sea bass, brought its head back to Cumming as a souvenir, and gave it to Junior. As a prank, Junior showed the huge fish head to the local forest ranger and told him he had caught the fish in the local lake. When the ranger asked where the rest of it was, Junior simply replied, "I got a big family and it fed us all."

That fish tale had come to the attention of a local radio station where Junior told his tall tale in an interview, the edited tape of which came to the attention of a Nashville record company. It was released as a single called "The World's Biggest Whopper" and became a regional hit. That led to Junior being signed by an agent who, not knowing quite what to do with a client having no act, had brought him to us that fateful morning in 1969 at the Holiday Inn.

One reporter asked if it was true that he had just two pairs of overalls, one for everyday and one for church, to which Junior replied: "Not anymore." He then opened his closet door to proudly reveal seven neatly hung bib overalls. "I got one for every day of the week."

When queried about what else had changed in his life since his newfound fame and fortune, Junior bemoaned all the autograph seekers. But he was proud that he could now afford a chandelier to hang in his house, "just like one of them Nashville hotels."

The press people were completely charmed by our star attraction's homespun wit, and the resulting stories in the local and national press were terrific. The line most quoted by all was his answer to the query "Do you have any complaints about your stay here at the Beverly Hills Hotel?" Junior had replied, "Only one. How come they got boy waitresses in the restaurant?"

\* \* \*

Later that year, Ralph Edwards decided that Junior would be an interesting subject for his series, *This Is Your Life*. As it turned out, he was an unforgettable subject. Edwards told us we would have to bring Junior to Los Angeles on some pretext so that he could be surprised by the host announcing, "Junior Samples, this is your life!"

We gave Junior a call and told him CBS wanted him to fly to the

Junior's album.

West Coast to tape some special promotional spots for the show. He reminded us that we had promised that he could bring his wife on the next trip, but we had to renege since Grace would be brought separately, along with his children, to shock him out of his wits when they appeared on Edwards' show. We told him the budget wouldn't allow it, and he grudgingly agreed to come anyway, after much coaxing.

The day after Junior's arrival, we paid him a visit in his room at the Roosevelt Hotel on Hollywood Boulevard, where Edwards billeted all his subjects. It was a bit of a comedown from his former accommodations in Beverly Hills, which we assumed was the reason Junior was sulking when we arrived. We were wrong.

The poor guy was worried sick because he couldn't reach his wife on the phone. We weren't about to tell him that Grace wasn't home because she was already on her way to L.A. with his children to surprise him on *This Is Your Life.* Poor Junior was concerned that something terrible might have happened to her, and there was no way we could relieve his anguish without giving everything away.

Junior was in a terrible stew for the next day and a half, not realizing that the cause of his worries was in a suite two floors below with the rest of his family, safe and sound and enjoying an endless feast delivered nonstop by room service. Junior, on the other hand, was in such a state that he couldn't eat a thing, which must have been quite a shock to his 400-pound bulk.

On the night of the show, we took Junior to a studio adjoining Ralph Edwards' stage supposedly to tape the fake promos. Bill Davis was there to direct them, so that Junior would be more at ease with someone he knew from *Hee Haw*.

After the first promo was done, Edwards finally appeared to spring his big surprise. A dazed Junior was then led onto the set of *This Is Your Life* as a delighted studio audience cheered at his appearance. When his wife was led out from the wings to join him, Junior broke down completely, howling and sobbing uncontrollably into a big red bandana he had pulled from one of his pockets. Each of his friends from Cumming, and every member of his family, was greeted with a fresh howl, followed by more non-stop tears. Junior wrung out his sodden red bandana so many times during the show, the studio floor became a major flood area.

After the show, there was a gala party at the Roosevelt Hotel. Downing a few stiff shots of bourbon, Junior finally regained his composure and had a wonderful time with his friends and family. Frank and I, along with Bill Davis, were not to be included in this love fest. Junior refused to even speak to us when we tried to wish him well. After all, we were the cause of all his pain and anguish over the past few days, and we were not to be forgiven. It was a full year before Junior Samples deigned to forgive us and speak to us again.

# 19

# A WEEKEND AS BIG AS YOUR FIST

*"You can't kill that show with a stick!"—Bob Wood, president of CBS, New York City, March 1971*

When we had returned to Los Angeles from Nashville after shooting the first 13 weeks of our first full season, Nick Vanoff was waiting at our Yongestreet office to put us right to work on a mammoth new project.

It had been Vanoff's dream for many years to produce a two-hour, star-studded variety special covering the entire breadth of American history, called *Swing Out, Sweet Land.* He had finally sold the idea to the brewers of Budweiser beer, and John Wayne had agreed to be the host. The show would be a co-production of Yongestreet and Wayne's Batjac Productions.

Paul Keyes, Dean Martin's jovial head writer, had been enlisted for the project because he was a close pal of practically every celebrity in town, making big name bookings a cinch. By the time we had finished the script in concert with Keyes, we had dozens of episodes with a lot of novelty casting for our all-star line-up: Lorne Greene would be George Washington; Jack Benny the man who finds the silver dollar Washington threw across the Potomac; Bing Crosby as Mark Twain; and Bob Hope, as himself, entertaining the troops at Valley Forge. We even snuck our own Roy Clark in as a banjo player at Andrew Jackson's inaugural.

Meanwhile, Bill Davis was in the editing bay at CBS churning out new episodes of *Hee Haw* for our debut in September. Things were going a lot faster since additional editing machines had been installed, and Davis had the format down pat. When *Hee Haw* returned that fall, in its new time slot at 8:30 P.M. on Tuesdays, it took its customary place in the Nielsen Top Ten.

We had little time to celebrate, since *Swing Out, Sweet Land* was already in production. It was a fun shoot, with only one particularly memorable incident.

John Wayne was to ride into an old western town at the beginning of a scene depicting the old Wild West. The town was Corriganville, an authentic setting outside Los Angeles that had been used in dozens of movie Westerns. Its streets were lined with spectators who had come for a glimpse of their hero, "The Duke."

When Wayne appeared, it was a stirring sight. He was in full western gear, riding down the street on his favorite pinto, looking every bit the gallant hero he had always been on the silver screen. The admiring onlookers stared in awed silence until, halfway down the street, a horrified gasp was heard when a gust of wind blew their idol's hat off revealing a pate that was as bald as a boiled egg. Needless to say, the Duke had his trusty toupee pasted on under his hat for the second take.

93

**A stupid moment in our writing room with me hawking photo proofs to a bemused Jack Burns, circa 1971.**

*Swing Out, Sweet Land* went on the air at the end of November and was a huge success, winning rave reviews and a subsequent Emmy. Needless to say, with *Hee Haw* more popular than ever, and a prestigious two-hour special to our credit, 1970 was a good year for Yongestreet Productions.

\* \* \*

For Frank and me, 1971 seemed destined to be just as fabulous as the year before. We both had beautiful homes in Beverly Hills; great families; plenty of money; a hit show that seemed it could go on forever; and a successful production company. We only had to go to Nashville twice a year, leaving us free to choose whatever other projects we might like to do, and we could spend the rest of our time just having fun. We were on a roll, and nothing could stop us now! Let's face it, for two guys in their early 40s, we were on top of the world.

At the beginning of 1971, Nick Vanoff introduced us to an affable young man named Andrew Wald, and suggested that we take him on as a general assistant. Andrew was a strapping lad with the approximate dimensions of "the Incredible Hulk," but with a decidedly sweet disposition.

Vanoff was a friend of Andrew's father, the celebrated movie producer Jerry Wald, who wanted his son to get some practical experience in the business. Vanoff was happy to take him on, as were we. Andrew proved his worth almost immediately when he suggested that a bunch of us go to New York in March for "the Fight of the Century" between Muhammad Ali and Joe Frazier at Madison Square Garden. Andrew said he could round up a bunch of our favorite celebrities for a wonderful lunch at the famed New York restaurant 21 before the fight, and a fantastic weekend would be had by all.

The Ali-Frazier fight was scheduled for Monday, March 8, 1971. We flew into New York the Friday before with Jack Burns and Pat McCormick, and checked into the St. Regis Hotel. The following day, Andrew Wald's VIP lunch was scheduled for noon in a private room at 21, so we all had an early night in eager anticipation.

We certainly weren't disappointed. When we arrived, the guests were milling around having pre-lunch cocktails. They included newsman Walter Cronkite, NFL commissioner Pete Rozelle, composer Henry Mancini, musician Bobby Short, famed band leader Artie Shaw, composer Alan Jay Lerner, and restaurateur Mike Romanoff. We happily joined in the milling and had short conversations with as many as possible.

I had known Artie Shaw from my days living in New York and was aware that, to him, a conversation was a monologue. As usual he was ruing that he had ever begun the beguine, and had made his clarinet into a lamp upon realizing that he had reached perfection on the instrument and was now a full-time intellectual.

Walter Cronkite said he was tired of doing the news every night and couldn't wait to retire. Mike Romanoff said he was sure his pal Sinatra would show up for the lunch. (He didn't.) David Frost's conversations sounded like interviews, while Bobby Short seemed at a total loss without his piano. Hank Mancini, as always, was a man of few words.

When lunch was served, I was lucky enough to be seated across from the amiable Bennett Cerf, publisher of Random House, who said he still missed putting on his tuxedo every Sunday night to be on the panel of the legendary TV show *What's My Line*. Several times, he repeated his mantra that the key to writing a successful book was to make it short and funny, the same formula that had made *Hee Haw* a hit.

The food was great, the talk was stimulating, and, amazingly enough, almost everybody had seen *Hee Haw* and actually liked it! I look back fondly at that lunch as one my favorite memories in a life that thankfully keeps getting longer at the speed of light.

We spent the rest of that weekend revisiting old haunts, most of them Irish pubs, in that great city that I had called home for twelve wonderful years.

\* \* \*

The following Monday morning, I got a call from Fred Silverman. Perry Lafferty had told him that Frank and I would be in town at the St. Regis, and he invited us to meet him for lunch, once again at 21. (Obviously, nobody who was anybody in Manhattan ever had lunch anywhere else—the Russian Tea Room must have been chopped liver to those in the know.)

Silverman said he would meet us there at 12:30, and I hoped he would have wonderful news about *Hee Haw*. I called Frank, but he was feeling under the weather so I went alone.

I arrived a bit early and went to the bar, where I encountered Bob Wood. He looked at me grimly and said, "The ratings came out this morning. Do you know where that damn show of yours is this week?"

"No, sir. I don't."

"It's a solid number nine, that's where it is!" he growled. At that point he went into a comical little dance, slamming his feet on the floor as if crushing deadly vipers.

"You can't kill that show with a stick!" he snarled.

At that point, Silverman arrived and rescued me, explaining that "Bob gets a little worked up when it comes to *Hee Haw*."

I pointed out that Wood was the one who picked us up for a full season, and we were doing a heck of a job. *Hee Haw* was the ninth most popular show in the country that week. The man damn well ought to be grateful, even if he hated the show.

Silverman agreed, but added that both he and Wood hated all the "shit-kicking" shows that made up the CBS Top Ten, and that changes would be made when the new season was announced.

The maitre'd seated Silverman and me at a choice table near the bar, and Silverman chortled smugly at the sight of his boss, Bob Wood, climbing the stairs to the "Siberia" of the second floor. Apparently, one-upmanship was alive and well at the "Tiffany Network."

During the ensuing four-martini lunch, I tried to find out what changes were to be made to the schedule, but Silverman was stolidly non-committal as he expressed his hatred of all things rural, his love of America, and his hero worship of John Wayne.

Since Yongestreet had produced The Duke's first special, Silverman asked if we could deliver Wayne as host of a CBS variety series, and guaranteed a firm 26-week commitment if we could pull it off. I told him I would talk to my partners and give it my best shot. We shook hands on it—in that golden age where a handshake deal really meant something—and proceeded to get properly smashed.

When I reeled out of 21 at about three that afternoon, Muhammad Ali was walking down the street with a big smile, a strapping bronze Adonis sparring playfully with a bunch of kids. Considering he would be in the ring for "the Fight of the Century" just a few hours later, my only thought was "Where but in New York? It certainly is one helluva town!"

* * *

The fight itself was quite a spectacle, if not in the ring then certainly ringside. From my humble seat, which seemed at least a half-mile from the action, I peered through binoculars at such luminaries as Barbra Streisand, Bill Cosby, and Sammy Davis, Jr. Former champs Jack Dempsey and Gene Tunney were also in the audience. Frank Sinatra seemed to be everywhere around the apron of the ring with a camera, as official photographer for *Life* magazine. This was pretty heady stuff for a rube from Toronto.

The excitement was electric, but the "Fight of the Century" didn't quite live up to its title. When Ali lost, the air seemed to be sucked out of Madison Square Garden and every one of its occupants—with the exception of the victorious Joe Frazier.

The following morning, we all flew back to L.A. savoring the events of a truly great weekend despite a truly bum ending—we had all been pulling for Ali.

* * *

Back in our Yongestreet offices, after I had filled my partners in on my lunch with Silverman, Nick had a meeting with Batjac Productions, John Wayne's company. Since Wayne's film career wasn't exactly blazing hot at that moment, there was a general feeling that something could be worked out. However, from a purely creative point of view, Frank and I had great difficulty visualizing a non-singing, non-dancing, non-comedic "Duke" Wayne hosting an hour-long variety show every week.

I left several messages for Fred Silverman over the next few days, but received no reply. When I finally reached him, he seemed to have cooled to the whole idea. Maybe Bob Wood had squelched it, thinking John Wayne was too rural because he did westerns in a cowboy hat. Whatever the reason, the handshake was apparently non-binding, according to Silverman because "we had a lot to drink at that lunch." For whatever reason, I must say Frank and I were actually relieved.

Now all we had to worry about was whether *Hee Haw* would be picked up for another season.

# 20

# "The Murder Game"

> *"It's really simple. We draw lots to see who gets killed, give him twenty minutes to hide, load our guns, hunt him down, and shoot to kill."—Bernard Glow in Nashville, 1971*

We were looking forward to taping the next 13 shows, since Nashville had become a comfortable home away from the standard showbiz atmosphere of Los Angeles. And we had become genuinely fond of our rustic cast of characters and the friendly, unpretentious people behind the cameras at WLAC. Because it was a tiny studio in a very small station, we became pals with all the technicians and with our hardworking stage hands with odd names, "Oot" Sullivan and an extremely large, bearded fellow we knew only as "Bear." There was also a very tall, older man, Charles Barnhardt, who had apparently missed out on the nickname lottery.

The people in the office were always busy typing and doing all those things that people in offices are always busy doing, so we didn't get to know them very well, except for Sam Lovullo, who we had given the title of producer; his amazingly proficient assistant, Marcia Minor, who had been with him since *The Jonathan Winters Show*; and, of course, our "Little Miss EECO," Sandy Liles.

To me, one of the most unforgettable people on the show, and certainly the most indispensable in those early days of *Hee Haw*, also happened to be one of the nicest people I had ever met. His name was Don Rich, the show's first musical director after our L.A. import, Bob Alberti, fled when he couldn't fathom the Nashville number-system of musical scoring.

Rich was lead guitarist with Buck Owens' "Buckaroos," which became our house band under his leadership for those first 12 summer shows. He was also indispensable to Buck, with whom he sang harmony, providing that special, unique sound that was largely responsible for Buck's steady stream of hit records in the 1960s. Rich was the kind of gentle, affable guy you just liked to spend time with, especially since he had a hearty laugh that made him a great audience for the zany antics of us writers.

Of course, we still had our resident toper in the paint shop, Gene Cross (alias Verne Gagne, the famous wrestler), none the worse for his beating at the gala City Club party in '69. Whatever his faults, he was still a heck of a painter and a lot of fun to have around.

Perhaps the unlikeliest member of our off-camera group was makeup artist Charles Nash. Nash was country to the bone, but the country happened to be Great Britain. It always made my head spin full circle after a chat with someone like Junior or Grandpa, with their homespun twang, to encounter this proper English gentleman, sporting a military moustache and impeccable tweed outfits, spouting phrases right out of a Jeeves and Wooster novel. Nash's references to his wife as "the Memsahib" and bombastic utterances such as "Pukka Gin!" and "Jolly good show!" were more suited to the British Raj in India than Nashville, Tennessee. He was just part of what made our motley group so distinctive, combined with Jack Burns' Boston-Irish bombast, and the northern cadences of all us Canadians. We had created our own little island of oddballs within the walls of WLAC-TV.

We didn't see much of Archie Campbell in the writers' room on that trip, presumably because he was conserving his energy by cutting down on commuting and spending more time at his theatre in Gatlinburg. But Archie kept sending us plenty of good material.

Gordie Tapp was busy with his television show in Toronto, but he planned to join us with reams of good routines for the General Store and the Cornfield when he arrived with the rest of our out-of-town cast.

We were just as pleased since our small room could only really comfortably accommodate me and Frank, along with Jack Burns, George Yanok, Tom Lutz, and Stan Ascough. Our job of coming up with new material for all the Cornfield County characters was getting easier by the day as we became more and more familiar with each of them.

It also helped that our local cast members, such as Minnie, Grandpa, and Stringbean, were always popping in with helpful suggestions. Our work load was additionally eased by the fact that there were quite a few comedy bits left over from the previous shoot, and much of the show had always been comprised of bloopers and out-takes that no one could possibly have scripted.

One of the highlights of each trip to Nashville was our outdoor film shoot. It was always fun to get out into the countryside with our director, Bill Davis, filming with a 16mm camera, as everybody did crazy sight gags as a way to cut away from the perfectly-lit studio stuff. Occasionally we would also import a really nutty novelty, like the dog we saw in the *National Enquirer* that could drive a car.

Nonetheless, we had a lot of work to do. Humor is probably the most difficult form of writing, not to mention performing. As British actor and director Sir Donald Wolfit is reputed to have said on his deathbed, "Dying is easy, comedy is hard."

*   *   *

Back at the King of the Road, nothing much had changed, except Jackie Mason was no longer in the penthouse nightclub. He had been replaced by more suitable, and no doubt less costly, local entertainers.

Bernie Glow greeted us on our arrival from Los Angeles, as weird as ever, ready to introduce us to the new game he had planned as our recreation director. Since he apparently lacked any other, more practical abilities, his job was to keep us entertained in the evenings after spending long days creating bucolic buffoonery for our large cast of comical cornhuskers.

At this point, you may well be wondering why we chose to limit our nightly amusements to the confines of the hotel, rather than going out on the town. Surely "Music City, USA" must offer all sorts of exciting after-dark entertainment. That may well be the case in the 21st century, but we're talking about way back in the 1970s when Nashville's night life was crammed into one narrow strip known as Printers Alley. It consisted of neon-lit honky tonks and strip joints, anchored by its prime attraction, Boots, featuring the "Yakety Sax" of Boots Randolph.

Another popular spot was Skull's Rainbow Lounge. Skull, the proprietor, was aptly named, since his head resembled that spooky Halloween prop of the same name. His place of business offered food and drink as well as entertainment by budding young country music hopefuls.

Skull had attached himself to *Hee Haw* as our number one fan from the very beginning, which was a mixed blessing. He took to wearing a pair of our novelty cartoon *Hee Haw* overalls day and night. Alas, the overalls, like Skull himself, were apparently rarely if ever laundered. Still, he was a pleasant, well-meaning fellow and it was nice to have such a dedicated fan in *Hee Haw*'s hometown.

The honky tonks along the strip, with their steady fare of middling country bands and singers, held little interest for us since we could enjoy the very best talent right in our own studio. We gave the strip joints a pass, since the cozy bar at the hotel had far more attractive women to look at, albeit clothed. And although Boots Randolph was an excellent musician, there's only so much yakety sax a body can stand. Of course, we regularly went out to dinner at several of Nashville's many excellent restaurants, but always returned to the comfort of our hotel for postprandial amusements.

Bernie Glow was positively atwitter (with either excitement or the effects of items he had ingested, chosen from his thick volume of apothecary delights) as he described "The Murder Game." Each of us was to write the name of a victim of our choosing on a slip of paper and place it in a hat. The person receiving the most votes would then be given 20 minutes to find a hiding place and would then hunted down and "murdered."

Glow distributed our weapons. Each of us received a realistic black toy pistol, with ammunition consisting of short wooden darts with suction cups on one end. When the chosen victim was found and hit with one of the darts, he would be considered "murdered."

The voting solemnly took place in a secluded part of the downstairs bar, with everyone marking their ballots and dropping them into the hat. The votes were then counted as the suspense mounted. Perhaps a better name for the game would have been "Paranoia," since nobody relishes being a victim. However, I think we all knew who would be the first to be chosen. It was, of course, the devisor of the game, although we vastly underrated the cunning and inventiveness of Bernie Glow once the chase was afoot.

After giving him his 20-minute head start to find a hiding place, we all picked up our weapons and spread out around the hotel, stalking our prey. The rules stipulated that the victim could not seek haven behind locked doors, thereby protecting the privacy of the guests in their rooms, and greatly narrowing his choice of places to hide. Nonetheless, an hour later Glow was nowhere to be found.

We hunters had agreed to meet in the lobby on an hourly basis until the subject of our search had been located and dealt with. After the first hour, we compared notes and apparently had covered every nook and cranny of the King of the Road. Our quarry was still at large.

As we pondered where Glow might be, a voice came over the paging system: "Would a member of the *Hee Haw* group please pick up the phone at the front desk." Stan Ascough rushed to answer the call. When he rejoined the group, he was shaking his head in disbelief.

"It was Bernie," he said. "He's mocking us. He says he's definitely in the hotel, but we have to use our brains to find him. Then he laughed like a maniac and hung up, but I think I know where he might be."

"Where?" we all asked in unison.

"I heard the sound of dishes rattling in the background. I think he's in the hotel kitchen."

"But I already looked there," someone said.

"Obviously not hard enough!"

So off we all scampered to the kitchen to give it a more thorough search. We even looked inside the larger cooking pots, reasoning that Glow was a little guy and anything's possible. We finally had the kitchen staff join the search, but we all came up empty.

While heading back the lobby, we heard ourselves being paged again. It was Glow, of course, cackling and having the time of his life.

"You'll never find me!" he said. "I am the master of my own game."

This time, music was heard in the background, so we all dashed for the elevator and headed up to the penthouse nightclub. We searched the entire room, peering under tables and behind the bandstand, but he just wasn't there. We then pondered how he could have moved from the ground-floor kitchen to the penthouse, so we spread out again and checked all the emergency stairways and main elevators to no avail. He was indeed the master of his own game.

Finally, the third and final call came from our quarry, who was gloating at his cleverness. The lack of any sound in the background, save for a faint whirring noise, led to someone finally coming up with the solution.

"There's one place we haven't looked! He must be using the service elevator in the kitchen."

We all immediately trooped to the kitchen and waited patiently by the service elevator door until it finally opened and revealed our prey. The poor fellow gaped at us in shock as we all shot him point blank with our suction-cupped ammo.

We all agreed it was a game well played and certainly worthy of future encores, and then retired to the bar for a well-earned round of strong drink.

After that, we played practically every night. Bernie Glow became the best and most popular victim by far, with his ability to find the most ingenious hiding places. Sure it was a nutty game, but it was fun and it kept our minds sharp.

Once the out-of-town *Hee Haw* cast took up residence at the hotel, things really got crazy. The sight of a bunch of grown men earnestly stalking around the hotel holding toy guns, with murderous intent in their eyes, was enough to unsettle even the staunchest of souls. At first sight, the pistols looked authentic if you didn't notice the suction cups sticking out of their muzzles.

Once, one of our party happened to be standing outside an elevator in the lobby as Buck Owens emerged. Owens held up his hands in surrender until he noticed the suction cup. Buck, not noted for a highly developed sense of whimsy, lowered his hands, gave the fake gunman a look of total disdain, shook his head sadly at the miscreant, and continued on his way.

Our fake posses got the biggest rise out of some of the female members of the cast, ranging from shrieks of fright to squeaks of alarm at the sight of what appeared to be lethal firearms. Others, like the worldlier Lulu Roman, just took it in stride, shooting us a "boys will be boys" expression. Lisa Todd, always the cool one, simply ignored us.

Roy Clark just laughed and thought we were nuts, but Junior got a real kick out of our nightly stalking and even asked to join in. Junior Samples had an inborn sense of fun. Like the rest of us, I suppose, Junior never wanted to join the real world and become a grown-up.

One of my most vivid memories of those early days in Nashville was the night Junior approached our table in the bar with an impish look on his face and, no doubt, several bourbons on his tab.

"I suppose you fellas think us big fat fellers have little tiny dickies," he said. "Well, that just ain't true. Take a look at this."

With that, Junior reached into the top of his bib overalls and pulled out what appeared to be the very large, pink head of what he would have us believe must be a five-foot long male member. We all just stared in total amazement as Junior let out a hearty guffaw and moved on to the next table still exhibiting what he must have found in a local joke shop. Bill Davis, who was sitting with us that night, just blinked his eyes in shock and made the perfect comment: "Sometimes," he said, "even hooligans blush."

\* \* \*

Meanwhile, back at the studio, everything was moving along at a rapid pace. Our musical guest stars had all been taped singing their latest hits, and for the first time some of them stayed around to appear in some of the comedy spots, particularly in the Cornfield. Gunilla Hutton sang a couple of numbers in addition to her regular role as Doc Campbell's Nurse Goodbody. The great Mickey Mantle even appeared as a special guest star.

The entire cast was in a wonderful mood. We were beginning to feel like a real family, and when it was time to go home we hugged and kissed and vowed that we would all be together again next fall. After all, *Hee Haw* was an enormous hit. How could we not go on into the unforeseeable future?

# 21

# THE GREAT CBS COUNTRY MASSACRE

---

*"They couldn't kill it with a stick so they cancelled it with a pencil."—Frank Peppiatt*

---

Talk about self-delusion! We should have seen it coming. My lunch with Fred Silverman in New York should have been a pretty good indicator that we were doomed.

As early as that February of 1971, a column in *Daily Variety*, predicting shows to be canceled, read: "Apparently doomed are such venerable rube sitcoms as 'Beverly Hillbillies,' 'Green Acres,' and 'Mayberry, RFD,' and such rural variety shows as the Jim Nabors entry and 'Hee Haw.' The latter and 'Mayberry,' however, are strongly resisting all citified notions with good ratings, and thus must be considered marginal."

It was that last sentence that kept our hopes up. Being marginal is a heck of a lot better than being canceled.

In late March, CBS announced its new schedule for the fall 1971–72 season. *Hee Haw* was not included. In a gutsy move by Bob Wood and Fred Silverman, the network had canceled most of their Top Twenty shows in order to "de-ruralize" its programming. How could they do this to us? We had created a fabulously successful show only to have it deleted simply because the cast wore overalls and had twangs?

We were still in Nashville taping what would be the show's final episodes on CBS when the news was released, but nobody had the heart to let us know until we had returned to L.A. Every one of the CBS country stars had been given the axe with the exception of Glen Campbell's "citified" variety show.

Bob Wood had announced that the new schedule represented the most extensive changes in the history of the network. Along with the *The Beverly Hillbillies*, *Mayberry R.F.D.*, *Green Acres*, and Jim Nabors, CBS also canceled *Lassie* and *Hogan's Heroes*, neither of which were at all rural, although it's true that Lassie didn't live in a city. The heartless bastards even dropped *The Ed Sullivan Show*, just one year shy of its 25th anniversary.

Strangely enough, Wood was counting on *All in the Family* to be the biggest lure for urban audiences in that upcoming season. It had finally made its debut following *Hee Haw* in January 1971 at 9:30 P.M. where it foundered with low ratings and a flood of criticism of the bigoted main character. Mind you, putting Archie Bunker after a rural family show like *Hee Haw* seemed like a pretty dumb move. However, the reaction to the pilot in the editing room, when we were assembling *Hee Haw* for that first summer back in 1969, gave us a pretty good indication that *Family* would be a hit.

Needless to say, Peppiatt and I were pretty depressed by the news. We started ruing that we hadn't done the Don Knotts series for NBC instead of beating a dead donkey. Then the news came that NBC had cancelled Don's show for the coming season. CBS, however, had renewed *The Doris Day Show* for a third season, so we could also rue not doing her show when we had had the chance.

Adding insult to injury, CBS sent us an accounting of their sale of *Hee Haw* for syndication in Australia. The network had reaped several hundred thousands of dollars from the sale, but after deducting costs for tapes, reels, and other miscellaneous items, our share turned out to be a measly five bucks. We demanded an audit, which CBS Business Affairs agreed to do. The result, a few weeks later, claimed that Yongestreet owed CBS money on the deal. We considered it creative bookkeeping at its bogus best.

As we sank further into a full funk, Perry Lafferty invited us to lunch and tried to cheer us up by telling us that CBS still loved us, and that Bob Wood had been forced to do what he did—it wasn't simply because he hated our show.

Each network, aside from having hundreds of individual affiliates around the country, also owned and operated a few choice TV stations (known in the trade as "O&O") in large metropolitan markets such as New York, Los Angeles, Boston, Philadelphia, and San Francisco. Naturally, these O&Os accounted for much of a network's profits, and were therefore of the utmost importance when it came to scheduling programming.

Even though *Hee Haw* and the rest of the rural comedies on CBS were wildly popular nationwide, they fared poorly in the big urban O&O markets. It was pretty obvious that in New York and Boston, sophisticated viewers would not savor the antics of hayseed bumpkins, while bib overalls hardly made a fashion statement in Los Angeles. The O&Os complained bitterly that their urban advertisers weren't buying into shows having little appeal to urban buyers of urban products.

Apparently, geezers were also no better off than cornhuskers. Metropolitan advertisers—other than Geritol and Polident—were seeking a younger audience than Ed Sullivan was delivering for CBS. Similarly, Lawrence Welk had just been given the boot by ABC, after 16 years of loyal service and high nationwide ratings. Even the kiddie market seemed to be taboo—thus the exit of *Lassie*. Hogan and his heroes, I was relieved to hear, were simple victims of low ratings and not a corporate decision that World War II was old hat.

Perry Lafferty then suggested that we start thinking about creating yet another new show that would appeal to both town and country viewers who were neither too young nor too old. With that in mind, and with Lafferty's good wishes, we walked out of CBS Television City and into an extremely uncertain future.

* * *

Back at Yongestreet, Nick Vanoff had some interesting news.

Vanoff was the business brain of our group, thank God, since Frank and I were strictly right-brain creative people who had previously left such things to agents and managers. Up to then, we'd had no need to consider affairs of commerce. We had always delivered the scripts and the shows in return for handsome paychecks, and so far life had been not only good to us but a lot of fun too. Now, however, the time had come to start paying attention to the business side of show business.

Vanoff filled us in on some developments that might possibly save *Hee Haw*. First of all, the networks had been ordered by the FCC to divest themselves of syndication rights to all their shows. In addition to that, the FCC ruled that individual stations must devote the hours between 6 P.M. and 8 P.M. to local news or local programming. The affiliates had largely depended on the networks to fill the bulk of those hours, and most stations around the country couldn't afford to fill all that time—officially known as "primetime access"—except for their regular local newscasts. Thus, hundreds of TV stations around the country were looking for syndicated programming to fill the gap. Lawrence Welk was the first to take advantage of this, and his show was already being offered to all those outlets, apparently with great success. So why couldn't we do the same thing with *Hee Haw*?

Vanoff suggested selling the show on the "barter system." We would offer the show to the stations for free, which is not as dumb as it sounds. Each show would have eight commercial positions, four for the local station and four for us. The station would sell its ad positions to local sponsors, and, hopefully, we would sell ours to national advertisers.

The only catch was that our four spots would be our only source of income to pay for the show and make a profit. It all depended on how much we could get for each of our four minutes. On top of that, we would have to pay to produce the first 13 shows out of our own pockets, an investment of well over a million bucks. It was a hell of a gamble.

Our manager, Bernie Brillstein, was dead set against it. He thought we could make a lot more money doing other shows. Thank God, Frank and I were still in demand as writers and producers. But once we had had a taste of owning a hit show, it was pretty hard to go back to just being hired hands. Brillstein wanted nothing to do with it. He thought we were absolutely nuts!

What the heck? We had nothing to lose but our shirts.

# 22

# SAVING OUR "ASS"

*"You guys should do what you want to do! Either way, you win or lose."—Sam Lovullo*

Following Lovullo's ringing malaprop endorsement, he and Nick Vanoff went to the annual spring meeting of the National Association of Television Program Executives (NATPE) in Chicago to find out how many stations wanted our show. Vanoff also enlisted the aid of his old friend, Alan Courtney, a former NBC vice-president and more recently president of Four Star Productions, who joined them on the trip.

It was obvious that almost everybody wanted *Hee Haw*, and our guys were deluged with offers from all the distributors who were practically salivating to syndicate the show for us. The catch was that they all wanted 40 percent off the top. Such an arrangement was obviously untenable, so Vanoff made the gutsy decision that we would do it all ourselves.

Back in L.A., wires were sent out to all the CBS affiliates who were broadcasting the show (*Hee Haw* was still in re-runs), plus every other television station in the country. It had never been done before and the reaction was overwhelming!

Practically all the CBS outlets, save for the O&Os, wanted to keep *Hee Haw* on the air, and a flock of affiliates of other networks—plus quite a few independents—were willing to sign on as well. Soon we had a really impressive network of outlets to air the show, with hundreds of stations printed on cards and pinned to a huge board in Sam Lovullo's office.

Vanoff's plan was to beam the show out of Nashville directly to all our stations at 7 P.M. every Saturday night. It was a hell of an exciting plan. We would have our very own *Hee Haw* network! Alan Courtney was so impressed he decided to join Yongestreet Productions and use his considerable prestige to help Vanoff sell spots to national advertisers in New York.

We raised enough money to finance the production of the first 13 shows by putting second mortgages on our homes and emptying our bank accounts. It would be the gamble of our lives. Against the advice of practically everyone, Peppiatt and I prepared to head back to Nashville and start putting shows together as if nothing had happened.

We vowed not to skimp on anything, though Jack Burns, the highest paid of all our writers, gracefully bowed out to lighten the load. Burns could always make a good living as a performer as he was soon to prove when he reunited with Avery Schreiber.

As a team, Burns and Schreiber had always been hilarious, best known for a routine that began years before when the two first met on the stage of Chicago's Second City. Burns played the fast-talking, opinionated Boston tourist seated in the back seat of a taxi driven by Schreiber, the world-weary cab driver. Not long after Burns left *Hee Haw*, they were not only playing Las Vegas but soon starring in their own TV series.

As Peppiatt and I headed off to Nashville in May 1971, Nick Vanoff and Alan Courtney flew to New York with high hopes of selling our four minutes to national advertisers at premium prices.

Vanoff and Courtney were indeed an odd couple. Physically, they were as different as Noël Coward's description of China and Japan: one very big, the other very small. Vanoff, a former professional dancer, was slight of stature and whippet-thin, with the temperament of a coiled spring. Courtney, on the other hand, was the very model of a powerful executive. He was quite tall, with a stocky build and a booming voice, combined with the confident manner of an Ivy League brahmin.

Their backgrounds were equally poles apart. Vanoff had come to America as the child of Greek immigrants who settled in Buffalo, N.Y., and grew up in humble quarters above his family's restaurant. In his late teens, he joined the Marines where his talent as a dancer flowered as a performer in camp shows. Following discharge, Vanoff had gone to New York seeking a career as a dancer on Broadway, and eked out a meager living as a member of various experimental ballet companies around town. He finally made it to Broadway in the original production of *Kiss Me, Kate*.

Courtney, on the other hand, was the child of a well-to-do California family who began his executive career when he became manager of a large, upscale movie palace. This was back in the days when armies of trained ushers wearing braided uniforms wielded flashlights with which to lead patrons to plush seats in enormous, darkened auditoriums, richly decorated not unlike the interior of Versailles, as thousands gazed at star-studded motion pictures on one gigantic silver screen.

By the early 1950s, when the growing competition of television forced the demise of the movie palace, Courtney turned his considerable management abilities to the new medium at NBC, where he quickly rose through the ranks at Rockefeller Center to become vice-president of programming.

Between dancing gigs, Vanoff had also turned to television, holding cue cards for *The Perry Como Show* at NBC. In time, he had become Como's associate producer. As a result, Vanoff abandoned the muse of Terpsichore in favor of this new, more lucrative career.

With both Vanoff and Courtney at NBC, their paths quite naturally crossed and they soon became good friends, an association that lasted over the years as both men carved out impressive careers. Vanoff became a highly successful producer, and Courtney became president of several major television companies. By merging their diverse talents and personalities, making our challenging enterprise a success would seem a slam dunk.

They were in for a rude awakening upon their arrival in New York.

* * *

Meanwhile, our arrival in Nashville was greeted with nothing but cheers for our bold plan to keep *Hee Haw* on the air. The members of the cast were all thrilled to be back, and everyone was still on board. We had even added a couple of fresh new faces, Barbi Benton and Misty Rowe.

Barbi Benton had gained fame as a *Playboy* centerfold in 1970 and as Hugh Hefner's constant companion for six years. She certainly added to the feminine quotient of the show, was wonderful to look at, and brought us loads of publicity.

Misty Rowe, however, was the real find. A blonde beauty with an adorable lisp, she

<u>Wire to TV Stations</u>

*April 5, 1971*

Because of the exciting response from stations, agencies,
sponsors and viewers, Yongestreet Productions will continue in production with new one-hour HEE HAW shows for
the Fall 1971-72 season.  These programs will maintain
the same high quality they delivered as the Number 15
Nielsen show for the 1970-71 season.  The programs will
be supplied to you without charge with 4 minutes of
commercials, leaving 4 additional minutes for you to
sell.

Please advise us by wire or phone:

(1)  If you can clear and can schedule a minimum of 26
     new HEE HAW shows and 26 repeats.

(2)  If so, can you clear 7:00 to 8:00 p.m. Saturday
     C.N.Y.T. in the event we elect to make a feed on
     an inter-connected basis.

(3)  If you have an alternative time period for broad-
     cast that you would prefer.

Subject to our securing necessary clearance, we will
confirm to you in ample time so that firm commitments can
be made by May 15.

Please contact Alan Courtney, Sam Lovullo, Frank Peppiatt,
John Aylesworth, or Nick Vanoff at 213-273-8290, 357 North
Canon Drive, Beverly Hills, California 90210.


                    (signed)    Alan Courtney, President
                                Yongestreet Program Services

**April 5, 1971, wire to TV stations from Alan Courtney, president, Yongestreet Program Ser-
vices, to supply programming to stations without charge after *Hee Haw* was canceled by the
network.**

*Ellen*

Rev. 5/24/71

HEE HAW TAPING SCHEDULE - MAY/JUNE 1971

TUESDAY, MAY 25

SAMMI SMITH

HAGERS

WEDNESDAY, MAY 26

GUNILLA HUTTON

ARCHIE

HAGERS

THURSDAY, MAY 27

CONWAY TWITTY (PFFT) - Archie

LORETTA LYNN

HAGERS

FRIDAY, MAY 28

DALE ROBERTSON (PFFT)

ARCHIE

NASHVILLE EDITION

SATURDAY, SUNDAY, MAY 29 & 30

OFF (FILM REMOTE)

MONDAY, MAY 31

ROY ROGERS (PFFT)

DALE EVANS

TUESDAY, JUNE 1

BUCK OWENS SONGS

WEDNESDAY, JUNE 2

BUCK SONGS

THURSDAY, JUNE 3

BUCK SONGS

FRIDAY, JUNE 4

BUCK SONGS W/SUSAN

SUSAN RAYE

KENNI HUSKY

BAKERSFIELD BRASS

**Copy of *Hee Haw* taping schedule for May/June 1971.**

had recently appeared in a movie as Marilyn Monroe. She had shown her comedy flair as Maid Marion in Mel Brooks' satirical Robin Hood TV series *When Things Were Rotten*.

It was obvious that cute little Misty would be the ideal foil for Junior Samples' Used Car Dealer spot, which we hadn't got around to using since Tom Lutz had first suggested it. I'm glad we waited.

On camera, Misty and Junior were simply made for each other. When it came time to tape, eight Edsels had been borrowed from a local collector to make up the set, bedecked with colorful pennants. The make-up people had painted a thin black moustache on Junior, adding the perfect touch as he tried to sell his worthless stock with a series of TV commercials aided by his adorable assistant, Misty. Each spot ended with a catch line that would soon sweep the country: "The number to call is BR 549."

Our musical guest stars were just as happy to see us back in Nashville as our regular cast. The line-up for the first year in syndication would include Roy Rogers and Dale Evans, always a lucky charm. Old friends included Loretta Lynn and Tammy Wynette, as well as a few new faces like Conway Twitty, Jeannie C. Riley ("Harper Valley P.T.A."), Brenda Lee, Porter Wagoner, and Dolly Parton.

Bud Wingard came up with a couple of funny new musical spots to highlight our growing contingent of beautiful girls, and the comedy was better than ever. The fact that we were paying for it all out of our own pockets gave us a wonderful pride of ownership, but we had to make a few sacrifices.

Considering our shaky future, Lovullo was lucky to make a deal with the local Howard Johnson motel as the new home for our cast and production people. We also saw fit to dispense with our recreation director, Bernie Glow, a definitely expendable expense. I have no idea what became of that funny little man. Perhaps he ended up following his true calling as an assistant pharmacist.

In any event, it was time to put away childish things and spend our free time simply enjoying evenings with the *Hee Haw* gang.

Everything was coming up roses in Music City. We could only hope that Nick Vanoff and Alan Courtney were having as fruitful a time in New York.

# 23

# "NEW YORK STATE OF MIND"

*"The networks have a responsibility not to air mindless rural pap like* Hee Haw*"—Fred Silverman, addressing the National Association of Broadcasters, 1971*

When Nick Vanoff and Alan Courtney arrived in New York City hoping to sell four minutes of time to national advertisers for the coming season of *Hee Haw*, they almost immediately ran into a brick wall of indifference.

Since canceling all their country shows, Bob Wood and Fred Silverman were continually casting scathing slurs on rural programming—*Hee Haw* in particular—as if they had saved the world by banishing everything with even a hint of hay in it. Their message was loud and clear: twangs were taboo and country was bad for the country. It was thus little wonder that Madison Avenue's reception was icy cold when Vanoff and Courtney approached to sell their rustic wares.

There were other problems as well. A lot of network advertisers had already pretty much firmed up their advertising schedule for 1971. The economy was down and, aside from Lawrence Welk, hour-long variety shows were a rarity in syndication. Most of the syndicated offerings were daytime talk shows such as *Donahue*, or half-hours on film like *Death Valley Days* and *Wild Kingdom*. Even *Lassie* had resurfaced with new shows.

The outlook was decidedly bleak. The few account executives to actually give Vanoff and Courtney an audience practically laughed in their faces at the outrageous possibility of a self-respecting national advertiser actually buying into a hayseed horror like *Hee Haw*. That hadn't been a problem when we were on CBS because that was a major network. We had now been demoted to the bargain basement of syndication.

Discouraged but still optimistic, these two esteemed and powerful men in the world of television, who had left their Beverly Hills mansions on a quest to sell a hit network show in transition, were now forced to share a room in a cheap midtown hotel. It was just downright humiliating. Vanoff, in particular, had spent many wonderful years in New York, but this wasn't one of them. He often looked back fondly at the fun times he'd had at the old Hudson Theater producing *The Steve Allen Show* with Bill Harbach.

In case you were wondering what had become of Harbach, our original fourth partner in Yongestreet productions, he bailed out on us the moment CBS cancelled *Hee Haw*. He was an inveterate New Yorker who had never really liked living in Los Angeles. Although he had enjoyed working with Vanoff on *The Hollywood Palace*, he had never gotten into the West Coast lifestyle. And although Harbach was fun to have around with his upbeat charm and quirky personality, he had never offered much input to the company.

When *Hee Haw* had come along, Harbach was completely baffled by the show's popularity. He loved show business, and to him *Hee Haw* was definitely not show business. He yearned to return to his tower in Manhattan, where Broadway played his kind of music and hillbillies belonged in "Li'l Abner" on the *Daily News'* comics page.

William O. Harbach was the son of Otto Harbach, the brilliant lyricist who provided the words to such classic songs as "Smoke Gets in Your Eyes." Lacking his father's creative talent and dyslectic as well, Harbach made up for any shortcomings with bounding energy and the stunning good looks of a movie star. In fact, MGM once signed him to a contract as a possible leading man, but after non-speaking parts in a couple of musicals, he was finally let go because he couldn't remember lines. He did, however, become friendly with just about every big name in Hollywood, a definite plus as a producer of early television variety programs.

In his beloved New York, Harbach had taken over *The Steve Allen Show* in the 1950s. Nick Vanoff became his associate producer, taking care of all the day-to-day chores of actually getting the show on the air. Meanwhile, Harbach charged around the office entertaining Steve Allen and the staff with his loony non-sequiturs, and lured top names to appear as guest stars on the show.

Unfortunately, Harbach's terrible memory extended to stars' names. To make up for this, he tried to remember them by what they were known for. For example, when Charlton Heston, star of the *The Ten Commandments*, appeared on the show, Harbach constantly referred to him as Chester Moses.

Comedian Bill Dana, a writer on the Allen show, recalled the time Harbach burst into the writer's room to announce that he had booked Ethel Waters and wanted them to come up with a sexy production number for her. Since sexy hardly fit the image of the matronly Miss Waters, they quickly learned from Vanoff that Harbach was referring to the glamorous swimming star, Esther Williams. In Harbach's mind, the combination of Esther and swimming had translated into Ethel Waters.

Another time, as Dana tells it, a friend called him to ask if Harbach was free for lunch. The reply was classic Harbach: "You bet! I'll meet you in five minutes at the corner of Walk and Don't Walk!" With that, he abruptly hung up the phone and rushed out the door. Harbach must have had a lonely lunch that day.

A few years later, when Vanoff and Harbach were co-producing *The Hollywood Palace*, Harbach was the scourge of stand-up comedians. In rehearsal, when they would run through their routines, Harbach would laugh heartily all the way through, and then yell out, "Pure gold! Cut it in half!"

Yet another time, while a magician who worked with dozens of birds was doing his act on the air, a loud crash was heard from backstage causing the frightened birds to fly out into the audience, liberally sprinkling everyone with what birds usually sprinkle on statues and people. Harbach immediately rushed out on stage and, thinking of the SPCA but mixing it up with the organization that collected his father's music royalties, he yelled out, "Call ASCAP!"

When Harbach opted out of Yongestreet, Vanoff bought Harbach's share of the company and then owned 50 percent, while Frank and I retained 25 percent each. Needless to say, we were a bit miffed that we weren't consulted about this arrangement. On the other hand, Vanoff was responsible for half our debts if things didn't work out. As we saw it, he was twice the gambler we were with twice the exposure, making his plight trying to sell ads for *Hee Haw* in New York even more pressing.

As for Bill Harbach, he was happy as a lark being back home in his beloved New

HEE HAW

Commercial Rundown

AGENCIES: Compton Advertising--Don McIntosh--Proctor & Gamble, Crisco
B.B.D. & O.--Don Schwab-Dodge
Valentine Smith--David Kennedy--Kids Magazine
Parkson Advertising--Irv Ross--Geritol

SHOW #3     PROD. # 71054     TELCO AIR DATE: 10/2/71

| Comm #1 | Station | (:60) |
|---|---|---|
| Comm #2 | Station | (:60) |
| Comm #3 | Public Service Annc. Driver Safety | (:30) |
| | Public Service Annc.-Technical Careers | (:30) |
| | or | |
| | * Kids Magazine TV-VS-60-2C | (:60) |
| Comm #4 | Public Service Annc.-Capt. Clean-up | (:30) |
| | Public Service Annc.-Love Poster | (:30) |
| | or | |
| | * Kids Magazine TV-VS-60-1C | (:60) |
| | STATION TIME & I.D. | (:33) |
| Comm #5 | Station | (:60) |
| Comm #6 | Station | (:60) |
| Comm #7A | Dodge-DT/1-72-30P-Softie | (:30) |
| #7B | Public Service Annc.-Down and Out | (:30) |
| | or | |
| | * Geritol-WJGE 0083 30 | (:30) |
| Comm #8A | Proctor & Gamble-Crisco  PG CCO 780 | (:30) |
| Comm #8B | Public Service Annc.-Love Poster | (:30) |
| | STATION TIME & I.D. | (1:04) |

* Only stations on Telco Feed and KTLA in Los Angeles received and
aired the "Kids Magazine" commercials in positions 3 & 4 and the
"Geritol" commercial in position 7B.  All others aired the public
service announcements as listed above.

**Commercial rundown for *Hee Haw* showing only two sponsors when the show began taping for syndication, 1971.**

York. He and Vanoff had dinner together once in a while during this treacherous time. Harbach expressed sympathy for Vanoff's plight, but still had not the slightest inkling why a show like *Hee Haw* could possibly be worth saving.

After about a month of seemingly endless humiliation, Vanoff and Courtney finally discerned a faint ray of light at the end of the tunnel. An account executive at Compton

## COMPTON ADVERTISING, INC.

*625 Madison Avenue, New York, N.Y. 10022*

TELEPHONE: *(212) 754-1100*

*Vice President*

Dear

In the 'first October' Nielsen pocketpiece there were 14 prime time network shows that didn't reach the 9,000,000 homes level (equivalent to a 14.5 rating).

But, believe it or not, a syndicated show reached that 9,000,000 level in its sixth week!

The show - "Hee Haw" - formerly on the CBS network, now in syndication, currently carried by 195 stations (over half of which are CBS affiliates).

Nielsen's documenting the show's progress, and it's pretty impressive to date as evidenced by the 9,000,000 figure - what makes it even better is the realistic, reasonable price tag the producers have put on it.

> For Jan./Feb./Mar. the price is $31,500 per :60 -
> half of that for a :30.

Based on its performance to date, the show is almost certain to average 10,000,000 homes in the January-March period - providing a homes CPM of $3.15. The prognosis for prime night network in this period looks to be in the $3.75-$3.90 area.

The price and CPM become even better if you buy an alternate week minute (or 1-:30 weekly) over the 8½ months January-September 1972:

> Estimated Homes   -   8,035,000
> Average :60 Price  -   $22,500
> Homes CPM         -   $2.80

That's why we call their pricing reasonable and realistic!

(cont'd.)

*₁N ADVERTISING, INC.*

Page -2-                          November 5, 1971

How about audience composition?

| Category | Viewers Per Set |
|----------|-----------------|
| Total Women | .82 |
| Total Men | .74 |
| 18-49 Women | .41 |
| 18-49 Men | .38 |
| 35+ Women | .62 |
| 35+ Men | .56 |

Despite all this, the show is having rough sledding this year - they started selling after a lot of network advertisers had firmed up for calendar 1971, the general economic picture wasn't too rosy, and a lot of us in the industry have somewhat of a "wait and see" attitude re syndicated shows this year.

What's our stake in this: Nothing personal, except one of our clients is in the show and we'd like to have it available for a long time to come. Also, we just hate to see a good effort like this go to waste, because of an unfortunate mixture of circumstances, especially when it's doing so exceptionally well.

One thing further you should know. Like all syndicated shows, "Hee Haw" isn't cleared everywhere - however, its 195 stations give it 82% U.S. coverage and it's carried in 45 of the top 50 markets. On a total U.S. basis it currently has a 28% share and if we relate that to only the area where the show is cleared its share is 34%. *Yongestreet continues to work on clearances and expects soon to add several more markets in the top 50.

Tnat's the story and, frankly, we're hoping you'll look twice at this property as you move into January 1972 (and beyond) network negotiations. The guy to call at Yongestreet is Nick Vanoff and the New York number: 212 - JU 6-5930.

For your use, attached is a spec sheet spelling out, in detail, current and future audience data for this show.

Cordially,

COMPTON ADVERTISING, INC.


Graham D. Hay, Vice President
Director, Network Relations

GDH:jhk

Att.

*The show is produced by Yongestreet Productions.


*Above and opposite:* **Form letter to interest advertisers, from Graham D. Hay, vice-president, director network relations, Compton Advertising, November 5, 1971.**

Advertising took pity on our two bloodied but unbowed heroes and threw them a bone. One of his clients was Proctor & Gamble, and one of P&G's many products was Crisco, the brand of shortening thought to be a favorite of Southern bumpkins. With this in mind, they agreed to buy two 30-second spots on the newly syndicated *Hee Haw* at bargain basement rates.

It wasn't much, but at least it was something.

# 24

# THE LONG WAIT

*"It ain't over 'til it's over."* — *Yogi Berra*

On our arrival back home in Los Angeles with enough material for thirteen new shows, we obviously couldn't work at CBS, so arrangements had been made to put the show together at a new, state-of-the art editing arm of the Technicolor organization Vidtronics.

When we arrived with our huge load of 2" tapes on reels the size of tires on a jumbo jet, our new editor took one look, shook his head in wonder, and promptly went to work. He turned out to be okay, although we greatly missed good old Marc Zappia, who had won *Hee Haw*'s one and only Emmy.

As far as Vidtronics was concerned, as Bill Davis put it, one dark room is pretty much the same as another. The biggest difference was simply that CBS was no longer footing the editing costs, and we were fast approaching the poverty of dormice.

Meanwhile, the news from New York was pretty disheartening. Aside from the slightly comical vision of the wiry Vanoff sharing one room in a cheesy hotel with the portly Courtney, it was downright discouraging that after all those weeks they had only succeeded in selling a couple of 30-second spots to the makers of canned lard. If things didn't improve, we would all be broke and homeless.

While Bill Davis was busily assembling the first and, we thought, the last *Hee Haw* shows, Frank and I remembered Perry Lafferty's advice to come up with a brand new show.

Back at Yongestreet, with Vanoff and Courtney in New York, the offices were like a ghost town. Lovullo was still finishing up in Nashville. That left only Max, our surly switchboard operator, and Dottie, Courtney's chirpy little secretary. Frank and I were between secretaries at the time, which was just as well since we would have had to pay her with IOUs.

Over the next week and a half, we finally came up with a concept for a new series. *Happy Days* had suffered from attracting an audience primarily made up of geezers, and *Hee Haw* was strictly for middle America, so we decided we had to create something reflecting the current tastes of hip urban viewers. After all, we had broken new ground in the 1960s when we wrote *Hullabaloo*, the first network show devoted to rock 'n' roll, so now we planned to do the same for the 1970s. We would call it *Hip Hip Today!* an hour filled with the latest musical groups and lots of smart satirical comedy.

We called in Jack Burns to help us write the cutting-edge sketches, and made a list of the hottest singles from *Billboard*'s Hot 100. The pilot script was completed in a little over two weeks. We then called Lafferty, who loved the title and the idea. He said he would set up a meeting for us with Fred Silverman, who was coming to the West Coast in a couple of weeks.

Naturally, we wanted to make the presentation as special as possible, and we suddenly remembered the successful audio pilot we had made for *Happy Days*. Why not do the same for *Hip Hip Today!*?

We rounded up our favorite comic performers and set a date to record the pilot the following week. To save money, we would use commercial singles of the latest musical hits to augment the comedy, and we made the best deal we could with a recording studio. The result was a slick, ultra-contemporary, and very funny sampler of hot rock and biting satire.

When Silverman came to town, Lafferty arranged a lunch meeting in his executive dining room. Looking back on it, it would now be utterly impossible for a couple of writer-producers to present a new show idea to the top brass of a network without going through all kinds of channels.

Back then there were four vice-presidents at each major network. Each VP had a staff of one (a secretary), and they had autonomy over their own individual departments: Drama, Sitcoms, Variety, and News. They were always available to hear new ideas, and if they found one they felt was worthy, they would pass it on to a senior vice-president in charge of programming and a decision would be made. At CBS, there were two senior VPs: Lafferty on the West Coast and Fred Silverman on the East. Both had only the president of the network—Bob Wood at CBS—above them.

Today, everything is run by committee. Each vice-president has a fleet of as many as 20 assistants, most of whom are young interns fresh out of TV school. None of the current VPs has the kind of autonomy we experienced back then. If you're lucky enough to get an appointment to pitch an idea, you get 20 different opinions of why your idea won't work. Nobody wants to take responsibility. The senior VPs are impossible to meet with until you go through the junior VPs and their minions. Apparently, only the president of a network can actually make a decision, and they're scared stiff they might make the wrong one and be replaced. It's a wonder anything new ever gets on the air!

All this has occurred since the major networks were taken over by large corporations, and therefore run much the same way as their corporate owners. The chance that two guys with an idea could just call up a senior VP and set up a meeting to pitch it, and then get an immediate decision, is nil. In the 21st century, the business of show is simply business. It would have been impossible to sell a show like *Hee Haw* if we had had to go through the current pecking order.

Fortunately for us it was 1971, and we had access to all the decision-makers. We were excited about the meeting and hoped that maybe Fred Silverman felt he owed us one for the ill-fated John Wayne affair.

And so it came to pass that with crossed fingers we went to CBS Television City for lunch with the man who might hold our future in the palm of his urban hand. We could only hope that the stench of *Hee Haw* wouldn't affect his judgment of our latest endeavor.

We needn't have worried. After a pleasant lunch, we played our sampler, Silverman chuckled in all the right places and enjoyed the music, and when it was over he turned to us with a big smile.

"I love it!" he said.

We practically fainted with relief.

"Bob Wood is coming out here at the end of the week, so let's all get together then and make a decision," he went on. "As far as I'm concerned, it's a hit!"

Frank and I were ecstatic! We called Nick Vanoff in New York with the good news.

"I wish I was having that kind of good luck here in New York," he said, his voice reflecting the agony of defeat. "Nobody's budging. If it weren't for the guys at Compton Advertising, I'd come home right now and forget the whole thing."

"No, you wouldn't," I said. "You're not the kind of guy who gives up easy."

"Yeah, I guess I'm not, damn it."

"If we can sell this show to Bob Wood, everything will be fine, Nick," said Frank, as cheerfully as possible.

"Good luck selling your new show, guys," he replied. "Now I gotta get back to work trying to save the last show you sold."

* * *

Our meeting with Bob Wood and Fred Silverman was set for a Friday afternoon. At the appointed hour, we walked into the conference room on the third floor of Television City. Wood and Silverman were waiting for us at one end of the conference table. Wood greeted us cordially, which rather surprised us. Silverman, our new ally, looked on with a smile and told Wood that we had come up with a really interesting concept for a new variety show. Without any preamble, we put our audio pilot tape of *Hip Hip Today!* into the big Ampex player in one corner of the room and let it roll.

I have no idea what Bob Wood was expecting, but his reaction as he listened was stoic. In spite of Silverman having chuckled in all the right places; Wood barely cracked a smile. The show might as well have been called *Hee Haw Today*.

At the end of the sampler tape, there was a long silence. It was finally broken by Bob Wood.

"I don't get it," he said.

We were a bit flustered by this reaction and tried to explain that, unlike *Hee Haw* or *Happy Days*, this show would reflect what was happening right now through smart, contemporary comedy and the very latest on the music scene.

Silverman came to our defense, saying he thought we did a hell of a good job, and the show certainly fit the new image of the network.

Unfortunately, the president of the network remained unimpressed. Perhaps he was stuck with a vision of that damn donkey braying in his head. He said he was sorry but he just wasn't sold on our concept. He thanked us for coming in, we all shook hands and he left the room, leaving three completely bewildered people staring at each other.

Finally Fred Silverman shrugged, expressing our mutual bewilderment. Like so many other worthy projects in the world of television that inexplicably never get on the air, this was simply yet another exercise in futility.

We never took the presentation to NBC or ABC. I guess we were pretty demoralized about the whole thing. Besides, our hearts still belonged to our first born—*Hee Haw*. Though slightly diminished, our hopes were still high. All we could do was wait and see what happened next.

# 25

# *HEE HAW*'S BACK!

---

*"The critics are unanimous, but watch it anyway."—Syndication promo, 1971*

---

*Hee Haw* was beamed out of Nashville to almost 200 television stations for its debut in syndication on September 18, 1971. We had no way of knowing how many people watched, since unlike the networks' overnight and weekly Nielsen reports, ratings for syndicated shows were issued monthly.

Most of our stations had scheduled the show from 7 to 8 P.M. on Saturdays. In a lot of markets, *The Lawrence Welk Show* was scheduled directly opposite us in that same time period. We could only hope our fans would outnumber the geezers who watched Welk.

All our stations were making out like bandits, with their four minutes of commercial time sold out at prime rates to local advertisers. Unfortunately, we had only two 30-second spots for Crisco, which barely paid for our editing costs. The remaining three minutes were filled by free public service announcements for the likes of Smokey the Bear and driver safety.

The show itself looked better than ever. We hadn't cut back on anything, and the audience reaction was great. Adoring fan mail poured in like never before, mostly thanking us for keeping the show on the air. The regional critics were turning soft, complimenting our bravery in sticking with a product even they had to admit was becoming a genuine piece of Americana.

Back in New York, however, we were still a laughingstock. How could intelligent, sophisticated television pros like the people at Yongestreet take such a gamble on a show that appealed only to backward hicks in the sticks? If it hadn't been for the friendly reception they had received at Compton Advertising, Nick Vanoff and Alan Courtney would have felt even more suicidal than they did when *Hee Haw* debuted that September in New York and appeared on a local independent station in a less-than-prime-time period, and Yongestreet was billed for the privilege.

Finally, in late October, the Nielsen ratings for syndicated shows were released. On November 5, 1971, Compton Advertising sent out a memo to other agencies stating that although 14 prime-time network shows had failed to reach the 9,000,000-homes level, the syndicated *Hee Haw* had reached 9,000,000 homes in only its sixth week. It was being carried by 195 stations, over half of which were CBS affiliates. In other words, we were a hit!

The Compton memo went on to say that in addition to having such a huge audience, *Hee Haw* also had a very reasonable price tag: $31,500 per 60-second spot, and half that for 30 seconds. Based on its performance to date, *Hee Haw* was almost certain to average

10,000,000 homes in the January-March period, which made it one hell of a buy for the coming year!

The memo was signed by Graham D. Hay, vice-president, director Network Relations. Mr. Hay added one personal plea on our behalf, for which I'll be eternally grateful:

> Despite all this, the show is having rough sledding this year—they started selling after a lot of network advertisers had firmed up for calendar 1971, the general economic picture wasn't too rosy, and a lot of us in the industry have somewhat of a "wait and see" attitude re syndicated shows this year.
>
> What's our stake in this? Nothing personal, except that one of our clients is in the show and we'd like to have it available for a long time to come. Also, we just hate to see a good effort like this go to waste, because of an unfortunate mixture of circumstances, especially when it's doing so exceptionally well.

Thanks to Mr. Hay's memo, *Hee Haw* was no longer a laughingstock. The doors along Madison Avenue were beginning to open wide to Mr. Vanoff and Mr. Courtney. We were Number One in syndication, with ratings almost equal to those we had enjoyed on the CBS network. By January, we would have a full slate of national advertisers and be able to make a victorious return to Nashville. We would have enough income to tape the next 13 shows for our first full season in syndication, with a second season virtually assured.

It would take a while to make back our original investment, but if *Hee Haw* held up in the ratings, our gamble would finally have paid off.

# 26

# HAPPY DAYS ARE HERE AGAIN

---

*"Hee Haw gets last laugh."*—Variety, *1972*

---

By January 1972, we were one of the hottest shows and the best buy in television. All across the nation, Saturday night was *Hee Haw* night in more than 10,000,000 homes. We were beating all the competition in syndication, including our biggest rival, Lawrence Welk.

Even so, we weren't completely out of the woods yet. We still needed more station clearances. Even though we almost equaled the ratings we had had the previous year on CBS, as of November we were carried in only 45 of the top 50 markets, having just over 80 percent of the country covered. We obviously needed more.

Alan Courtney was now officially president of Yongestreet Program Services. Since he and Vanoff had returned from New York, Courtney had been diligently calling TV stations trying to improve our coverage. We could hear his booming voice from his office down the hall for eight hours a day, wheedling and cajoling recalcitrant big-city station after station to put *Hee Haw* on their schedules.

*Hee Haw*'s success was literally going to Courtney's head. One morning, he announced that he was shopping for a toupee to cover his bald dome.

"I've found one that you can actually swim in," he told us.

"Gee, it must be enormous," said Peppiatt, with mock awe.

The next day, Courtney appeared wearing what looked like a lemon soufflé on his head, matching his flaxen fringe. We stifled our laughter, since he seemed extremely pleased with his new head cozy. He was still wearing it when I last saw him years later. Heck, whatever made him happy.

Courtney was an amazing salesman. He managed to get us on the air in cities like Boston and Philadelphia, where our show had little drawing power. In fact, we were shocked when word got to us that we had one very unlikely fan in Boston—Arthur Fiedler, the legendary conductor of the Boston Pops Orchestra.

The truth was we had legions of unlikely viewers. While in New York for the Ali-Frazier fight, Walter Cronkite and Bennett Cerf had said they had seen the show and got a kick out of it. Sammy Davis, Jr., thought we were a hoot and came to Nashville to be on one of our shows, as did my favorite comic, Alan King. Even President George H.W. Bush actually appeared in one of our trade magazine ads!

One of *Hee Haw*'s most memorable fans wasn't a well known personality at all. He was a retired farmer in his late 90s who popped up one night on NBC's *Tonight Show Starring Johnny Carson*. Carson introduced him as "the world's oldest *Hee Haw* fan."

I watched in amazement as our ancient groupie strode briskly to Carson's couch, attired in overalls and a peaked cap, to tell America that among the highlights of his long life was watching *Hee Haw* every Saturday night. He was a remarkably spry old codger with a lively wit, bragging that he had never needed to wear glasses to read. He insisted on proving the point by reading names out of the Los Angeles phone book with his eagle eyes, sans lenses.

Naturally, we immediately booked him to be a guest on *Hee Haw*. About a week later, he strode intro our office at WLAC filled with eager anticipation at the thought of meeting our cast in person. Before granting his wish, our bespectacled group of writers insisted on having him read names out of the Nashville phone book with his unaided eyeballs. After reeling off a column from a page selected at random, we naturally asked him how he had retained such excellent eyesight at such an advanced age.

"It's real simple, boys," he replied, pointing to the peak on his cap. "My pappy told me that if I always wore a cap with a long beak on it, I'd never need eye glasses. And by granny he was right! It's a little late for you fellas, but be sure to tell your young'uns."

We took him down to the studio, introduced him to the whole *Hee Haw* gang, let him do a few jokes in the Cornfield, gave him a full "SA-LUTE!" and sent him on his way, a happy man.

Over the years, I've found that our harshest critics have been people who had never seen the show and simply didn't like the idea of it. In any case, we were now a big hit in syndication. Alan Courtney was steadily making headway toward full coverage of the entire USA, Nick Vanoff was making plans to help refill our depleted coffers with new shows to produce, and it was time for us to head back to Nashville.

* * *

Upon our triumphant return to Nashville we were greeted by an ever-expanding cast. George Lindsey dropped into the studio one day, a refugee from the cancelled *Mayberry R.F.D.* on which he played Goober Pyle. Naturally, we asked him to join our show, and he was a perfect fit. We built him a replica of "Goober's Garage," just like the one he had run in fictional Mayberry, and he moved right in for the next 20 years. Being a talented actor and comedian, Lindsey played a lot of other characters on our show. However, despite a background that included roles in two Broadway musicals, *All American* and *Wonderful Town*, George Lindsey would forever be known as just plain old "Goober."

Another addition was beautiful young actress name Marianne Gordon. She was from Athens, Georgia, with the accent and appearance of a genuine upper-crust Southern belle. When she auditioned for us in L.A., we hired her on the spot, and wrote a bunch of spots featuring her on a swing in front of an ante-bellum mansion dressed like Scarlet O'Hara and doing spoiled rich girl monologues.

Marianne was a true delight, and of course she joined with the other girls in the show for all the musical numbers. By this time, we realized that pretty girls in abbreviated "Daisy Mae" outfits were a big draw for our millions of male viewers, while not being a turn-off to the women in our audience, since they were always used in wholesome, entertaining ways.

One other new cast member who wandered into the studio one day was a man named Harry Cole. He did a character called "Weepin' Willie." Cole had loads of very funny material about terrible things that had happened to him which he delivered while crying into a big bandana like the one Junior had used on *This Is Your Life*. Cole was with us for four

**George "Goober" Lindsey (left), the indispensable Marcia Minor, and guest star Johnny Bench, famed Cincinnati Reds catcher, in the *Hee Haw* studio at WLAC, 1973.**

years. I have no idea whatever became of him. He was like so many characters that appeared on *Hee Haw* over the years who just seemed to drift in and out, never to be heard from again.

One of the musical guests making her debut during that season was a multi-talented little blonde bombshell named Barbara Mandrell, who certainly would be heard from again and again for years to come.

Our other musical guests included Tammy Wynette, George Jones, Waylon Jennings, Bobby Goldsboro, and Hank Thompson. They were the cream of the country crop, always brilliantly directed and lit by our terrific technical staff.

One thing I've neglected to give the necessary credit to, during those formative years of *Hee Haw*, is the lighting. Our musical numbers looked so crisp, in startlingly vivid color, that network variety shows were using them as examples of sheer "state of the art." The credit for this must go to our original lighting designer, Bob Boatman, and later to Leard Davis. Watching the DVDs of those early shows today, it's almost startling how bright and fresh everything looks. It's especially amazing considering the limited resources of our tiny studio at WLAC. To my mind, the combination of Bill Davis' artistry as a director and Bob Boatman's brilliant lighting made *Hee Haw* not only a commercial but also an artistic success.

**John Aylesworth with Roni Stoneman at Lulu's Truck Stop, 1974.**

Our writing staff had become leaner during that 1972 trip to Nashville. Stan Ascough and George Yanok had moved on; Archie Campbell and Gordie Tapp mostly sent in their spots by mail from Gatlinburg and Toronto; and Don Harron always brought his material for KORN news with him when the rest of the cast arrived.

Our small writer's room at WLAC was then inhabited only by me and Frank, Tom Lutz, and Bud Wingard. This wasn't a problem, since by that time all the comedy pieces were pretty well set. Wingard's musical segments, as well as additional guest stars, were taking up more time each week. We did sometimes add something new, such as Archie Campbell as "Justice O'Peace" and "Lulu's Truck Stop," but essentially the format wouldn't vary much in the years to come. Even the Cornfield had been extended by building a "Mini-Cornfield" in one corner of the studio so that our musical guest stars could join in the fun between taping their numbers.

When we had completed shooting the last 13 shows of our first syndicated season and headed for the airport, it was the first time we had the luxury of knowing we would definitely be back. The news from L.A. was getting better and better, and nobody could cancel us ever again.

Roy Clark even recorded a hit single on his 1972 album *Roy Clark Live!* called "Lawrence Welk-Hee Haw Counter-Revolution Polka," that included lyrics about the possible network cancellation of the show and its stubborn refusal to go off the air.

*Hee Haw* was here to stay!

# 27

# MOONLIGHTING

*"You're going to Nashville to do WHAT?"—Julie Andrews, October 1972*

Talk about a change of pace!

Having just left Cornfield County, Nick Vanoff hit us with the news that he had made a deal for Yongestreet to produce the classiest upscale variety series in television history, in partnership with Julie Andrews' Jewel Productions. Sir Lew Grade, the British impresario, had been trying to get Julie to do a television series for three years, to be distributed worldwide by his ATV (Associated Television) company.

Julie had finally relented and agreed to do 24 one-hour shows for the 1972–73 season, for which she would be paid $1,000,000. Sir Lew made a deal with the ABC network to broadcast the series in the United States, and the ABC Los Angeles facilities would be utilized for the actual production. Vanoff then made a deal with Julie to produce the show, for enough money to refill our depleted coffers from the *Hee Haw* syndication caper.

*The Julie Andrews Hour* would be broadcast on ABC at 10 every Wednesday night beginning September 13. This gave us the full summer to put her show together and shoot the first few episodes. Bill Harbach would return from New York to co-produce with Nick Vanoff, while Frank and I would serve as writing supervisors, leaving us plenty of time for the care and feeding of *Hee Haw*. Can life get any better?

Bill Davis would direct the show, meaning we would have to suspend production on the Andrews show for a few weeks in the fall in order for Davis, Frank, and me to fulfill our duties in Nashville. We were sure we could find a way to accommodate that when the time came. We spent June and July putting together all kinds of ideas for the show, and we were getting really excited about the whole project. Now, all we had to do was finally meet with our star, Julie Andrews.

Vanoff, Frank and I met with Julie and her husband, Blake Edwards, on a July afternoon at their palatial home in Brentwood. Blake was the noted writer-director of such movie classics as *Breakfast at Tiffany's*, *Days of Wine and Roses*, and the wildly successful Inspector Clouseau series with Peter Sellers, *The Pink Panther* and *Shot in the Dark*. At the time of our meeting, Blake had hit a bit of a slump in his career, leaving him somewhat morose and at liberty to offer his input regarding the show, which would become a mixed blessing.

The meeting, however, was quite pleasant. Both Julie and Blake were receptive to most of our ideas. Since Julie was basically a singer-actress and not noted for her comic abilities, we suggested a back-up team of Alice Ghostley and Rich Little to perform with her in comedy sketches. Unlike our experience with *Hee Haw* and country comedy, we already knew all the mainstream comic actors and those two seemed best suited to work with Julie.

We would do a series of funny vignettes based on Julie's early days in New York as a Broadway performer, with Alice Ghostley as her odd-ball roommate. Rich Little, at that time, was the best young impressionist in the business, and could be anybody we wanted him to be.

Since we would need the best possible musical support, it was agreed that Nelson Riddle, one of Frank Sinatra's finest arranger-conductors, would be the ideal musical director. Tony Charmoli was also available as choreographer, and Andy Williams' brother Dick was agreed upon to be choral director.

Vanoff had convinced ABC to build a special theatre-studio to accommodate a large audience for Julie's show in their downtown facilities. There was little doubt in anyone's mind that this was to be the finest, most lavish variety show ever to appear on television. We parted that afternoon in a giddy mood of total elation.

Rich Little and Alice Ghostley were quickly signed for the show. We were lucky enough to get Bob Ellison, one of the best comedy writers we ever worked with, to join Frank and me in writing the scripts. Since Julie was British and apparently had no flaws, we based the New York sketches on the premise of her roommate, Alice Ghostley, being insanely jealous—"...she's so perfect!"

We lined up the best possible musical guest stars for the series, including Harry Belafonte, Peggy Lee, Sammy Davis, Jr., Steve Lawrence, Eydie Gorme, and one of Julie's co-stars from Broadway's *Camelot*, Robert Goulet. We also added a few surprise non-singing stars, like James Stewart, Sid Caesar, and Carl Reiner.

For the very first show, we decided there should be no guests at all. It would be all Julie. It would give her a chance to introduce herself to her audience and recreate all the characters she had made her own on stage and screen, from Eliza Doolittle to Mary Poppins to Maria Von Trapp.

*The Julie Andrews Hour* debuted on September 13, 1972. The critics raved. It was an unforgettable tour de force, as far from *Hee Haw* as Pluto from Mars. Take that, Bob Wood!

In the weeks that followed, Alice Ghostley and Rich Little were introduced. The New York sketches with Julie and Alice were funny, Rich was terrific, the guest stars made Julie shine, and the production numbers were fabulous.

The first sign of trouble came after the third show, when Julie announced that she didn't want to do the New York sketches with Alice any more. The reason she gave was that she wasn't really perfect. We tried to explain that Alice was simply reflecting the public perception of Julie's many talents and proper British bearing, and the audiences were really enjoying the comedy of it. But Julie was adamant that she no longer wished to be perfect.

The loss of the New York sketches left the show with a dearth of comedy. We decided to make use of this with protracted comedic production numbers. One that went over particularly well was based on the hit song of that year, "I've Got a Brand New Pair of Roller Skates." Julie was cast as Helen Wheels, America's top roller derby queen, and the story line was that of "All About Eve," involving an ingénue trying to take Helen Wheels' place at the top. Carl Reiner was a guest that week, and with Julie, Alice, and Rich in top form it went over very well. As a result, we did several similar pieces when we had comedy guests such as Sid Caesar.

When it came time for our five-week hiatus to Nashville and *Hee Haw*, Julie was somewhat shocked, to say the least, that her writers and director had a double life in the boonies. Blake, on the other hand, just laughed at the irony. I think by that time Julie needed some time away from the show. I think we all did.

When we resumed production, Bob Ellison had left to write and produce a special with Alan King in New York, and we were joined by our old friend, Jack Burns, to finish off the season.

There were other writers on the show, of course, but they specialized only in jokes. Unlike *Hee Haw*, however, this show didn't need jokes. It needed concepts. Jack Burns contributed a number of short dramatic vignettes for Julie to perform with guest stars who were also actors. It was a great way to showcase Julie's versatility.

There were several problems that plagued the show from the very beginning. Julie's solo numbers were always visually magnificent and she sang like an angel, but they were also among the show's biggest production problems. With an unemployed Blake Edwards watching everything on a monitor in his wife's dressing room and rarely satisfied with her performance, her numbers had to be re-shot again and again. Often this resulted in taping sessions lasting well into the wee hours of the morning. Blake was certainly a brilliant movie director, but in television unnecessary multiple re-takes simply demoralize everyone.

Some of the guest stars had problems with Julie, who at the best of times seemed to have difficulty loosening up. Harry Belafonte was a memorable case in point when he came to our office to complain that during their duet spot she was making calypso sound like madrigals.

When Sammy Davis, Jr., was on the show, he convinced us that he could make our star really "get down" with a medley of funky tunes. When it was taped, Sammy just shrugged and said, "Sorry, guys."

Despite all the problems, it was a hell of a show. In 1973, it won a Golden Globe and five Emmys, including one for our own Bill Davis. What it failed to win was an audience. Unfortunately, the ratings were abysmal.

Perhaps the 10 P.M. time slot was wrong for a family show like *The Julie Andrews Hour*. This theory was borne out by the fact that one of Julie's shows dedicated to Walt Disney was moved to 8 P.M. and the ratings went through the roof. Alas, ABC learned nothing from this, and moved us back to 10 P.M. for the rest of the season. While *Hee Haw* remained number one in syndication, Julie's show languished near the bottom of all network shows.

Frank and I were very proud of *The Julie Andrews Hour*, and it was a pleasant change of pace from Cornfield County. Julie was a very nice lady and never less than charming. As for Blake, his frustrations were understandable. After all, the guy was a genuine auteur, and he was simply doing what he thought best for his wife and the show. He was never less than supportive through it all. I'm pleased for him that his career soon got back into gear with a series of hit movies such as *Ten* with Dudley Moore and *Victor Victoria* starring Julie.

Unfortunately, Julie's series ran for only one season due to the poor ratings. If any show deserves to be preserved and released on DVD (as Time Warner did for *Hee Haw*), especially now that Julie has lost that magnificent singing voice, it would be *The Julie Andrews Hour*. Then, hopefully, it would get the audience it so richly deserved.

# 28

# *HEE HAW*—THE NEXT SIX YEARS

*"If you mix the oldest jokes known to Western man with the newest computer technology, add a banjo, a guitar and a few pretty girls, it will come out Hee Haw."*—John Fergus Ryan, Country Music Magazine, *September 1973*

In the fall of 1973, *Hee Haw* was riding high. The ratings in syndication were still astronomical, we were gaining outlets in major markets, all our minutes were sold out to national advertisers, and it seemed as if we could go on forever.

It was also that fall that *Hee Haw* suffered its first tragedy. Stringbean and his wife Estelle were brutally murdered on Saturday night, November 10, as they were returning to their home in Ridgetop, Tennessee, from String's regular session at the Grand Ole Opry.

It was general knowledge that Stringbean, having grown up during the Great Depression, didn't trust banks and kept all his money in his overalls or hidden in his house. On that fateful night, two low-life cousins named Brown had already ransacked every room at String's home, finding nothing but a chainsaw and some guns. Consequently, they lay in wait for String and his wife to arrive. When they walked in the door and discovered the cousins waiting for them, Stringbean tried to put up a fight but both he and Estelle were shot dead.

As fate would have it, the bodies were discovered the next morning by String's best friend in the world, Grandpa Jones. Needless to say, it was a somber taping session that fall. It was strange to see String's real name, David Akeman, in all the newspaper stories. To all of us he was, and always would be, just plain Stringbean.

The scarecrow remained in the Cornfield for the entire run of the series, an empty suit of rags on a stick, as a lasting memorial to dear old String. To this day, it still stands in our original Cornfield, preserved for all time in Nashville's Country Music Hall of Fame.

One of the few bright spots during our fall taping in 1973 was the appearance of Roni Stoneman. She was discovered by *Hee Haw* during an appearance at Printers Alley, playing banjo and singing songs from her days as a member of the legendary Stoneman Family, a touring musical group led by her father, "Pop" Stoneman. In 1925, Pop made the first million-selling country music recording, "The Sinking of the Titanic." Roni was one of 23 children, only a few of whom survived to maturity.

Aside from her considerable talent playing banjo, Roni was a very funny, scrawny little lady, with a big gap in her teeth and a comical, raspy voice. Gordie Tapp conceived a new spot for *Hee Haw* the moment he saw her. It was a series of funny vignettes with Roni and Gordie as a bickering country couple living in a tumble-down shack. It was called "The Naggers," and was an immediate hit. Roni also replaced Stringbean in the *Hee*

*Haw* banjo quartet, featuring Roy Clark, Grandpa Jones, and the amazing Bobby Thompson from our band.

We needed another funny lady on the show, since we had lost Lulu due to a drug bust in Dallas. She had been raised in an orphanage and had a pretty tough time of it, suffering the taunts of other kids for being overweight. She claimed she was never adopted because, in her words, "People don't adopt fat kids."

After she left the orphanage at the age of 18, Lulu had eased her pain with drugs and a great sense of humor, even becoming a novelty stripper at the Busy Bee Lounge in Dallas. Jack McFadden, Buck Owens' manager, saw her there one night and recommended her to us for a spot on *Hee Haw*. Lulu later admitted she had been "messed up on drugs and almost missed it" when she auditioned for us, but we had no idea of the seriousness of her problem. We just knew that Lulu was funny and we wanted her on the show.

Lulu was an expert comedienne and never less than completely professional with me. Now, after the Dallas bust, she would be sorely missed. We hoped she would someday be back, if our largely Bible-belt audience could forgive her transgressions. But Roni Stoneman could fill the bill— if not in girth, then certainly in mirth.

The show was also changing by the 1973–74 season. What started as a fast-paced country *Laugh-In*, with non-stop jokes and sketches interrupted only by a couple of guest stars singing their latest hits, had now metamorphosed into more of a musical-comedy show. This was due largely to the input of Bud Wingard's numbers for the increasingly popular female members of our cast, numbers with amusing verses such as "Gossipy" and our "Hee Haw All-Girl Jug Band," led by Minnie Pearl.

Wingard also contributed a very funny musical piece for the men, "Gloom, Despair and Agony on Me." All of this was fine with me and Frank, as long as the show kept its focus on comedy, either sung or spoken. Though musical guest stars were still an important ingredient, it was comedy that

*Top:* **John Aylesworth with Roy Clark, circa 1973.** *Bottom:* **Still a family affair—Linda Aylesworth, John's eldest, enjoying the sunshine with George "Goober" Lindsey, circa 1974.**

made the show a hit and we intended to make sure it stayed that way. If the comedy was musical, so much the better.

One of the funniest and most endearing musical moments on the show was when Grandpa Jones and his wife Ramona strapped bells on their hands, arms, legs, and feet to play tunes like "Bells of St. Mary's" and other old favorites. I just have to smile warmly when I recall the two of them shaking those bells with every part of their bodies. They were a sweet old couple, and our audience just couldn't get enough of them.

The increasing emphasis on music actually turned out to be a blessing in 1973, due to the fact that we had lost Bill Davis as our director. The reasons for this are still somewhat vague in my mind. I was on a cruise at the time, while Davis was on vacation in Hawaii. On our return, he had been replaced by our lighting designer, Bob Boatman. Bob had been angling for the job over the past season, telling us how he had studied Davis' camera patterns for musical numbers which made each number shine along with Boatman's brilliant lighting.

When Davis and I inquired about this abrupt change, vague excuses were made, most of which seemed to do with money. As a founding member of our team, Davis was getting handsome raises each season. But his contract had lapsed, and it was too late to do anything about the decision since Boatman had already been signed to a new contract as director.

Frank didn't seem to share my misgivings, but as it turned out we lost a great lighting man and gained a neophyte director. It was a classic case of money decisions taking precedence over artistic decisions. Boatman did handle the musical numbers just as Bill Davis would have, but when it came to the comedy sketches, I felt he left much to be desired.

In all fairness, comedy is a tough thing for a director to shoot. It's something that can't be studied or learned, just as I believe comedy itself can't be taught. You either have an inborn talent for it or you don't. Davis did.

As an example, if a comedy piece involves two people, most directors figure if they have more than one camera they should cut back and forth to a close-up of each person as they deliver a line. But then you miss the reaction of the other person to what's being said.

A good comedy director will instinctively stay on a two-shot for the entire routine. Think of Abbott and Costello's classic "Who's on first?" If you cut back and forth, you would miss most of Costello's growing befuddlement as Abbott explains the strange names of the baseball players. It would completely ruin the flow of the piece, especially the visual stimulus for the viewer's laughter. Boatman, through no fault of his own, simply believed that every camera at his disposal should be used on all occasions.

Bob Boatman was very nice man, and everyone on the show liked him very much. Happily, he was a fast learner, the show didn't suffer unduly, and the audience certainly didn't complain. But in the long run, our *modus operandi* increasingly became "the more musical pieces, the better."

Meanwhile, when in Los Angeles we did everything we could to promote *Hee Haw*. In 1974, Vanoff, Frank and I reunited with our old boss, Perry Como, to write and produce his Easter special for NBC. We made sure to book Grandpa Jones and Minnie Pearl for the show, and especially Archie Campbell. It was a running gag that Perry had once been

*Opposite, top:* (Left to right) Nick Vanoff, Perry Como, John Aylesworth, and Grandpa Jones, *The Perry Como Easter Special*, 1974. *Opposite, bottom:* "Where's Waldo?" See if you can find Aylesworth and Peppiatt among the whole *Hee Haw* cast and crew, circa 1974. (Hint: standing near the back on the left side.) (Courtesy Gaylord Program Services, Inc.)

a barber, so it was a natural to have Archie give him a haircut while doing one of his routines. It was a great show, and gave *Hee Haw* a nice boost on a network special.

Back in Nashville that same year, yet another element was added to our ever-changing show. In the very beginning, in the summer of 1969, we were told that it was traditional to end all country TV shows with a hymn. We didn't want to do that because *Hee Haw* was a comedy show; we felt that a hymn would be too somber as a closer.

We stuck to our guns until Tennessee Ernie Ford appeared as a guest in 1973 and put together a gospel quartet with himself, Buck Owens, Roy Clark and Grandpa Jones. We got so much positive reaction from the viewers that starting with the 1974–75 season every show ended with a hymn. The reason we waited that long was simply that Tennessee Ernie sang bass, and it wasn't until the fall of 1974 that we added a bass singer to the cast in the person of the jovial, rotund, and huggable Kenny Price.

Kenny had been on the show as a guest star the year before, singing his hit single "The Sheriff of Boone County." He was such a natural comedian, we just had to hire him as a regular. He played—you guessed it—the Sheriff of Cornfield County.

Another regular added that year was the equally jovial and rotund, and completely nuts, Gailard Sartain. Kenny and Gailard became fast friends, sharing a passion for fun, food, and strong drink.

Gailard was a particularly fortunate find, due to his extensive background in zany comedy. He was brought to our attention by Roy Clark's manager, Jim Halsey. Both Clark and Halsey lived in Tulsa, Oklahoma, where, beginning in 1970, Gailard became the star of a local late-night weekend television show. It was called "The Uncanny Film Festival Camp

**Gailard Sartain (partially hidden, left) and John Aylesworth playing post office with Minnie Pearl and Grandpa Jones, 1975.**

**Gailard Sartain (front) with the Hager Twins and Nick Vanoff's sister, Sandy Zajak, 1973.**

Meeting," featuring hilarious lunacy presided over by Gailard, who adopted the persona of "Dr. Mazeppa Pompazoidi."

Gailard's comedy on that show was wrapped around showings of old horror movies and 1930s musicals. A talented artist as well, Gailard painted the artwork for one of fellow Tulsan Leon Russell's most memorable LP albums. Russell returned the favor by often dropping into Mazeppa's show to jam with the likes of Eric Clapton.

Gailard's show became a cult hit everywhere in Oklahoma that was able to pick up the signal from Tulsa. The show could have gone on indefinitely, but it ended a scant three years after its inception when Gailard became a regular on *Hee Haw*. He left behind his manic cohorts on the show, Gary Busey—who later starred in *The Buddy Holly Story*—and Jim Millaway—aka "Sherman Oaks."

After experimenting with several characters for Gailard to play on *Hee Haw*, we finally found the perfect spot for his wildly inventive comedy mind. Gordie Tapp's General Store spot was becoming a bit time-worn, so we spruced it up by casting Gailard as Gordie's bumbling assistant, Maynard. Utilizing a meek little voice, wearing a funny little peaked cap and a tiny bow tie, Maynard made the spots hilariously brand new with Gordie acting as the perfect straight man.

As I recall, it was about that time our success in syndication enabled Sam Lovullo to

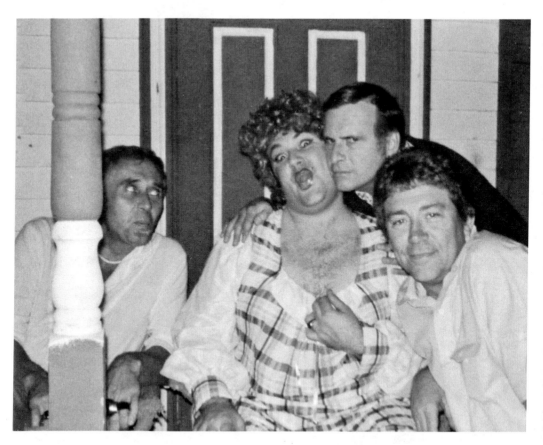

**Frank Peppiatt (left), John Aylesworth (first from right), and Tom Lutz (right) with Gailard Sartain in drag for a skit, 1976.**

move us from the lowly Howard Johnson motel to the much superior and spanking new Maxwell House Hotel. This unaccustomed luxury raised the spirits of all involved.

One of my favorite memories from the old Howard Johnson's was when I solved the mystery of why the food in the restaurant was always cold when it was served. After being presented with a tepid bowl of clam chowder one evening for the umpteenth time, I inspected the heat lamps over the kitchen counter that were supposed to keep the food hot until the waitresses picked up the plates. The mystery was solved—they weren't heat lamps at all, but 40-watt bulbs.

Another memorable culinary tale goes back to our stay at the Holiday Inn that first summer in Nashville. At breakfast one morning, my partner Frank found a very large cockroach in his waffle. When he pointed this out to the waitress, she simply shrugged knowingly and said, "They must have sprayed the kitchen." Needless to say, Frank skipped breakfast that morning.

But those days were behind us now. The food at the Maxwell House was as good as their namesake's coffee ... "good to the last drop." Aside from the shocking death of Stringbean and the loss of Bill Davis, the 1973–74 season went very smoothly indeed, with the addition of Gailard Sartain and Kenny Price making our *Hee Haw* family complete once again, save for the unfortunate absence of Lulu Roman. We even had our old rival Johnny Cash on the show as a guest star!

\* \* \*

The following year, another tragedy struck. Don Rich, the lead guitarist with the Buckaroos, was killed in a motorcycle accident. Although we were all extremely fond of

**Gailard Sartain as Maynard with Gordie Tapp in *Hee Haw*'s General Store, circa 1975.**

Rich, Buck Owens was struck the hardest. He had not only lost his best friend but the heart and soul of his band. Without those distinctive harmonies he and Rich made on all those gold records in the past, Buck never had another hit.

As for *Hee Haw*, we owed Rich a great debt. During that first summer of 1969, he got the show off the ground as our first musical director. Besides, he was genuinely one of the good guys. He would be sorely missed.

On a brighter note, Lulu's parole had ended in Dallas, she had become a born-again Christian thereby winning forgiveness from the Bible belt, and we welcomed her back with open arms. She was just as funny as ever, and we immediately put her together with Gailard Sartain in a new spot called "Lulu's Truck Stop." Gailard played the fry cook while Lulu tended the counter as various cast members dropped in for some very funny bits, generally concerning the lousy food. It became one of the highlights of the show for years to come.

As you know by now, we had two taping sessions for each new season, one in the spring and one in the fall. Most of the time, there were plenty of bits left over from the first session to be mixed in with the second in the editing room.

In the 1974–75 season, Archie was still wearing his jet black toupee during the

first session while the face beneath was showing definite signs of encroaching age. Archie took note of this, and when we arrived for the second session, he had switched to a snow white toupee. Needless to say this would cause no end of consternation when it came time to edit the second set of 13 shows, since Archie's leftover material from the first taping would make it seem that he had aged 20 years in a nanosecond.

Archie claimed that his hair just naturally turned white since our last taping, forgetting that his rug had flipped off the year before during one of his bits, affording us all to have a good look at the shiny dome that lay beneath. When we reminded him, old Arch turned a deep crimson and made us promise not to tell a soul outside

**John Aylesworth's oldest son, Robert, manning a mike at WLAC, 1975.**

the studio. He claimed that even his wife didn't know he wore a toupee, which seemed a bit unlikely.

Archie apologized profusely and offered to go back to his black rug for the current taping, but we let him off the hook and decided to just make do with what we had. The strange thing is, Archie's black toupee did show up in the second half of the season, sometimes right after his brand new white one, but nobody seemed to notice. Maybe the audience thought it was just a weird sight gag.

We had always had surprise guests on *Hee Haw*, like the time in 1972 when the great Dizzy Dean dropped by to visit the Barber Shop. We also started to have some really oddball guests. Barbi Benton brought her boss from *Playboy* to the set at one point, and it was quite a sight to see Hugh Hefner hopping into the Cornfield wearing a bunny suit.

We even had an inexplicable visit from Ernest Borgnine. Sometimes they would be booked as guests, like President Jimmy Carter's goofball brother Billy, and sometimes they would just happen to be in town and decide to drop by the set, as in the case of Lorne Greene and Alan King. We just stayed loose all through the 1970s, and everybody was having a dandy time.

One day, a pre-country Kenny Rogers wandered onto the set. His group, The First Edition, had recently broken up and he was somewhat pressed for cash. As I recall, he had

**Baseball great Dizzy Dean in the Barber Shop with director Bill Davis (left), producer Sam Lovullo (first from right), and *Hee Haw* host Roy Clark (right), 1972.**

come to see if he could sell a couple of Arabian horses he owned to Buck Owens, who lived on a ranch in Bakersfield, California.

Our musical director by that time was George Richie, who was very well connected with the music industry in Nashville. Richie told Rogers he had the perfect song for him. Frank and I had known Rogers back in L.A., so we asked him to be on the show. I don't know if Buck ever bought those horses, but the song George Richie gave Rogers to sing on *Hee Haw* became a huge hit when Rogers recorded it a few weeks later. It made him a very rich man. The song was "Lucille," the first of a long string of successful hit records that put Kenny right on top of world of country music.

"Lucille" wasn't the only prize Kenny found on *Hee Haw*. He became immediately smitten with our own Mary Ann Gordon, who soon became Mrs. Kenny Rogers. As for George Richie, he later married

**John Aylesworth with Lorne Greene on the *Hee Haw* set at WLAC, 1977.**

Tammy Wynette, but he will always be remembered by the *Hee Haw* gang as the guy who gave Kenny Rogers "Lucille."

In 1978, Richie left the show to become Tammy's husband and manager. His replacement as musical director was a man named Charlie McCoy, a consummate musician who had been a guest star on the show several times in the past playing his harmonica, on which he was a true virtuoso. McCoy was an inspired addition to the show, and our band took to him immediately. He stayed with us to the very end of our run, a tremendously creative force, and, like Don Rich, one of the good guys.

One of my favorite memories during those years was the ritual that always came late in the afternoon every Friday. Five o'clock was the official quitting time, but often we would run late. Everyone on the show was well paid, but the big money came on weekends when most of our cast would make personal appearances around the country. Consequently, as the hour approached 5, everyone would start nervously looking at their watches and taking turns saying, "I got a plane to catch!" They always seemed to catch their flights, since

*Opposite, top:* **Grandpa Walton (actor Will Geer, center) visits *Hee Haw* at WLAC, 1976. In the front, from left, Frank Peppiatt, Roy Clark, Will Geer, John Aylesworth, and Buck Owens. In the background, from left, Lisa Todd, Jim Hager, Misty Rowe, and Marianne Rogers, among others.** *Opposite, bottom:* **Archie Campbell, Roy Clark, and John Aylesworth with President Jimmy Carter's brother, Billy (in the barber chair), 1978.**

**Frank Peppiatt and John Aylesworth relaxing on the *Hee Haw* set, 1976.**

*Top:* **Party time with Marcia Minor (first from left), Gunilla Hutton (second from left), Francesca Peppiatt (first from right) and Cathy Baker (right), 1976. My profuse apologies to the lovely woman on the left whose name I cannot recall).** *Bottom:* **(Front, left to right) Buck Owens, John Aylesworth, Sam Lovullo, and Roy Clark, getting an award from the Nashville Chamber of Commerce, 1976.**

the airport was close by and back in the seventies there was no security to hold them up. Nonetheless, the ritual continued every Friday afternoon year after year.

One Friday I was sitting next to Kenny Price just as he was beginning to fret about missing his plane. I asked him where he would be playing that weekend.

"I got three big dates," he replied. "I got two concerts booked in London and Rome, and a matinee in Paris."

Obviously impressed, I said, "Country music is popular in places like that?"

He looked at as if I was nuts and said, "Well, sure."

Then I asked how he was going to get back to Nashville all the way from Europe by Monday morning.

"Who's talking about Europe?" he replied. "I'm playing London, Kentucky; Rome, Georgia; and Paris, Texas."

*Top:* **(Left to right) Archie Campbell, Kenny Price, and Gordie Tapp, 1976).** *Bottom:* **John Aylesworth and his pal, huggable Kenny Price, 1978.**

As I write about those days so long ago in Nashville, I realize how very much I miss them. As time went on, our evenings were no longer consumed with game playing but just having great times in the bar laughing and enjoying ourselves with our great cast of amiable, funny, companionable people.

Throughout the 1970s, one year just seemed to meld into the next with no network to worry about and rock solid ratings. We had gone through three hound dawgs, starting with Kingfish the Wonder Dog, who had a great talent for doing nothing but just lying there. He was followed by Beauregard, who belonged to our technical director, Joe Hostettler, and possessed much the same talent as his predecessor. Then came Beauregard, Jr., who had a habit of getting up and walking away after a punch line, as if making a critical comment.

In the late seventies, we added two more people to the cast. One was Buck Trent, who was a whiz on the banjo and would do little comic songs he would make up on the spur of the moment.

The other new addition

was the beautiful and very funny Linda Thompson, who was living with Elvis Presley at the time. She told us how Elvis loved the show and wanted to be on it if only the colonel, his manager, would let him. Linda fit in perfectly with the other *Hee Haw* girls, and we kept hoping that someday she could convince Elvis to bypass the colonel and pop up on *Hee Haw*. Alas, he never made it.

Occasionally, an especially interesting new cast member would really shake things up. That was the case in the fall of 1975.

# 29

# JOHN HENRY FAULK

*"As he puffed his pipe on the set of* Hee Haw *recently, Faulk said he could only describe this new chance to play his once-familiar role as a front porch philosopher as 'exhilarating.'"*—Los Angeles Times, *November 1975*

As a Canadian citizen living in Toronto during the 1950s, I was appalled at the news stories coming from our neighbor to the south about the McCarthy "witch hunts." Over the years, whenever that dreadful era was discussed on radio or television, the name John Henry Faulk kept coming up. He was always described as a CBS radio commentator who was blacklisted after being accused by a right-wing vigilante group of pro–Communist sympathies.

Although Faulk professed his innocence, CBS fired him. At that point, Faulk became one of the few to fight back by suing his accusers for libel, enlisting the aid of the famous Louis Nizer as his attorney. After six long years of battle, costing him his marriage and every penny he had, Faulk finally cleared his name. The jury awarded him a record $3.5 million which, after paying legal fees and past debts, left him with about $75,000. After that, he sank into obscurity, but not before writing a book about his experience called *Fear on Trial*.

Since he was always referred to as a CBS radio commentator, I assumed that John Henry Faulk must have been some sort of cosmopolitan news analyst commenting on the events of the day for CBS radio in New York. I hadn't read the book, but when it was announced that CBS was going to be showing a dramatization of it, I looked forward to watching.

On the night of October 2, 1975, *Fear on Trial* was aired starring William Devane as Faulk, and George C. Scott as his attorney, Louis Nizer. The film began with a scene depicting Faulk at a microphone doing his radio show in New York.

John Henry Faulk wasn't a news commentator at all. He was a folksy good old boy with a Texas twang, spinning comical down-home tales of life in the heartland. My first reaction was simply "This guy has got to be on *Hee Haw*!" He would be a natural, and with all the press coverage leading up to the film of his story, it could be a bonanza of great publicity for our show. Better still, it would give a guy whose career had been ruined by false accusations another chance. It was a win-win situation.

The next day, I called CBS and got the telephone number of the man who had written the television film, David Rintels. He told me he was furious that the film ended with an announcement that Faulk was now employed by a Dallas radio station. That was far from the truth.

146

John Henry was, in fact, let go after only four months by that Dallas station and was now eking out a meager living on an 8-acre farm in Madisonville, Texas. Since that one gig in Dallas, Faulk had never been offered another job in broadcasting. I told Mr. Rintels that I was about to remedy that situation. He gave me John Henry's phone number.

I was pretty excited making that call. I vividly remember it as if it were yesterday. A male voice answered the phone with a tentative "Hello," as if he hadn't had a call in a long time.

"I'd like to speak to John Henry Faulk," I said.

"This is John Henry speaking," was the reply.

I then asked him if he'd ever watched *Hee Haw*.

"Well, sure. Every Saturday night. It's my favorite show," he said.

"Mr. Faulk, I'm calling to ask if you'd like to be on the show every week."

There was a long pause. "Is this some kind of joke?"

I told him that I was an executive producer of *Hee Haw*, and after watching *Fear on Trial* the night before, I was convinced he would be a natural to tell some of those folksy tales from his radio show in New York to a national audience on television.

He was totally flabbergasted.

Finally, he said, "I'd be honored. This is the only good news I've had in over ten years."

I asked him to gather up at least 13 funny stories, and that we would be sending him plane tickets to Nashville for the taping of the show in a couple of weeks. He thanked me profusely, and said he had better go tell his wife and kids the news. I said I ought to be thanking him, and I had better go tell our publicity people to spread the news to the press.

It was a big story. The next day it was in every newspaper in the land. Major

## A Break for John Henry Faulk

As co-creator, with Frank Peppiatt, of "Hee Haw," I would like to point out that John Henry Faulk was not rehired by CBS to appear on our show, as you stated (NEWS-MAKERS, Nov. 3). In fact, "Hee Haw" itself was "fired" by that network in 1971 at the height of its success—a victim of the "hillbilly" purge. "Hee Haw" now flourishes at the top of the prime-time access chart in syndication. John Henry was not so lucky, and it was our pleasure as independent producers to be able to offer him the kind of employment he so richly deserves.

JOHN AYLESWORTH
Yongestreet Productions
Beverly Hills, Calif.

*Top:* **John Henry Faulk makes his debut on** *Hee Haw* **in 1975.** *Bottom:* **Letter to the editor from John Aylesworth,** *TV Guide,* **June 5–11, 1993, in response to the Cheers for** *Hee Haw***'s Silver Series. "After 25 years of sneers, it's great to get cheers."**

*Top:* John Henry Faulk tells a tall tale to John Aylesworth (left), Sam Lovullo (standing, right), and Archie Campbell (seated, right), 1975. *Bottom:* John Aylesworth, Grandpa Jones, and John Henry Faulk on the set of *Hee Haw*, 1975.

news services and newsmagazines were sending reporters out to Madisonville for interviews and photographs. As a result, a lot more facts came to light.

According to *Newsweek*, CBS paid Faulk a mere $8,000 for the film rights to his book, but the network didn't feel any other restitution was in order. A CBS spokesman was quoted as saying, "There are no plans to give John Henry Faulk his job back."

George C. Scott, as Louis Nizer, summed up Faulk's meager prospects for employment in network broadcasting in the film's closing scene. "He's won a great victory," Scott mused, "but he's still a controversial man."

When I picked John Henry up at the airport on his arrival in Nashville, he was almost delirious with joy. "This is all like a dream. I still can't hardly believe it's happening."

But happening it was. The young man depicted by William Devane on television was now 62, and the intervening years had not been kind to him. Dressed in jeans, a western shirt, and a cowboy hat, he seemed a bit frail, but his spirit was lively and he was raring to get started on his long-awaited new career.

WLAC was crawling with reporters when we arrived, and the next several hours were taken up with multiple interviews in the small station cafeteria. The *Los Angeles Times* ran a long story on him by Aleene MacMinn in their Sunday magazine section. She reported that Faulk was now remarried and that he and his present wife had a six-and-a-half year old son. "He's the only baby born under Medicare in the state of Texas," John Henry quipped.

The article went on to quote its subject about his new job:

Humor gives you a proper way of saying something to our society. It's always been my concept that a very essential role was played by the humorist in America. This is the way you puncture the humbug, the pretense, the pomposity that passes for posturing statesmanship; reduce these people to what they are. However you might feel about the Bill of Rights and the Constitution, they make you a beneficiary in perpetuity in principals, ideals, and they place an obligation on you. So many people today forget that there are generations that are going to inherit this earth. And if we leave a bob-tailed, ragged planet floating in space, what will our names be called?

That was the tenor of most of the interviews. The Cold War was still raging and some of our older cast members still looked on John Henry with suspicion, but he was a cheerful soul who pretty soon won everybody over.

Not only did Faulk bring the show tons of publicity, but he added a new kind of respect for *Hee Haw* nationwide. His humorous pieces, delivered with the cast gathered around him, were not only amusing but taught a few lessons about this country's Constitution and government.

Unfortunately, he was only with us for about five seasons until his health began to fail and he retired from the show in 1981. John Henry Faulk died in 1990 in his hometown, Austin, Texas. The downtown branch of the Austin Public Library is named in his honor.

We were proud to have him with us for a while.

# 30

# "KEEP ON TRUCKIN'"

*"In a moment, you'll witness the strange, the macabre, and the silly."—Rod Serling, 1975*

An interesting year for the team of Peppiatt and Aylesworth was 1975. John Henry Faulk had joined our cast, Lulu Roman had returned to the show, *Hee Haw* had hit its stride, and people we would never expect to see in bib overalls were popping up in the Cornfield. After six successful years, we had relaxed our rule of barring mainstream "city" guests, but only if they appeared as surprise cameos.

This is the story of one who was willing but, sadly, never made it.

It began when the ABC network in Los Angeles offered us a chance to experiment with something poles apart from our six years of corny shenanigans. An ABC vice-president named Frank Brill approached us with an offer we couldn't refuse.

Brill asked us to write and produce a series of four one-hour variety shows to be aired in the summer of 1975. We had known Brill for a number of years, and he was quite aware of the fact that Frank and I were slightly nuts. He set no ground rules, except that he wanted it to be different from any other show. He gave us a completely free hand to do whatever we wanted. It was a comedy writer's dream, so naturally we jumped at the chance.

We had been wanting to utilize the zany Gailard Sartain in something other than *Hee Haw* for quite some time, so our first thought was to build the show around him. Gailard could certainly set the tone for a completely off-the-wall hour of urban comedy. It would be a total change of pace. Now all we had to do was write the scripts. To help accomplish this happy chore, we enlisted the aid of a puckish young wag named George Bloom, who turned out to be the perfect choice.

After much discussion, we finally settled on a concept. We would call it *Keep on Truckin'* and we would augment Gailard with a company of bright young comics. The premise was that they would all be on a tour of the ABC facilities when their tour guide was paged, leaving them in a deserted studio packed with all kinds of sets for everything from a soap opera to a game show.

Naturally, the cast would go wild, using each of the sets for a variety of satirical sketches. We envisioned a spoof of *Masterpiece Theater*; a wildlife show hosted by a lion exhibiting the strange habits of people; a goofy game show; a disaster series featuring a runaway bus full of screaming passengers, encountering everything from earthquakes to a rampaging flea circus; and a show featuring "endangered species" such as the Big-Band Leader, the Drugstore Cowboy, and the Shepherd.

We had the time of our lives writing all this lunacy, and assembled a terrific cast to

**Laurel and Hardy (John Aylesworth and Gailard Sartain) amuse George "Goober" Lindsey in Goober's Garage, circa 1978.**

work along with Gailard. They included the brilliant writer-comic Franklyn Ajaye, known as "The Jazz Comedian"; Jack Riley, from *The Bob Newhart Show*; cute little Didi Conn, from *Grease*; Fred Travalena, a wonderful young impressionist; ventriloquist Wayland Flowers and his outrageous puppet, Madame; the very funny monologist Jeannine Burnier; and Charles Fleischer, who later became the voice of Roger Rabbit.

Since our cast, talented as they were, lacked star power, we realized we would need some kind of drawing card to induce people to watch this hour of mirthful madness. We all gave this a great deal of thought and then, suddenly, I had an epiphany.

I had recently become quite friendly with Rod Serling, whom I had met on a cruise to Tahiti. I was surprised to find the creator of *The Twilight Zone* was not at all like the grim persona he presented as narrator of that series. In fact, Serling was a lot of fun and had an odd-ball sense of humor. Who better to host our show and display his never-before-seen comical side?

I called Serling at home that evening, and he readily agreed to give it a whirl. Our first day of taping, we seated Serling in the studio's empty audience bleachers. We ran through the lines we had written for him on cue cards for the four different openings we had planned, supplied him with a few props, and rolled tape.

The following is the opening of the first show:

"Good evening. I'm Rod Serling, inviting you to once again activate your imagination and suspend credulity for the next sixty minutes. I'm sitting here in a deserted tele-

# Cover Story

Gaylard Sartain is shown acting as a muscled male to bored Rhilo Fahir in "Keep On Truckin'" which is shown at 7 p.m. Saturday on Channel 13.

# "Truckin'" Seen As Active Gallery

"A twilight gallery of contemporary comedy, laughter and whackadoony."

That's how "Keep on Truckin'," the new comedy-variety summer series, starring 14 new entertainer-zanies, is described by Rod Serling, who will introduce each of the series' four one-hour programs, premiering on Saturday, at 7 p.m. on Channel 13.

The multi-talented resident company includes comics, impressionists, singers, dancers and stunt people who will carry on a rapid-fire barrage of broad buffoonery and sly satire for 60 minutes each week.

Members of the troupe are Franklin Ajaye, Rhona Bates, Kathrine Baumann, Jeannine Burnier, Didi Conn, Charles Fleischer, Wayland Flowers, Larry Ragland, Marion Ramsey, Rhilo Fahir, Jack Riley, Fred Travalena, Gaylard

Sartain and Richard Lee Sung.

On tap for the premiere show are such varied vignettes as a scene from "Bus Stop '75," the super disaster film of the century; "The Endangered Species," an interview with a forgotten hero of the past; "Wild People," a look at people as animals, acting out their roles; and "The Housewife," a monologue by a long-suffering wife whose husband, while physically present, is mentally withdrawn.

Also on the uproarious agenda: an impression of Howard Cosell and a look at a number of new sports for television; the first appearance on TV of a new singing group, the Karl Malden Singers; a visit to an underground radio station, WHIP; "Experimental Theatre," in which narrators describe

films for Public TV; "Sitting in for Johnny," a series of impressions of guest hosts, and "Ziegfeld Auditions," a sketch which showcases the diverse talents of several members of the resident troupe.

## Meara Starring In Own Show

Anne Meara will have her own series starting in September. Does that mean her marriage to Jerry Stiller is shaky? No. This season, she will play a highly out-of-the-ordinary lawyer named Kate McShane. Husband Jerry Stiller (they were a comedy team — Stiller and Meara) will have no role in the production, but this is not indicative of any marital problems.

Anne and Jerry and their two children, Amy and Benjy, are a very close, very happy family. Although this was a "mixed marriage" (different-religions), this has never caused them problems. In fact, by forming the basis for their humor as a comedy team,

it is what brought them to stardom. (Actually, Anne converted to reform Judaism when their first child was born.)

So why is Anne undertaking this series alone?

Because it is a three-dimensional role which will demand "the very best I have to offer" and will therefore be personally as well as financially rewarding.

As for Jerry's attitude, he says he wants Anne to do whatever is best for her career. "These days in show business, you diversify," he says. "And I'm pleased to see Anne's career growing: As a husband first and a performer second, I'm glad to see my wife fullfilled."

"TV Times," *El Paso Times*, week of July 6, 1975, cover story for *Keep On Truckin'*, one of the few to run the Rod Serling PR after his death.

```
"Mr. John Aylesworth, please."
```

**CRABTREE STUDIO/**      1812 GROSS ROAD • TELEPHONE (214) 328-2653\*\*

**DALLAS\***

```
                         September 15, 1975

     Dear John:

          Sorry I haven't written you sooner but...well,
     I just didn't know what to say.  As you can imagine
     the drawing with Rod Serling front and center was
     caught and thrown out by most of the editors.  Three
     did use it.  I enclose the clips.

     There will be no charge on this one.  Lets try another
     later on.  Best wishes,
```

\*Texas. 75228

**Note from Tom Crabtree, Crabtree Studio, Dallas, regarding the PR for Rod Serling's hosting of** *Keep On Truckin'* **which was pulled by most editors after his untimely death, 1975.**

vision studio. I should be home, but my wife is mad at me and I love to hang out in spooky places. In a moment, you'll witness the strange, the macabre, and the silly. Join me and watch what happens."

At that point, Serling put on a pair of "Groucho glasses," with outrageous nose and mustache, and turned to his right as our cast entered the studio being led by their tour guide.

Serling delivered his lines with total solemnity. It was all we could do not to burst out laughing, which would surely have ruined the take. Later, after we had taped all four shows, we would edit in each of Serling's openings. When he finished the fourth one, we all thanked him profusely. He said he'd had a good time doing it, and at that point I asked him if he would ever consider coming to Nashville to do a surprise cameo in the Cornfield on *Hee Haw*.

"Sure," he replied. "Now that I've completely blown my image, why not?"

When we screened the completed shows for the network, the ABC publicity people were ecstatic. Serling's openings would surely get all kinds of coverage in the press, while providing the perfect set-up for such a crazy show. An air date was set for early July, and a cartoon montage depicting some of the highlights, with Serling's image featured in the center, was sent out to all the newspapers for the front covers of their weekly TV supplements.

Exactly two weeks before the premiere, bad news hit us like a bolt of lightening. Rod Serling had suddenly died of a heart attack at the age of 50, much too soon. The writer of *Requiem for a Heavyweight*, and creator of *The Twilight Zone*, was gone.

It was quickly decided to drop the introductions he had taped for *Keep on Truckin'*. It was a pity since he had gotten such a kick out of doing it, and television audiences would now never get to see his lighter side. As for the show itself, it sank like a stone without Serling's set-ups and was quickly forgotten.

To this day, I still crack up at the idea of Rod Serling popping up in the Cornfield. I think he would have loved it, and I know the audience would have as well.

# "THE BIG EVENT"—*HEE HAW*'S TENTH ANNIVERSARY CELEBRATION

*"A decade of success hasn't deprived* Hee Haw *of its corn. Its 10th anniversary special—an $800,000, two-hour music and comedy bash airing at 8 P.M. Sunday on NBC—is fresh evidence that this popular and durable syndicated series still has straw in the seat of its pants."—Howard Rosenberg,* Los Angeles Times, *October 20, 1978*

In 1976, NBC introduced a new series of movies and specials under the blanket title of "The Big Event." It was scheduled to be broadcast every Sunday night at 8 and was generally a great success, depending on the content. Among the first few shows were such offerings as *Gone with the Wind*, and *Old Blue Eyes Is Back* starring Frank Sinatra. Obviously, it was difficult to find such big ticket items every week, and the ratings varied depending on the drawing power of the film or star being presented.

During the summer of 1978, while the show was casting about for likely events to fill the two-hour Sunday time period, Peppiatt and I decided that a tenth anniversary celebration of *Hee Haw* ought to be a fitting entry. Admittedly, since the show had begun in 1969, it would be a year early. On the other hand, who counts? Besides, if we waited a whole year, "The Big Event" might not still be on the air.

We took the idea to Alan Courtney, whose past affiliation with NBC made him the likeliest of our group to present the idea. He thought they would buy it in a minute. When he made the call to his contact at NBC, it actually took a whole 10 minutes to make the deal but, once again, who counts?

The next day, a date was set and we made plans to shoot the special in September. It would air on November 22, 1978.

We decided to shoot the show in front of a live audience at the Grand Ole Opry, which had moved from the Ryman Auditorium to a new location at WSM, the station that had broadcast the Opry on radio since its inception. WSM had built a brand new facility from which it would televise the Opry every week.

It was an enormous studio, with plush seats replacing the old wooden pews that accommodated audiences at the Ryman. The whole operation was now under the auspices of a new entity called Opryland Productions, situated between the lavish, recently-built Opryland Hotel and a sprawling Opryland Amusement Park.

# State of Tennessee
## County of Davidson

# FATE THOMAS
*Sheriff of Davidson County*

TO *John Aylesworth*

## GREETINGS:

REPOSING FULL TRUST IN YOUR PRUDENCE, INTEGRITY AND ABILITY, I DO,
BY VIRTUE OF THE POWER AND AUTHORITY IN ME VESTED AS SHERIFF OF
DAVIDSON COUNTY, TENNESSEE, HEREBY COMMISSION YOU AN

*Honorary Deputy Sheriff for*
*Davidson County, Tennessee*

In testimony whereof, I have thereunto
set my hand and caused the Seal of
Davidson County, Tennessee, to be
affixed at Nashville, Tennessee, this

*tenth* _____ day

of ____ *July* ____ in the year

of our Lord One Thousand, Nine

Hundred and *Seventy-seven*

*Fate Thomas*
Sheriff

Official naming of John Aylesworth as "Honorary Deputy Sheriff for Davidson County, Tennessee," issued by Fate Thomas, sheriff of Davidson County, which came with an honorary badge that saved me from several speeding tickets in Tennessee.

The whole *Hee Haw* **gang on stage for the 10th anniversary special, 1978. First row, left to right: Buck Owens, Roy Clark, Cathy Baker (kneeling) with Beauregard the Wonder Dog; second row, left to right: Lisa Todd, Minnie Pearl, Gunilla Hutton, Archie Campbell, Gordie Tapp, Grandpa Jones, George Lindsey, Don Harron; third row, left to right: Misty Rowe, Jim Hager, John Hager, Junior Samples, Lulu Roman, Marianne Gordon, Jimmie Riddle, Jackie Phelps; fourth row, left to right: John Henry Faulk, Buck Trent, Gailard Sartain, Roni Stoneman; and fifth row, left to right: Joe Babcock, Wendy Suits, Dolores Edgin, Kenny Price, Hurshel Wiginton, Linda Thompson.** *Picture courtesy of Gaylord Program Services, Inc.*

Sam Lovullo made all the necessary arrangements for taping our anniversary show and booking the guest stars. Our cast and production people would stay at the Opryland Hotel. Altogether, it was going to be a heck of an operation.

We asked Bill Davis to come back as director, along with Gene McAvoy as scenic designer, and we let Bob Boatman share the production credit with Lovullo. Peppiatt and I would be executive producers and write the script with Bud Wingard, Tom Lutz, and a bright new addition to our group, Dave Cox.

We had Herb Klynn do some special animation for us, with our *Hee Haw* donkey dressed in a tuxedo to introduce the show, and the letters of our title coming to life and singing the opening theme. We wanted everything to be first class, and decided that everybody but the members of our regular cast should wear tuxes and evening gowns. All our guest stars were happy to oblige, including Tennessee Ernie Ford, Roy Rogers

*Top:* **Blowing out the candles on our 10th anniversary cake. (From left, Nashville Edition singer Hershel Wiginton, John Aylesworth, Frank Peppiatt, Sam Lovullo, Roy Clark, Gunilla Hutton, Buck Owens, Cathy Baker, and my memory fails me (sorry!), 1978.** *Bottom:* **George Burns and John Aylesworth at a social event at the home of Jim Backus, circa 1978 (other guests unidentified).**

and Dale Evans, Loretta Lynn, Charley Pride, Crystal Gayle, Barbara Mandrell, Kenny Rogers, Tom T. Hall, Ronnie Milsap, Mel Tillis, Conway Twitty, and, of course, Tammy Wynette.

Our regulars, by contrast, would be dressed as we always saw them on *Hee Haw*. It just didn't make sense for Minnie to wear her trademark hat with the price tag on top of an evening gown, and Junior Samples in anything but overalls was unthinkable.

It was Peppiatt's notion to have each of our regulars run downstage from their familiar settings placed across the back of the stage—Archie from the Barber Shop, Gordie and Gailard from the General Store, etc.—as their names and their hometowns were announced. They would then take their places in formation with each other like a football team.

The applause was thunderous as each one was introduced: from Bulls Gap, Tennessee ... Archie Campbell; from London, Ontario ...Gordie Tapp; from Botlenburg, Sweden ...Gunilla Hutton; from Niagra, Tennessee ...Grandpa Jones; from Grinders Switch, Tennessee ... Minnie Pearl; from Cumming, Georgia ...Junior Samples; from Santa Barbara, California ... Lisa Todd; from Toronto, Canada ... Don Harron as Charlie Farqueson; from Pilot Point, Texas ... Lulu Roman; from Jasper, Alabama ... George "Goober" Lindsey; from Chicago, Illinois ... Jim and Jon Hager; from Athens, Georgia ... Marianne Gordon; from Suffolk, Virginia, and Dyersburg, Tennessee ... Jimmy Riddle and Jackie Phelps; from San Gabriel, California ... Misty Rowe; from Tulsa, Oklahoma ... Gailard Sartain; from Galax, Virginia ... Roni Stoneman; from Spartanburg, South Carolina ... Buck Trent; from Covington, Kentucky ... Kenny Price; from Memphis, Tennessee ... Linda Thompson; from Austin, Texas ... John Henry Faulk; from Edinburg, Texas ... Cathy Baker; from

**Buck Owens and John Aylesworth in consultation with "Doc" Archie Campbell at WLAC, 1979.**

# Congressional Record

United States
of America    PROCEEDINGS AND DEBATES OF THE 95*th* CONGRESS, SECOND SESSION

*Vol. 124*    WASHINGTON, WEDNESDAY, SEPTEMBER 13, 1978    *No. 142*

## *Senate*

### "HEE HAW"

Mr. SASSER. Mr. President, I would like to call to the attention of my colleagues the 10th anniversary of the nationally syndicated television show "Hee Haw." As my fellow Senators know, "Hee Haw" is produced in Nashville, and, as they say on the show, we Tennesseans are "right proud" of the show, the performers and the staff.

The 10th anniversary show of "Hee Haw" is scheduled to be aired on October 22 on the NBC television network. This appearance will mark a return to network television for "Hee Haw" which began as a CBS network television show in 1969. In that year, the show rose to the number 16 position in the national ratings. Despite that rating, the first year show was cancelled by the network.

The following year, the creators of "Hee Haw," Frank Peppiatt and John Aylesworth, along with their partner, Nick Vanoff, decided to create their own network to air the series, which after a year of network exposure had a well-earned national following. At great personal risk and expense, these gentlemen financed the entire cost of production for "Hee Haw's" second year.

The foresight of the producers of "Hee Haw" has paid off many times over. The show has consistently been, by rating and demographic standards, one of the most successful syndicated television series. It is seen 52 times a year on 220 stations in the United States and Canada.

Mr. President, the people of Nashville and Tennessee are justly proud of "Hee Haw." The show has brought recognition of Tennessee's contributions to the Nation's music industry and it has shown that quality television shows can be produced in Tennessee.

I am proud of "Hee Haw" and of its Tennessee origin, and I want to take this opportunity to commend and congratulate the producers of the series, the production staff, the stars of the show, the guest artists, and all those other people who have contributed so much to the success of this all American television show. I look forward to viewing the 10th anniversary show of "Hee Haw" on October 22.

A Congressional "Sa-lute" to *Hee Haw* on its 10th anniversary, 1978.

*Top:* Tennessee governor Ray Blanton (left) presenting "Honorary Citizen" plaques to (left to right) John Aylesworth, Frank Peppiatt, Nick Vanoff, and Sam Lovullo on Hee Haw's 10th anniversary, 1978. *Bottom:* (Left to right) Peppiatt, Vanoff, and Aylesworth making a fast getaway after receiving copies of the *Congressional Record* honoring *Hee Haw*'s 10th anniversary, 1978.

Nashville ... Beauregard, the Wonder Dog; and from Sherma, Texas, and Meherrin, Virginia ... Buck Owens and Roy Clark. Whew!

This was the very first time *Hee Haw* had been taped in front of a live audience, and the reaction was thrilling. The laughter confirmed that everything we had assumed was hilarious was actually hilarious.

Don Harron's KORN newscaster, old Charlie Farqueson, always wrote his own material and had some of the sharpest jokes in every show, but we had often wondered if our viewers could fully understand him due to his exaggerated rural Canadian accent. We would wonder no more. When he did his routine for our capacity audience of native Nashvillians, it was one of the comedy highlights of the evening.

In fact, all the comedy pieces were received with gales of genuine laughter, from Archie's reprise of his classic "That's good, that's bad" routine with Roy in the barbershop, to John Henry Faulk's folksy monologue, to a montage of Junior Samples' funniest moments from the past nine years, to Grandpa Jones and Ramona tying on their bells to play "My Bonnie Lies Over the Ocean."

What really gave the show its soul were moments such as Grandpa's touching tribute to his best friend Stringbean, and Buck Owens' heartfelt appreciation of Don Rich with a medley of the hits they had done together.

In addition, each cast member had a chance to say "What *Hee Haw* Means to Me," and Tennessee Ernie wound things up by leading our cast and guest stars in a stirring closing rendition of "Will the Circle Be Unbroken."

Altogether, the show was a lasting testament to all we had accomplished since that first summer of 1969. As *People Weekly* said in October 1978, "Ten years, one network and 20,000 impossibly corny jokes ago, the first *Hee Haw* was televised." It was heartening to learn that Time-Life recently issued an indelible record of the occasion on a DVD so that future generations can see what *Hee Haw* was all about.

At the time, we were proud to hear that Senator James Sasser of Tennessee had read a tribute to our 10th anniversary into the Congressional Record. It began:

> Mr. President, I would like to call to the attention of my colleagues the tenth anniversary of the nationally syndicated show *Hee Haw*. As my fellow senators know, *Hee Haw* is produced in Nashville and, as they say on the show, we Tennesseans are "right proud" of the show, the performers and the staff.

Immediately after we had taped the special, we attended a huge party that had been arranged to honor us in the ballroom at the Opryland Hotel. It was a grand occasion, climaxing with Governor Ray Blanton calling Frank, Nick Vanoff, Sam Lovullo and me to the stage, where he thanked us for bringing *Hee Haw* to his state and presented each of us with plaques proclaiming us to be honorary Tennesseans.

It was a most impressive ceremony, and the fact that Governor Blanton had to be dragged from his office, kicking and screaming, a few months later to stop his end-of-term signing frenzy pardoning scores of convicted murderers for cash doesn't detract one bit from that golden memory. (He was probably dissatisfied with his pension, and a guy's gotta do what a guy's gotta do.)

In any case, it was a great show, even though the enormous Opry stage made us all yearn to get back to our cozy little nest at WLAC which, as it turned out, was on borrowed time.

# 32

# THE "HEE HAW THEATER"

> *"I'm telling you, Branson's gonna be a big attraction someday and there ought to be a Hee Haw Theater there."—Tom Lutz, 1979*

In the fall of 1979, Tom Lutz invited me to visit him and his wife in a new house he had built in the Ozark Mountains. I had known Lutz since *The Jonathan Winters Show*, when he and his partner, Stan Ascough, supplied and held the cue cards. We all became good friends, and they provided the same service for *Hee Haw* in Nashville the following summer.

Lutz and Ascough were very bright guys and soon joined our writing staff. Now, 10 years later, Lutz was still writing for *Hee Haw*. I happily accepted his invitation since I had never been to the Ozarks.

I flew to Springfield, Missouri, on a Friday, where Lutz picked me up. We drove for several hours through some of the most breathtaking landscape I had ever seen.

Lutz's house had been designed by a student of famed architect Frank Lloyd Wright. It was a graceful structure blending into the wilderness surrounding it. His wife, Mindy, was a charming, beautiful young woman I had met several times before, and I was looking forward to a restful weekend of good jazz on Lutz's state-of-the-art stereo equipment, wonderful meals provided by Mindy, and plenty of good talk.

All this came to pass until that Sunday morning, when Lutz said he planned to take me on a drive that afternoon to a place called Branson, a town he felt I just had to see because he had a plan that would make *Hee Haw* immortal. I was quite naturally intrigued, so off we went just past noon.

After a half-hour drive through the exquisite countryside, Lutz turned onto a two-lane road identified as Highway 76. For about 20 minutes, we passed dozens of fishing lodges facing a man-made lake that, Lutz informed me, was a fisherman's dream come true. The traffic was dense on the narrow highway, and I began to wonder what a popular fishing hole could possibly have to do with the immortality of *Hee Haw*.

At the far end of the lake, we passed a sign welcoming us to Branson, Missouri. On either side of the road, the brush had been cleared to accommodate row upon row of enormous barn-like structures. Each of them had large, hand-painted signs hanging over their front entrances, announcing what one could expect to find within: "BALDKNOBBERS HILLBILLY JAMBOREE," "PRESLEY'S COUNTRY JUBILEE," "PLUMMER FAMILY MUSIC SHOW," and "FOGGY RIVER BOYS."

"My God!" I said. "It's like a hillbilly Vegas."

"That's exactly what it is, without the gambling," Lutz replied.

163

He went on to explain that all those people who came for the fishing, whole families of them, needed something to do at night. All those huge barns were packed every night with audiences eager for entertainment. The shows were mostly just good old no-frills country music, mixed in with comedy of the "blacked-out teeth and barnyard" variety that made *Hee Haw* look like Noël Coward.

According to Lutz, it was all pretty primitive, but the audiences really ate it up. Apparently, it wasn't just the fishing folk who came to these shows. People from miles around would make the trip on weekends to see the Baldknobbers and the Presleys, and it was a sure bet that every one of them were *Hee Haw* fans. They would come to Branson even if it meant missing one of our shows on a Saturday night.

At this point, I realized what Lutz had in mind for making *Hee Haw* immortal. He obviously wanted to open a Hee Haw Theater in Branson. He already had the plans drawn up for the construction of the building, and he was convinced it would be so successful that even the fish would come to see it.

When I asked where the talent would come from, Lutz said there were tons of really good local musicians and cloggers for production elements. All we would need to make it special would be an act from *Hee Haw*, like Grandpa Jones, Lulu Roman, Roni Stoneman, or the Hager Twins to play a couple of weeks each and rotate them so there would always be a *Hee Haw* performer to headline the show. Not only would it be the hottest ticket in town, but it would be the flashiest theatre Branson had ever seen, with our donkey logo up in lights out front, luring thousands of paying customers

By the time Lutz finished his pitch, he had me convinced. It could be a gold mine! Long after the TV show left the airwaves, the Hee Haw Theater would keep the money rolling in to keep us wealthy in our dotage. It couldn't miss.

Okay, I'm an easy mark. But now I had to convince my partners, those poor souls who hadn't yet been steeped in the wonders of the Ozarks.

Frank Peppiatt thought the idea was great. Nick Vanoff was skeptical—he didn't trust anything that existed in that great wilderness between New York and Los Angeles. (The only exception was Nashville, since that's where the money came from.) I explained that the theater building wouldn't cost that much, considering our current cash flow from *Hee Haw*, and finally Vanoff suggested that we send someone from our business management office to Branson to check out whether the idea was financially viable.

Forthwith, an accountant in a business suit and carrying a briefcase was dispatched to the wilds of Missouri on a one-man safari to compile a full report. On his return, the outlook was less than gung-ho. He nit-picked that the town didn't even have a decent hotel, forcing him to stay in a smelly fishing camp. He complained that the only access was a two-lane highway, and therefore the location was not conducive to large numbers of people flocking through town. He actually attended one of the shows and was shocked by its crude vulgarity. It was also mid-week, and therefore had less than a full house. He felt it would harm the *Hee Haw* image even being in the same vicinity as such low-life operations. His final recommendation was simply to forget about it, which Vanoff and Frank were quite willing to do.

I, however, in the belief that accountants and business people in general feel it their duty to take a dim view of anything the least bit chancy—and would have told Edison he was wasting his time fooling around with light bulbs—decided to fly Tom Lutz to L.A. to make his own pitch. He had certainly sold me on the idea.

Lutz was happy to make the trip, bringing with him his plans for the theater building. He made one hell of a presentation, offering to operate the theater himself for only a small percentage of the profits. It was a hard sale but finally everybody agreed to give it a try. Even our business manager, a conservative follow named Al Rettig, invested in it. If it didn't work, I would be the guilty party which I didn't mind one bit. I was convinced it would be, if not a goldmine, at least a lasting annuity.

By late spring, the theater had been constructed and was ready to announce its grand opening. As I recall, Grandpa Jones was to be the headliner, and since we were taping in Nashville that month, I decided it would be fun to rent a Learjet for the occasion and fly a bunch of us to Branson on a Friday night after the day's taping.

On our arrival, I was heartened to see our donkey logo all lit up in front of the brand new Hee Haw Theater. There were over 1000 seats, all of them filled with paying customers.

Lutz greeted us with a big smile, bursting with pride at his achievement. He then introduced us to an attractive local woman he had hired to help him manage the operation. Since every seat was happily taken, our party sat in folding chairs at the back to enjoy the show. Al Rettig had even flown in from Los Angeles to join us.

The adequate house band played an overture of country tunes to herald the entrance of Grandpa and his banjo, to thunderous applause. Grandpa then did his act and that was the whole show. The audience loved it, but I wondered what had happened to the promised cloggers and other production elements Lutz had mentioned in his sales pitch. I asked him about that, and he said not to worry. "I'm working on it." I worried.

A few weeks later, as the profits from the theater began to roll in, Al Rettig sent a man named Marv Blanton, one of his most trusted colleagues, to Branson to hire a local accountant to keep an eye on things. By that time, Lulu Roman had replaced Grandpa as the headliner. Blanton went to see the show, and once again the only show was a local band and Lulu's act.

The checks kept coming in for the rest of the summer, so obviously the paying customers were happy with what they were seeing. However, when the checks suddenly stopped after Labor Day, yet another fact Lutz had neglected to mention in his sales pitch came to light. Everything in Branson closed down for the winter. Our Branson accountant informed Blanton that from Labor Day to Memorial Day you could shoot a cannon down Highway 76 without hitting anything but cold air. However, we were told the theater had done extremely well considering that a late spring opening had made it a short season.

About midway through the following summer, the receipts were beginning to drop compared to the previous summer. We began to hear tales of unrest among the *Hee Haw* headliners. Once again, our representative went to Branson to see what was going on.

The rest of the story is painful to relate. Apparently Lutz had become smitten with the woman he had hired to help run the operation; his wife got wind of this and promptly left him. Lutz had apparently succumbed to large amounts of strong drink, and the theater was rapidly going to wrack and ruin with most of the lights illuminating the donkey logo either broken or burned out. Lutz had been a great salesman, but obviously a disaster as a manager. Before any action could be taken, he disappeared. Nobody knew where he had gone.

The theater was closed down and sold shortly after at a considerable loss. The greatest loss, of course, is what could have been. Today, Branson is a booming year-round operation with 52 theatres containing over 60,000 sold-out seats, including Andy Williams' Moon River Theater, acrobats from China, an Imax, and—inexplicably—a show starring Russian comedian Yakov Smirnoff that has been running successfully since 1991.

Ironically, the Baldknobbers and the Presleys are still going strong in their original barns. One can only imagine how successful the Hee Haw Theater would be in Branson today. I imagine it often, usually at three in the morning after a bad dream when I can't get back to sleep.

I only heard from Tom Lutz once after that. It was in the form a note from Dallas clipped to a newspaper clipping about a series I had just produced for ABC. It began: "Dear John, Sorry I haven't written sooner but ... well, I just didn't know what to say." I'll bet he didn't!

What's the moral of this sad tale? Damned if I know. If I did, I'd never take a chance on anything again. I sure do miss that annuity.

# 33

# THE HEE HAW HONEYS

*"You guys should do a spin-off with the* Hee Haw *girls. I'll supply the advertisers and the station clearances—you supply the show."—Henry Siegel, Lexington Broadcasting, 1978*

Henry Siegel was a pioneer in the world of advertising, and had been among the few
denizens of Madison Avenue to be of help to Nick Vanoff and Alan Courtney while they
were seeking national advertisers for the syndication of *Hee Haw*. A few years later, he
formed his own syndication and production company, Lexington Broadcasting Services.

When Siegel suggested a *Hee Haw* spin-off, Yongestreet had just finished producing
two seasons of *Sonny and Cher* for CBS, leaving Frank and me free to try something new.
After meeting with Siegel, we went to work trying to come up with a concept for a pilot
with the aid of two promising young writers from Chicago, Barry Adelman and Barry Silver, who had been on the writing staff of *Sonny and Cher.*

We finally settled on an idea for a half-hour sitcom that would be as unlike the *Hee
Haw* format as possible. We called it *The Hee Haw Honeys*, which would be the name of
a singing group made up of three pretty young women who traveled the country in a Winnebago playing in small clubs. The series would follow their progress, as they hoped to
finally end up in Nashville and get their big break on *Hee Haw*. If you think that sounds
like a pretty flimsy premise for a series, you would be absolutely right. Henry Siegel, however, thought it was just fine and said he would finance the pilot.

We held auditions and found three very attractive young singers to play the Hee Haw
Honeys, and cast our resident *Hee Haw* teddy bear, Kenny Price, to play their manager
and driver of the Winnebago. We shot the pilot in Nashville, but it was so terrible we didn't
show it to anyone. The Honeys were pretty good singers individually, but as a trio they
sounded awful. Only one of the girls was a really good actress, and the comedy fell flat
except for one scene with Gailard Sartain as a drunken heckler in one of the clubs. Kenny
Price was his likeable self but badly miscast. We had totally goofed, and immediately went
back to the drawing board.

Our next attempt at a concept made a lot more sense. We would make the Hee Haw
Honeys a Nashville family named Honey who ran a restaurant that featured entertainment
from guest stars like Loretta Lynn and The Oak Ridge Boys. For insurance, we would cast
some of our own dependable *Hee Haw* regulars in all the parts but one.

Lulu Roman and Kenny Price would play Lulu and Kenny Honey. Their offspring
would be Willie Billie Honey as the chef in the kitchen, played by Gailard Sartain, and
their daughters would wait tables and occasionally sing with the house band. Misty Rowe

would play one of the daughters, while the other would be the immensely talented young singer-actress we had cast in the previous pilot, Kathy Lee Johnson. (You know her better today as Kathy Lee Gifford, Regis Philbin's former sparring partner.)

The pilot was terrific. Kathy Lee and Misty worked well together, and Lulu and Kenny made a terrific team. Gailard had a chance to let loose his unique manic comedy style with all the props in the kitchen, while the guest stars added marquee value and a relief from the comedy, much like *Hee Haw* itself.

We shot 26 half-hour episodes at WLAC during *Hee Haw*'s off season, and everything worked like a charm. Kenny and Lulu were naturals as a couple, and Gailard had never been funnier than in the sketches he did in the kitchen. Misty and Kathy Lee were both charming and beautiful. The two Barrys, Adelman and Silver, were a joy to work with and came up with some terrific material. The show was a winner from the moment it hit the air in September 1978.

Unfortunately, *The Hee Haw Honeys* was a victim of its own success. Since Lexington Broadcasting was in charge of its distribution, it was often scheduled as a lead-in to *Hee Haw*, sometimes on rival stations in the same time slot. In the ratings, it was beginning to eat into *Hee Haw*'s hitherto unrivaled popularity. We were in the uncanny position of successfully competing with ourselves!

That summer, Vanoff insisted that we stop production of T*he Hee Haw Honeys* in order to protect the mother lode, *Hee Haw* itself. Henry Siegel was suicidal. He begged us for at least one more season of *Honeys*. This first production distributed by his brand-new company was a huge success, and now we were taking it away from him. We felt bad for him, but what could we do?

When Siegel finally realized that we couldn't be swayed, he asked us to at least come up with another show idea to keep his company afloat. About a week later, I suddenly recalled Woody Allen's *What's Up, Tiger Lily*, a big hit comedy back it the 1960s. Allen had

*Top:* (Left to right) **Gailard Sartain, writer Barry Adelman and John Aylesworth, circa 1980.** *Bottom:* **Gailard Sartain and Kenny Price during taping of *Hee Haw Honeys*, 1978.**

**(Left to right) Writer Barry Adelman, Frank Peppiatt, and writer Barry Silver during a taping of** *Hee Haw Honeys* **at WLAC, Nashville, 1978.**

taken a Japanese action movie and written new dialogue to be dubbed in with American voices doing very funny lines. Why not get a bunch of foreign public domain films and do the same thing as a series?

Frank agreed that it was a good idea if we could find the right kind of movies. We hired a researcher to find out what was available and ended up with a list of about ten. The problem was that none of them were action movies.

We watched them all and found only one film that offered any possibilities at all. It was a ponderous Greek period film that appeared to be a biography of Socrates, with the somber, bearded hero wandering around ancient Greece making speeches to angry crowds that jeered him. The only action was a big fire near the end. We thought it might be funny to make the hero an aspiring comic and turn the speeches into terrible monologues causing the crowds to jeer, which would explain why he was so somber as he wandered around ancient Greece. We'd call it *Shecky the Greek*.

Henry Siegel thought it was tremendous idea, which only goes to show how desper-

**(Left to right) John Aylesworth, Barry Adelman, Frank Peppiatt, and Barry Silver on location in Nashville for *Hee Haw Honeys*, 1978.**

ate he was. We wrote a script and got a bunch of our funny pals, including Rich Little, to do the voices. We delivered it to Siegel who had a terrific poster made up to publicize it.

The problem was that after the first 10 minutes of watching a somber Greek walking around in a toga with no action, regardless of how funny the sound track was, it was pretty damn boring. By the time you got to the big fire near the end, you would be asleep. Consequently, *Shecky the Greek* was never sold, but Lexington Broadcasting went on to syndicate several other shows until it went bankrupt in 1992.

Anyway, you win some, you lose some. If there was just the right film with lots of action, I still think it could work. Hmmmm, I wonder...

# 34

# GRADY NUTT—"THE PRIME MINISTER OF HUMOR"

---

*"A lot of people ask how an ordained minister can be funny. I'm supposed to be different than other people. When I slam my thumb in a car door, I can't cuss like lay people. Well, that's not fair. To say, 'Verily and behold, I have slammed my thumb,' does not cross my mind."—Grady Nutt*

---

In the spring of 1979, Bud Wingard saw a very funny man on *The Mike Douglas Show* who happened to be a Baptist minister. When Bud mentioned it to us, we asked him to track the guy down and ask him to come to Nashville for an audition. If he was as funny as Bud said he was, we thought it would be a great novelty to have a comical minister on *Hee Haw*.

About a week later, Bud ushered a very tall man with an infectious smile into our office and introduced him to us as Grady Nutt. We asked him if Nutt was his real name and he said it was. He even spelled it for us—"N-U-T-T"—then added, "The second 't' is important. Without it, I'm just like the rest of you."

We knew right away that this guy was special, and asked him if he would do one of his routines on camera. He said he would be happy to, so we took him into the studio, waited for a break in the taping, introduced him to the cast and crew, set him in front of a camera, and went into the control room to watch his routine. Bob Boatman gave him the cue to start, and for the next five minutes he had everybody in stitches with a story about his first Sunday as a preacher.

We had the same thrill of discovery we had felt the first time we saw Junior Samples on camera. This guy was dynamite! When we asked him how many routines he had like that, he replied, "As many as you'd like." He wasn't kidding. Grady was on every show for the next three years, and each story was funnier than the last one.

Grady was the kind of jovial, exuberant man it was just fun to be around. He exuded a warm feeling of good humor and well-being, and that came across on the tube. He was likeable and hilarious at the same time, a valuable commodity in the world of comedy. It didn't take long to start thinking that Grady should have a show of his own.

Back in Los Angeles, I called my old friend and mentor, Perry Lafferty, who had recently moved to NBC along with his East Coast counterpart, Fred Silverman. When I told Lafferty about Grady, he became intrigued with the idea of a sitcom starring a comical Baptist minister. He set up a meeting for the following week, when Silverman would be in town, to hear what I had in mind.

171

Peppiatt was out of town, so I set up a session with the two Barrys to help come up with a concept and a title for the projected show. We finally decided that Grady should be what he actually had been in the past, the pastor of a middle–America church. He would have a quirky staff, including a stuffy, humorless assistant pastor, and a smart, feisty secretary to play off.

Some of the story lines would involve problems at the church but, not unlike Dick Van Dyke's show, a lot of the action would be home-oriented, revolving around his wife and troublesome teenage daughter. Admittedly, these are merely the bare bones of what the show could be. The Van Dyke reference was simply anticipating the inevitable question that always comes up when pitching a new show: "What's it like?"

For the title, after several attempts at satirical play-on-words attempts, we decided on *Reverend Grady*.

The main selling point, of course, was Grady Nutt himself. Lafferty had set up a lunch meeting for that Thursday, and I made sure to bring a cassette of Grady's funniest routines from *Hee Haw*. I thought it best to wow them with the cassette right off the bat. We could then discuss the rest as we ate.

It turned out to be exactly the right thing to do. Both Lafferty and Silverman were appropriately dazzled by Grady's brilliant routines, and the rest was easy. A deal to develop a pilot was settled even before the appetizers were served. Now all we needed was a script.

The two Barrys and I batted around all kinds of ideas for the pilot, and after a couple of days we finally settled on a simple plot line: A member of Grady's congregation has suddenly passed away, and Grady has to prepare a eulogy for him. The problem is that the deceased was a terrible person who nobody liked, not even his dog. A sub-plot involved Grady's concerns over his daughter's somewhat dim-witted boyfriend, allowing for the mandatory touching family moment between Grady and his daughter. The climax of the show would be the eulogy, in which Grady cleverly extols the few positive things he is able to glean from his parishioner's not-overly-bereaved widow, making the wretched man sound like the salt of the earth.

When we finished writing the pilot, it turned out to be as funny as we had hoped, an ideal vehicle with which to introduce Reverend Grady. We even threw in a next-door neighbor, just a regular guy named Joe. He and Grady are good pals, and their scenes illustrate his easy relationship to lay people. We figured we had all the angles covered.

Both Grady and the network were happy with the script, and we had the good fortune to acquire the services of Jack Shea, one of the top sitcom directors in the business.

The casting went just as smoothly. Considering that Grady's wife was a charming woman named Eleanor, it was proof that our luck was holding when the first person to audition was Elinor Donahue, who had played Robert Young's daughter, pretty little "Princess," on *Father Knows Best*. Maturity had made her even more appealing, and when she read with Grady there was no doubt in anyone's mind that Elinor was definitely Eleanor.

The rest of the casting went just as easily, including Peggy Pope, a veteran of films and sitcoms who was a natural as Grady's secretary; a cute young actress named Debby Lynn as his daughter; and Candy Azzara, hilarious as the deceased's non-grieving widow.

A taping date was set for mid–April, and after a week of rehearsal we were asked to do a full run-through in the rehearsal hall for the NBC vice-president of Situation Comedy Development, Saul Ilson. Ilson was a fellow Canadian writer from Toronto, and I had worked with him on several shows before we both moved to the States. In Los Angeles, he had teamed up with Ernie Chambers to produce several top variety series, including *The Smothers Brothers*.

**(Left to right) Writer Barry Silver, John Aylesworth, and writer Barry Adelman** pray for the success of *Reverend Grady*, 1981.

# Bansley Productions, Inc.

March 11, 1981

Mr. Saul Ilson
National Broadcasting Company
3000 W. Alameda
Burbank, California

Dear Saul:

We hope this script contains all the elements you
need to convince Mr. Silverman.  Grady is the
central character.  The story revolves around the
family core group and is home oriented.  We have
added a funny little "salt-and-pepper" kid.  The
situation could happen to anybody, not just a
minister, and would have fit very well into the
old Dick VanDyke series.  We have shown Grady
to be competent and in control in the office
situation, but fun at home.

The new title on the script - "FOR GOODNESS SAKE!"
- would be our choice, but here are some alternates:

> "HEAVEN HELP US"
> "COUNT YOUR BLESSINGS"
> "ALWAYS ON SUNDAY"
> "HIGH SPIRITS"
> "GLORY BE!"

We are anxiously awaiting your reaction.

Yours,

John Aylesworth

cc:  Richard Heller
     Michael Klein
     Perry Simon

JA/r

357 North Canon Drive
Beverly Hills, California 90210

Letter from John Aylesworth's Bansley Productions, Inc., to Saul Ilson, NBC, regarding Grady
Nutt's show and possible titles for the pilot episode, 1981.

```
"REVEREND GRADY"

SHOW #0527

CAST LIST
```

| ROLE | ACTOR | DRESSING ROOM # |
|------|-------|-----------------|
| REVEREND GRADY..............GRADY NUTT | | _____ |
| ELLIE.....................ELINOR DONAHUE | | _____ |
| BECKY.....................DEBBY LYNN | | _____ |
| REV. JEREMY HAWKINS........EDWARD MARSHALL | | _____ |
| LIZ.......................PEGGY POPE | | _____ |
| JOE.......................RALEIGH BOND | | _____ |
| RANDY.....................MICHAEL DUDIKOFF | | _____ |
| WILLIE....................MARGARET WHEELER | | _____ |
| MONA THOMPSON..............CANDY AZZARA | | _____ |
| 93-YEAR OLD LADY...........BILLIE JACKMAN | | _____ |

**Reverend Grady cast list for the pilot episode.**

We were all excited with what we had accomplished in rehearsal, and at the appointed time Ilson walked into the rehearsal hall trailed by eight extremely young assistants. Even back then, youthful demographics were important to networks. Somehow, I suppose, having very young interns was supposed to help lure a youthful audience. I had a brief conversation with Ilson and introduced him to Grady. Then he and his entourage sat down in a row of chairs. Each produced a note pad and pencil. Jack Shea introduced the cast and set up the opening scene.

From the moment the first line was spoken, Ilson and the interns began feverishly whispering to one another while scribbling on their note pads. This continued throughout the entire run-through, to the annoyance of the cast which nonetheless performed the entire half-hour show to perfection. Alas, from beginning to end, it would have been impossible for our small audience to have seen or heard a thing, as the whispering and scribbling didn't stop even once from the beginning to the end of the performance. In fact, they had to be told that the run-through was over, to which they reacted with some surprise.

At that point, without acknowledging the cast for a job well done, they simply sat in

**The cast of the pilot for *Reverend Grady*—left to right Peggy Pope, Edward Marshall, Elinor Donahue, Grady Nutt, Debby Lynn, and Raleigh Bond—1981.**

silence for a few seconds until Ilson looked at Jack Shea, the two Barrys, and me, and said, "We have notes." He then gestured to the doorway of an adjoining room into which he and his entourage promptly disappeared.

Jack Shea and I apologized to the cast for the rudeness of their audience, which they graciously dismissed as if it happened every day. We then joined Ilson and his apprentices in the next room, followed by the Barrys. I was steaming as I walked in, appalled at their rude behavior. I pointed out to Ilson that it would be ludicrous to give us notes since he and his assistants had neither seen nor heard the run-through since they had whispered and scribbled non-stop during the entire performance.

The young lackeys looked shocked. Ilson stared at me for about 20 seconds, before standing up and saying, "Okay ... no notes." He quickly left the room, trailed by his entourage.

I turned to Shea, who was a veteran of many pilots, and asked, "Is this how they always watch run-throughs?"

"Pretty much," he replied.

I suppose they had to justify their existence in some way, but I wondered how anything could ever make it through such a system unscathed.

We went back to the rehearsal hall and informed everyone that there were to be no changes and that a dress rehearsal, followed by the actual taping of the show, would take place the next day in front of a live audience in the NBC studios.

The result was everything we could have hoped for. Grady did the audience warm-up and it was a brilliant performance. He was at his hilarious best. The taping went beautifully. Following that, we did some minor editing to include transition shots of a Baptist church we had found in Burbank, and presented the final result to NBC.

Later that week, the pilot was screened for the network brass and the reaction was unanimously favorable, the general reaction being that they had a hit on their hands. There was, however, one more important step before any decision could be made.

Apparently, since network executives couldn't be expected to trust their own opinions, the pilot had to be "tested." That involved screening it for groups of ordinary people, selected at random, who would then fill out cards giving their opinion of the show. This was a practice that had existed since the late 1960s.

If *Hee Haw* had to go through this ritual, I'm sure it would never have made it to the air. Luckily, that show's first episode had been delivered just a few short days before its debut, leaving no time for testing. That allowed the home audience to show their approval through the Nielsen ratings. Lucky for us.

Unfortunately, *Heaven Help Us* didn't have that luxury. The reactions of the test audiences were mixed. Though they agreed it was funny, several were put off by the subject of "death," the catalyst for the eulogy and the whole point of the plot. Others didn't think the actor playing Grady Nutt was believable as a Baptist minister (go figure), and that the show was mocking religion.

**The Reverend Grady in all his spiritual splendor.**

We were subsequently told by the network that we should re-shoot the opening of the show with Grady introducing himself to the audience as an ordained Baptist minister, and the title should be changed to *The Grady Nutt Show*. Obviously, nothing could be done about the "death" aspect, since the whole plot line depended on it.

Grady flew in from his home in Louisville, Kentucky, to tape the new opening. We changed the title graphics to *The Grady Nutt Show*, and delivered the revised pilot to the network. It was tested once more, yielding much more positive results, and we were asked to write outlines for five more episodes, which we happily did. Fred Silverman let it be known that the show was a prime contender as a midseason replacement. We were thrilled.

That fall, Grady resumed his role on *Hee Haw* as the "Prime Minister of Humor," and was funnier than ever.

Tragically, on November 23,

1982, a stormy night, Grady died in a chartered airplane crash trying to make it home to Eleanor and his two young sons for Thanksgiving, after an engagement in Alabama.

We'll never know what the future might have held for this decent and very special man. His legacy remains in the dozens of episodes in which he appeared on *Hee Haw* between 1979 and 1982, and one long forgotten pilot for NBC.

Grady still lives in the hearts of everyone who knew him, and whose spirits were lifted by his unique brand of comedy.

# HEE HAW—THE MOVIE

*"When* Hee Haw *goes off the air, it'll be forgotten forever unless we make it into a movie."—Bill Davis, 1979*

Our partner Nick Vanoff was always looking for a new challenge. In the case of *Hee Haw*, when it had been cancelled by CBS, he had leapt into the breach and rescued it from oblivion through his Herculean effort to sell the show into syndication. Nick had gone through months of unaccustomed humiliation in New York to save the show, even though I've always thought he was somewhat embarrassed to be identified with *Hee Haw*.

Nick certainly wasn't a snob, being a street kid from Buffalo. On the other hand, *Hee Haw* was never mentioned in his bios. As a former Broadway dancer, his social circle included the likes of Martha Graham, Leonard Bernstein, and Alan J. Lerner, not exactly the kind of crowd you'd expect to have a knee-slapping good time guffawing at the antics of a bunch of rubes in a cornfield.

I'm not even sure if Nick ever actually watched the show he had done so much to save. And other than our 20th anniversary special, he had never come to Nashville. Considering Nick's distinguished career in New York and Los Angeles, *Hee Haw* hardly fit into the picture. It was simply the challenge to save it that had compelled him to action.

In 1970, while the future of *Hee Haw* still looked golden at CBS, Nick's newest compulsion was to produce a movie. I guess he figured that as long as he was in the movie capital of the world, he ought to be in pictures.

As a starter, Nick got Yongestreet involved in a British film that was to star Oscar-winner Patricia Neal, who had just miraculously recovered from a debilitating stroke. Her husband, Roald Dahl, was a successful author whose works included dozens of classic adult short stories, as well as books for children that included *Charlie and the Chocolate Factory* and *James and the Giant Peach*.

Dahl had recently written a film script for his wife to return to the screen after her prolonged absence. It was an adult thriller called *The Night Digger*. Nick gave us copies of the screenplay and suggested that we finance the production. It was a wonderful script, so we agreed.

Nick asked his old friend, Alan Courtney, who was yet to join our company and was between jobs at the time, to protect our interests in London while the picture was being shot. Alan happily accepted the assignment and his subsequent reports were glowing.

The shooting went well. When a rough-cut was assembled, Courtney flew back with a copy to get our reactions. It was a very good little thriller, but the biggest thrill for Frank and me was seeing our "Yongestreet Productions" credit at the end of a movie.

When the final product was completed, with a wonderful score by Alfred Hitchcock's favorite composer, Bernard Herrmann, we screened it for Jim Aubrey, who was then president of MGM. He was quite impressed and bought the film for distribution by his studio.

The film was well received by the critics and the public, we made a profit, and that was the end of Yongestreet's involvement in the world of feature films. Frank and I had our hands full with *Hee Haw* and a Don Knotts special, so we never thought much about making movies after that.

Nick, however, had been severely bitten by the cinema bug. Yet it wasn't until 1976, when *Hee Haw* was a solid success in syndication, that Nick plunged back into the movie scene, going into partnership with real estate mogul Saul Pick and leasing the old Columbia Studios lot at Sunset Boulevard and Gower Street in Hollywood.

The corner at Sunset and Gower was known as "Gower Gulch," harking back to the 1930s, when cowboy actors and extras used to hang around in ten-gallon hats and wooly chaps hoping to be cast in westerns at Columbia or the nearby Republic Pictures and RKO studios.

The Columbia lot had seen better days. Most of the stages had been converted to indoor tennis courts, but Nick welcomed the challenge to restore the studios that had produced all those classic Frank Capra films, like *Mr. Smith Goes to Washington* and *It Happened One Night*. He was determined to restore the Sunset-Gower lot into a thriving motion picture production center once again, getting rid of the tennis courts and refurbishing the sound stages to attract independent film productions. Alas, the only takers were a few television soap operas.

Personally, I've always thought Nick's real motive for wanting to lease the lot was to be able to claim the still-existing office and enormous desk of the legendary head of Columbia Pictures, Harry Cohn, as his own. Of all the famous movie moguls of the 1930s and 1940s, Cohn was the most tyrannical and bombastic. Nick was neither, but being somewhat short of stature—at about 5'7"—he could now sit at Harry's huge old desk in Harry's huge old office and imagine himself as a big-time movie mogul.

**All that's left of *Hee Haw—The Movie*.**

Since the facility was situated at Sunset and Gower, Nick and his new partner named their acquisition, with an appalling lack of imagination, "Sunset-Gower Studios." We always used to kid him that since his partner was Saul Pick, he should have named it "PickNick Studios."

Since our editing bills for *Hee Haw* at Vidtronics were escalating, Nick decided to utilize part of his space at Sunset-Gower for an editing bay. In 1977, we all invested in enough equipment to set up a primitive operation in one of the empty buildings on the lot.

We were fortunate enough to obtain the services of Terry Climer, a bright young tape editor from one of the networks, and we did all our own editing from that point on. We had no idea that within a few years this humble operation would grow into a $17 million state-of-the-art post-production center across the street from Sunset-Gower. It would become the envy of every other facility in town.

The only thing Nick wasn't doing with his new studio was making movies. In 1979, we decided to help him do just that. With *Hee Haw* pretty much settled into a foolproof routine at WLAC, and still at the top of the heap in syndication, Bill Davis suggested the time was right to make *Hee Haw—The Movie.* After all, our cast wasn't getting any younger, so while everybody was still alive and kicking, why not immortalize the show on film?

We got one of our original and best writers, Jack Burns, to work on a screenplay with us. In less than a month we had a finished product that we all agreed had captured the spirit of the show and would make a hell of a funny movie.

The screenplay opened with a series of intriguing dramatic vignettes taking place in New York, Las Vegas, and Washington, D.C., with narration by none other than Orson Welles. The vignettes ended with his great voice saying: "Any one of the scenes you have just witnessed would make a great story. Unfortunately, you're stuck with the one you apparently came to see. Ladies and gentlemen ... this is *Hee Haw—The Movie!*" The title then filled the screen as we heard the *Hee Haw* theme music, under which Welles is heard grumbling, "God! The things I do for money."

The story line was simple: An ancient, enormously wealthy *Hee Haw* fan dies laughing while watching the show and leaves his immense fortune to the cast. He had ordered the executor of his will to send telegrams to each castmember, stating that they all must be at the Tennessee State Fair in 24 hours to claim the money, otherwise it would go to his only living relative, a greedy nephew named Rollo. There was one important stipulation— they all had to travel by land since their benefactor didn't like airplanes. When the telegrams are delivered, the chase is on. Basically, the plot is a goofy rustic version of *It's a Mad, Mad, Mad, Mad World.*

Buck and Roy head for Nashville on horseback. Junior drives his tractor. Grandpa and Minnie get their telegram while they're out fishing in Pa's outboard motor boat which mysteriously can also travel on land. Gordie and Gailard hail a taxi. Doc Campbell and Nurse Goodbody take an ambulance. The Hager twins ride a tandem bicycle, and Lulu decides to run all the way, hoping to lose a few pounds.

Naturally, each of them encounters outlandish obstacles set up by the greedy nephew, to be played by the legendary comic-actor Paul Lynde. They all finally make it, with a climactic chase scene involving the whole *Hee Haw* gang in a runaway roller coaster car that flies off its tracks and careens through the fairgrounds. Okay, it didn't make much sense, but who would care as long as it was funny?

Everybody loved the screenplay, which was—if I say so myself—pretty damn hilarious. Bill Davis said he could direct the movie in Tennessee, a right-to-work state, for less than $5 million. Since that was a pittance for a full-length movie, and Yongestreet could easily afford it, we thought Nick would be thrilled. He wasn't.

"There's an old show business rule, fellas. Never put your own money in your own show," said Nick.

"But isn't that what we did to save *Hee Haw*?"

"That was different," said Nick.

"Why was it different?"

"It just was."

It wasn't, but we were in no mood to argue. Once again rising to the challenge, Nick vowed to find investors and get the movie made.

After several failed attempts, Nick finally gave the script to Ray Stark, a powerful producer, whose Raystar Productions had ties to a major studio. Stark loved the screen-play and offered to produce the movie with guaranteed distribution by Columbia Pictures and a large percentage of the profits for Yongestreet.

Naturally, we got all excited at the prospect, but Nick finally scotched the deal by insisting that our percentage should be based on the gross, not the net. Because of studio accounting methods, a percentage of net would end up meaning little or no money for Yongestreet.

Peppiatt and I didn't really care, as long as the movie got made. Nick, however, was adamant. He promised us he would find another way, but he never did.

Because Nick had always been the business expert in our organization, we had always gone along with his decisions. This was the only time since I had known him that Vanoff had failed to meet a challenge. I guess we should have followed our gut instinct and made the damn thing ourselves. It's a decision I'll always regret.

*Hee Haw—The Movie* was never made.

# 36

# THE END OF THE BEGINNING

---

*"I Told You I Loved You, Now Get Out"—Old Woody Herman song, written by John Frigo*

---

In December 1979, we were told by the management of WLAC that we could no longer use their facilities to do *Hee Haw*. We hadn't done anything wrong, they had loved having us there, but a corporate decision had been made to no longer rent their facilities to outside shows. They would revert to being simply the local CBS affiliate in Nashville.

After 10 happy years in our cozy little nest at WLAC, we were being evicted. Sam Lovullo tried everything to change their minds, but they just wouldn't budge. We had already taped the first 13 shows in the spring, and now we had to find a new home to complete the season.

The studios at Opryland were available, but as we had learned from doing the tenth anniversary special at their facilities, the atmosphere would be completely different. Everyone would have their own individual dressing rooms, the studios were enormous compared to what we were used to, and we were concerned that we would lose the close family feeling we had enjoyed for so long at WLAC.

As Reverend Grady Nutt wrote in his book, *So Good, So Far*, commenting on his first days as a *Hee Haw* regular, "It is a crazy, relaxed, and fun group. The feeling is 'vintage family.' I am allowed and encouraged to be myself. I love it. I am at home."

Over the years, Peppiatt and I had written or produced dozens of variety shows in large network studios, and the only times the entire cast came together would be at the first script reading and later in the rehearsal hall. Otherwise, everybody would stay in their dressing rooms on tape days, and only meet on stage when they were called. Consequently, the people on a show never really got to know one another.

The only time I had experienced anything like our time at WLAC was when Peppiatt and I were writing *The Perry Como Show* at the Ziegfeld Theater in New York. The Ziegfeld was an intimate little theater, and our cast of regular performers would gather together in the seats and chat during rehearsals. We would usually sit with them, and consequently everybody on the show—which included Paul Lynde, Kaye Ballard, and Don Adams—became close friends. Perry himself added to the family feeling when, during run-throughs of dance numbers, he would also come and join the group.

After two happy years at the Ziegfeld, the theater was sold by its owner, Billy Rose, and the show was forced to move to NBC's Brooklyn studios in 1963. Everything changed. The Brooklyn studios were huge and antiseptic, not unlike the studios at Opryland.

We didn't see much of each other that third Como year. The whole spirit of the show seemed to go downhill. About mid-season, Perry decided to retire from weekly television at the end of that season. I've always believed he made that decision in response to the show's move to Brooklyn.

In 1980, our situation was eerily familiar. Those chilly Brooklyn studios had nothing on the Opryland complex. I had the feeling that this might be the beginning of the end for our happy *Hee Haw* family.

After saying our sad goodbyes to Oot, Bear, Charles, and all our other friends at WLAC, we bravely decided to make the best of our sterile new location. Somehow, *Hee*

## GEORGE BURNS

April 18, 1980

Dear John-

        I'm very organized.  You sent me a note, now I'm sending you one.  The only difference is yours is on yellow paper and mine is one white.

        Anyway, when I get to Nashville we'll all have a drink together, and possibly some grits.

        Love to you and Ann.

George Burns' response to Aylesworth's request that Burns visit *Hee Haw* during a Nashville visit, April 1980.

The *Hee Haw* trailer at Opryland with George "Goober" Lindsey in drag, 1981.

*Haw* would survive this major upheaval with a smile on our faces and a country song in our hearts.

The whole building was so cavernous and sterile it was hard to believe we were still in Nashville. To add to that feeling, I was walking through the corridors of the Opryland complex one day and came upon a large sign posted outside one of the studio doors. In stark block letters it read, "No admittance! Do not open door."

I couldn't imagine what could possibly be going on inside that would be so top secret. When I asked someone who happened to be walking by, I was amazed to hear that the illustrious choreographer, George Balanchine, was taping a ballet for PBS and demanded complete privacy. Balanchine at the Opry, practically next door to *Hee Haw*? As Grandpa would say, "Outrageous!"

To make matters even worse, there was no office space for our production staff in the Opryland facility. Consequently, we were forced to work out of a trailer that was set up on blocks in the parking lot just outside the entrance to the studios.

But were we downhearted? You bet your sweet donkey we were! However, we were determined to make the best of things.

We didn't start our spring taping until June, due to the move. Since old habits are hard to break, we used the big new studio exactly the same way we had used the tiny one at WLAC. All the comedy segments were taped separately in units of 13 each, and the guest stars did all their numbers in one long session either before or after the comedy. It just made sense to keep doing what we had always done. After all, it had worked like a charm for ten years, so why change now just because the new studio was ten times as big?

Unfortunately, our new home had no place for all the cast members to gather, so they didn't see much of each other. It had a whole different feeling from what we were already referring to as "the old days." We didn't even get together for script readings or rehearsals like other shows did, since everything was on cue cards and we never rehearsed.

Luckily, the shows themselves didn't seem to suffer. When they went on the air, they looked pretty much like they always did. Our ratings stayed rock solid, and there were no viewer complaints. Maybe it wasn't the beginning of the end.

Perhaps it was simply the end of the beginning.

*Opposite, top:* **A crowded gathering in the *Hee Haw* trailer at Opryland, including (left to right) Butch Smith, the video guy, Garry Flood the cue card guy, Bill Williams, tech director/producer Sam Lovullo, writer Bud Wingard, stage manager Stephen Schepman, and general all-around get-things done guy John Gallagher, during the wrap party, fall 1981.** *Opposite, bottom:* **A cow visits the *Hee Haw* production staff, including left to right Sandy Liles, Susan Rettig, Francesca Peppiatt, Betsy Haney, Marcia Minor, and John Gallagher, in the parking lot at Opryland, circa 1981.**

# 37

# THE BEGINNING OF THE END

*"Youngstreet Prods.,* Hee Haw *library sold to Gaylord"*—Daily Variety *head-line—November 17, 1981*
*"*Hee Haw *Has the Last Laugh"—Chester Goolrick,* Wall Street Journal, *July 22, 1981*

After the move to Opryland, the show had settled into a set format. It was a success-ful format, to be sure, but there were no more surprises. We were all getting older.

Frank Peppiatt and I were in our fifties. The Lord only knows how old Grandpa and Minnie were. Junior's teeth were falling out. And Archie was showing up less and less, staying in Gatlinburg and leaving the writing to his son. It felt like the good times were a thing of the past.

There were no more larks like "The Murder Game," and all the other crazy stuff we used to do to while away the evenings. Like most families, we had all grown up and didn't see all that much of each other any more. The only time everybody got together was in the studio on Cornfield day, or in the hotel bar. As that great country poet Hoyt Axton once told me, "There are only three things you can count on in life: women rule the world, cowboy hats blow off in the wind, and things change."

Most of our guest stars were jumping up in a special "mini-cornfield" during music tape days to do jokes with either Buck or Roy. "Pffft, You Were Gone" had become a fun spot in which to inject stars like Johnny Cash, Kenny Rogers, or Loretta Lynn. They would stand with their backs to the camera while Gordie sang the verse, then turn around to reveal themselves and sing along, often ending with a pie in the face.

We had broken our rule of never having urban guest stars, since more and more celebri-ties—like comedian Alan King, Sammy Davis, Jr., Ruth Buzzi from *Laugh-In,* Lorne Greene from *Bonanza,* and comedian-singer Phil Harris were visiting Nashville, often to record country albums. Since *Hee Haw* was no longer a "hillbilly abomination" and was now considered an "American classic," everybody wanted to get into the act.

Gailard Sartain was still as goofy as ever, so we still had a few laughs when we would get together with him and the ever jovial Kenny Price after hours. Still, coming to Nashville for the tapings just wasn't as much fun anymore.

Of course, Peppiatt and I were grateful. *Hee Haw* had been awfully good to us. It had made us rich beyond our wildest dreams, and given us more fun and excitement than we ever could have imagined. It had also saved us from our former lives as journeyman writ-ers, going from show to show for productions that were not our own. We had also made lasting friendships with wonderful people in a part of the country we would have simply

*Top:* The entire *Hee Haw* production staff, with Roy Acuff (second row, fourth from right) and Grandpa Jones (sitting in front), 1980. *Bottom:* "Pickin' and Grinnin'" with Buck Owens and Roy Clark, circa 1980. (Courtesy of Gaylord Program Services, Inc.)

flown over as we shuffled back and forth between L.A. and New York where we worked with stars we would probably never meet again.

I asked Lisa Todd if she was still "chanting" to keep the show on the air, since I had always believed *Hee Haw* would never die as long as Lisa kept chanting. She said she was, so I felt we were doomed to keep making the trek to the chilly environs of Opryland twice a year for the rest of our lives.

**Director Bob Boatman (front, left) with the whole *Hee Haw* cast and crew at Opryland, circa 1981. First row, left to right: Dale Sellers, Bob Boatman, Faye Sloan; second row, left to right: Joe Babcock, Ricky June Page, Gene Evans, Sam Lovullo, Hurshel Wiginton; third row, left to right: Elizabeth Linneman, Ed Sunley; fourth row, left to right: Sandy Zajack, John Aylesworth, Ann Aylesworth, Richard Mahoney, Cathy Baker, Caren Daay, Bob Derryberry, Don Rich, Dolores Edgin, Bobby Thompson; fifth row, left to right: Bud Wingard, Bill Knaggs, Buck Owens, Roy Clark, Oot Sullivan, Jackie Phelps, Jimmie Riddle, Jerry Wiggins, Ron Jackson; sixth row, left to right: Sandy Liles, Harry Cole, Gailard Sartain, Marianne Gordon, Jenne Ferrell, Archie Campbell, Marcia Minor, Barbi Benton, Doyle Singer, Charles Barnhart, Kenneth Demonbreun; seventh row, left to right: John Sprague, Steve Schepman, Truett Smith, Joe Hostettler, Reed Skinner; eighth row, left to right: Tom Lutz, Mindy Lutz, Bobby Trull, John Gallagher, John Hager, Unknown, Jim Hager, Lisa Todd, Grandpa Jones, Gunilla Hutton, Gordie Tapp, Misty Rowe, Junior Samples, Don Harron, Roni Stoneman, Buck Trent, Gerald Brightman (with guitar); last row, left to right: Alan Fuqua, Bob Bowker, Unknown, Richard Kennedy, Dan Newman. (Caren Daay was into numerology and would change the spelling of her name almost every taping, the spelling listed for her is from a spring 1974 script.) (Courtesy Gaylord Program Services, Inc.)**

*Top:* **Grandpa Jones (seated, left) and Archie Campbell (seated, center) in drag, with Roni Stoneman (seated, right) and Lisa Todd (standing, right) in the *Hee Haw* Beauty Parlor, circa 1981. *Bottom:* Gailard Sartain (left) and Archie Campbell in drag in the *Hee Haw* Beauty Parlor with Misty Rowe, circa 1981.**

The fact remained, however, that 12 years after *Hee Haw*'s exciting beginning, we were simply starting to get lazy and possibly a little bored. Consequently, we were not at all upset when, in the summer of 1981, Nick Vanoff told us he was negotiating to sell the show to a company called Gaylord, a name that at once conjured up for me an image of riverboat gamblers. To the contrary, the Gaylord organization had apparently made a vast fortune in newspaper publishing and real estate.

Ed Gaylord, Sr., the patriarch of the Gaylord family, had recently died at the age of 101. The business had been passed on to his son, Ed Gaylord, Jr., who wanted to branch out into the entertainment business. It was a Southern company, headquartered in Oklahoma, so *Hee Haw* fit the image they wanted to project and they were anxious to acquire the show.

Vanoff and the Gaylord representatives were simply dickering over price, something we were happy to leave in Vanoff's capable hands since he was still the only Yongestreet partner possessing full use of the practical left side of his brain.

In November 1981, the deal was finally made for an ungodly amount of money. Gaylord had bought not only *Hee Haw*, with its library of 352 shows, but the package also included Yongestreet Productions itself! I'm convinced the Gaylord people had no idea that the name referred to the main street of Toronto. Even *Daily Variety* misspelled it "Youngstreet" in their headline announcing the sale, but it made Frank and me a bit sad to be losing our little company, named in homage to our hometown.

At the official signing of all the documents, we finally met Ed Gaylord, Jr., in person. As I recall, he was a slightly-built man who appeared to be somewhere in his sixties. What struck me most was his melancholy demeanor. He appeared to have rarely, if ever, smiled. Perhaps the interminable wait to get control of the company until Mr. Gaylord, Sr., finally left the building at the age of 101 would put anybody in a pretty sour mood. If it were me, I wouldn't exactly be a barrel of laughs either.

Since Frank and I had always been the company wags, we did everything we could to jolly Ed, Jr., into a smile, but to no avail. The best we got was the occasional "heh" in response to our increasingly desperate quips and antics. He was certainly cordial enough, but the toughest audience we had ever faced.

Since the deal stipulated that Frank and I would continue as executive producers of the show, as well as continue

**Grandpa Jones dressed as "Grandma" Jones, circa 1981.**

with our writing chores, we were filled with a whole new flood of enthusiasm to make the show better than ever. Barry Adelman joined our writing staff, the other Barry (Silver) having forsaken the Thalian muse and gone home to Chicago. Adelman is a brilliant comedy writer and together we tried to instill a renewed zest to the familiar *Hee Haw* format.

For one thing, we had all but forgotten the fun we used to have doing outdoor film pieces to be inserted into each show. We decided to shoot a series of episodes featuring the two most physical members of our comedy troupe, Gailard Sartain and George "Goober" Lindsey. We called it "Goober and Gailard in Hollywood," a series of filmed vignettes in which the two bumpkins would get into all sorts of comical situations in "Tinsel Town." Both George and Gailard were extremely competitive, each trying to outdo one another in every scene, which made each episode a comic gem.

We also increased the use of our animated bits, such as the disapproving skunk that would hold his nose after a bad joke, as well as our chorus line of dancing pigs. Sam Lovullo put together what he called "The Million Dollar Band," fea-

"Miss" Gailard Sartain strikes a sexy pose, circa 1981.

turing Nashville's top musicians: Floyd Kramer on piano, Boots Randolph on sax, Johnny Gimble on fiddle, Chet Atkins on guitar, and our own Roy Clark and Charlie McCoy on banjo and harmonica. It became a popular semi-regular feature of the show.

After a long hiatus, we also wanted to revive "The Culhanes of Cornfield County," and managed to emulate the inspired goofiness that Jack Burns had originally instilled into his creation. It was great fun to see Grandpa, Lulu, Junior, and Gordie back on their old divan in that Victorian setting, delivering their deadpan gibberish after so many years.

We decided to book a few really off-beat guests, like Ethel Merman, who tried to pass off a number from *Annie Get Your Gun* as a country song. Perhaps the most surreal booking was Henny Youngman, the New York comic known as "the King of the One-Liners." We put him in the Cornfield, all by himself, reeling off an endless stream of jokes, intercut with Charley Farqueson at KORN reporting on a strange alien creature that had landed in the cornfield and couldn't stop doing one-liners. He was finally chased away by our animated pack of angry hound dogs.

We also tried to restore some of the bygone sense of community we used to have by inviting large numbers of cast members out to dinner. This involved a long motorcade of cars.

One night, whoever was driving the lead car got hopelessly lost on the way to the

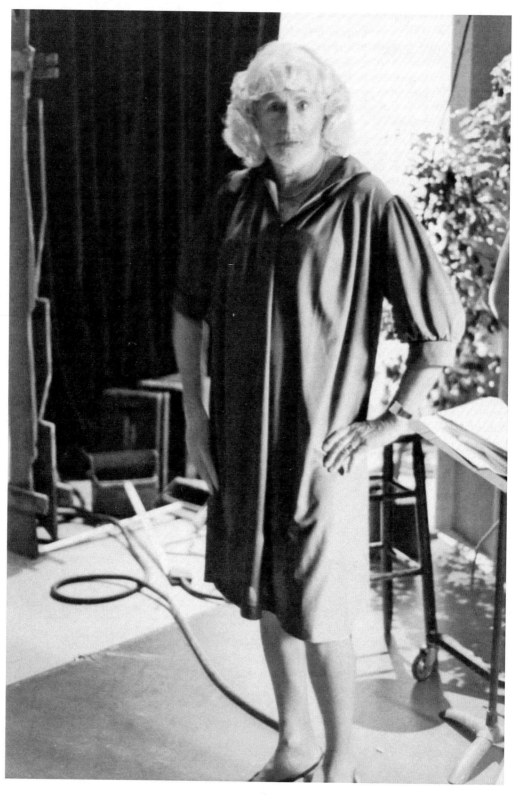

KORN's Don Harron in drag for the *Hee Haw* Beauty Parlor sketch, circa 1981.

restaurant. Consequently, the dozen or so cars following him ended up driving through all the twisting lanes on the campus of Vanderbilt University. At one point, I recall driving down three long flights of concrete stairs, after which we were all laughing so hysterically we finally came to a halt to get our bearings. We never did find the restaurant, and ended up eating at some roadside diner. It was all worth it for the laughs, but that was the end of the motorcade idea.

After a year of frenetic activity, we finally had to accept the fact that the move to Opryland had made it impossible to rekindle the original spirit of a show that had been born in a tiny studio and nurtured by a necessarily close-knit family for ten wonderful years at little old WLAC.

* * *

Back in Los Angeles, since Yongestreet Productions had been sold, we prepared to vacate our offices on Canon Drive in Beverly Hills and go our separate ways. Vanoff, of course, was already ensconced in the legendary Harry Cohn's office at Sunset-Gower. Frank had an office at NBC, where he was producing *The Barbara Mandrell Show* between spring and fall trips to Nashville.

I was now not only without a partner but without an office. I ended up leasing a space in a high-rise on Sunset Boulevard, where Barry Adelman and I proceeded to cook up ideas for new series while we awaited a mid-season decision on *The Grady Nutt Show*.

The odds against getting a new show on the air are astronomical. Even if you do, the odds that it will be a hit are about equal to winning the lottery. Nick Vanoff always said that a hit show is one that's on the air, which is cold comfort in a business that has little patience for anything that doesn't get big numbers in the first two weeks. A show like *Hee Haw* is a once-in-a-lifetime phenomenon.

Actually, I've been lucky enough to hit the programming jackpot twice in my lifetime, which is about as likely as being hit by lightening on a sunny day. The first was a panel show I created in Canada back in the 1950s. Like *Hee Haw*, it was a summer replacement show. The network was the Canadian Broadcasting Corporation, and the show was an immediate hit.

It was called *Front Page Challenge*, and it stayed on the air for 38 years. I never got any royalties from that show after I stopped being actively involved and moved to New York, since technically I was employed by the CBC when I created it. Still, it was kind of a thrill to have been responsible for something like that, and I was always a special guest on the anniversary shows every 10 years.

I probably should have quit while I was ahead, but I started to become obsessed with having one more home run. The closest I came to that was inspired by a stroll through Opryland Park one day on a lunch break while we were taping *Hee Haw* in 1980.

I discovered the Roy Acuff Theater near the entrance to the park, a compact little playhouse reminiscent of the old Ziegfeld Theater in New York. Since Nick Vanoff had enjoyed great success for many years in the similarly compact El Capitan Theater on Vine Street in Los Angeles by renaming it "The Hollywood Palace," I thought why not rename the Roy Acuff Theater for a series to be called *The Nashville Palace*?

How could it miss?

# 38

## THE NASHVILLE PALACE

*"Basically, it's a highfalutin'* Hee Haw*"—sales pitch to ABC, 1980*

Barry Adelman and I wrote a presentation for the new show. It would be an upscale country-variety show. In the tradition of *The Hollywood Palace*, there would be a different big name star as host each week with the hottest country acts as guest performers.

We would have our own honky-tonk with a mechanical bull and line-dancing, patterned after Gilley's in the 1980 hit movie *Urban Cowboy*, and plenty of laughs from our "Nashville Palace Comedy Company" mixing with the guest stars. Slim Pickens would be the off-camera announcer, with lots of by-play with that week's guest host.

We added a weekly satire of the hit prime-time soap *Dallas*, and we would have colorful big production numbers featuring our "Dixie Dozen Dancers."

We pitched the show to ABC and got a deal for a pilot.

Adelman and I went to Nashville hoping to find some new local comedy talent to form a cast of regulars for the new show. We arrived on a Friday. After checking into a hotel, we searched the entertainment page in the local newspaper to see if there were any comedy performances that weekend.

We found an ad for a local musical-comedy revue, so we phoned and ordered tickets for that Saturday evening. We were fully expecting a lot of banjo and fiddle playing along with a bit of cornball humor. We were just hoping to find some new comedy performers the likes of Stringbean and Minnie Pearl.

To our utter amazement, the revue was more Second City than *Hee Haw*. Polished satirical sketches, monologues, and amusing sophisticated songs were performed by four very talented, attractive young people. Terri Gardner was a pretty blonde with a lovely singing voice and excellent comedy delivery. Harry Murphy was humorously urbane and slightly arch. Donna Siegel was earthy and boisterous. And Chuck Bulot, more of a utility performer, very nicely filled out the quartet.

They had written all the material themselves and, while some of it could have been stronger, it was a delightfully urbane evening. Since *Nashville Palace* was to be more upscale than *Hee Haw*, we had miraculously found the new show's comedy family just 24 hours after our arrival!

After the show, we met with the four members of the cast and told them about the *Palace*. Naturally, they were as excited as we were. We got their addresses and phone numbers and told them we would be in touch to finalize a deal for their appearance in the pilot.

Adelman and I spent a leisurely Sunday strolling through Opryland Park. It was a fun place with all kinds of rides, an old west railroad, the General Jackson steamboat, and a full-scale musical production with talented young musicians, singers and dancers. We could certainly use them on the *Palace*, and got the name of the choreographer. Things were shaping up nicely for our new show, with plenty of local talent to spare.

On Monday, we flew back to Los Angeles and went to work on a script for the pilot. We both agreed that Roy Clark would be ideal as our first guest host. We wrote a funny satire of *Dallas*, which was still a hot show in 1981. We had chosen Jerry Clower, a heavy-set, blustery, middle-aged country comedian, to play the nasty billionaire J.R., since Clower was wildly popular with rural audiences and perfect for the part.

The rest of the *Dallas* family would be played by our four young Nashville comedy discoveries. They would also be given set characters to play in "Boots," our honky-tonk section. Terri Gardner would be the cute, garrulous young cowgirl who would adoringly bug our guest stars; the urbane Harry Murphy would be the "dude" urban cowboy; Donna Siegel would play the boisterous, man-hungry, good-time gal; and the bearded, macho Chuck Bulot would belie his menacing appearance with a high-pitched milquetoast voice.

I got Sam Lovullo and Marcia Minor on board to book the guest musical acts and take care of the producing chores, while I acted as executive producer and head writer. Bill Davis wasn't available, so I hired another equally talented director, Stan Harris, along with *Hee Haw* alum Ellen Brown as associate director. Gene McAvoy would come back to Nashville to supply the sets, and *Hee Haw*'s Leard Davis signed on as lighting director. It was a first-class staff. Now all we had to do was tape the pilot.

McAvoy did a marvelous job of transforming the front of the Roy Acuff Theatre into the Nashville Palace, where the opening production number would take place with our Dixie Dozen Dancers. The stage itself had a background of the Nashville skyline, and looked terrific.

Rehearsals went smoothly with our Nashville comedy players, who more than lived up to all our expectations. Jerry Clower was as funny as we had hoped in the *Dallas* sketch. Roy Clark, as always, was a joy to work with and a perfect choice to host the pilot. Slim Pickens was a total pleasure to have on board as our kibitzing announcer.

The actual taping came off like a dream. It was everything we had hoped it would be. The audience was well-dressed and highly appreciative of all the comedy and music. When we got back to Los Angeles, there was very little editing or sweetening to be done, and the completed pilot was delivered to ABC less than two months after we had gotten the green light.

The network was elated after screening the show. They scheduled it to be aired as a special, with plenty of promotion. It was broadcast about a month later. The reviews were good and the ratings put the special in the Top Twenty. We naturally assumed there would be a pick-up for a series, but after a few months the network decided that the show didn't quite fit the image of a network known for *Happy Days*, *Laverne & Shirley*, and *The Love Boat*.

Undaunted, we immediately pitched the show to NBC. They were impressed with the pilot and the numbers it had received, and thought it might do well following *Barbara Mandrell & the Mandrell Sisters*, an equally upscale country show on Saturday nights. Consequently, we got an order for five shows, the first of which would be aired in October 1981.

First, we booked guest hosts for each of the five shows. Roy Clark, of course, would return as host of the premier episode. Other hosts included The Oak Ridge Boys, Joe Namath, and the ever-dependable Roy Rogers and Dale Evans.

Among the guest performers would be our own Grady Nutt and Goober Lindsey, along with Andy Griffith for comedy, plus music by Tammy Wynette, George Jones, Mickey Gilley, Tom T. Hall, and Larry Gatlin, each one a class act.

Since *Dallas* was coming to the end of its run, we wrote a series of new comedy sketches featuring Hamilton Camp, one of my favorite comic actors. Unlike *Hee Haw*, each show was taped in sequence, in front of a live audience.

All five shows were as good as we could possibly make them, but my personal favorite was the one hosted by Roy and Dale. It turned out to be kind of a classic, reuniting Roy with the Sons of the Pioneers, a group with which he got his start as a singer back in the 1930s when he was still Leonard Slye. We had them gathered around a campfire as Roy joined them in a medley of their greatest hits, ending with "Tumbling Tumbleweeds."

Then Pat Buttram, Gene Autry's old movie sidekick, made an entrance. Since Roy was known as "King of the Cowboys," Pat had a surprise for him. At that point, a whole stagecoach full of old cowboy movie stars rolled on stage to pay homage to the "King."

One by one, as Buttram introduced them, the cowboy stars got out of the stagecoach and walked downstage to shake Roy's hand. First, there was George Montgomery, followed by Jock Mahoney, Sunset Carson, Eddie Dean, Rex Allen, Monte Montana, Lash Larue, and "Iron Eyes" Cody. Altogether, it was a wonderful, tear-inducing sequence.

As a special surprise for me, Gene McAvoy had painted "Aylesworth Stagecoach Line" on the side of the coach. What a thrill!

It was a great showcase for Roy and Dale. Roy did a yodeling number, and Dale talked him into doing his old sharpshooting act. They were both getting on in years, and it became a fitting tribute. There wasn't a dry eye in the house when they closed the show with "Happy Trails to You." Roy and Dale are gone now, along with Pat Buttram and all those old movie cowboys. It was an hour I'll never forget.

The other four shows were just as good in their own way, and a lot of fun to write and produce. Unfortunately, when they hit the air that October on a Saturday night, the ratings were a disaster. Everybody was shocked, considering that the pilot had been a big hit on ABC.

To me, the reason seemed pretty simple. With *Hee Haw* airing at 7 P.M., and *Barbara Mandrell* at 8 P.M., followed by *The Nashville Palace* at 9 P.M., there was just too much country for one night. On top of that, maybe audiences just weren't ready for an upscale *Hee Haw*, when they already had the genuine article two hours earlier.

*The Nashville Palace* simply disappeared after those five shows were aired and was never seen again. A year later, *Barbara Mandrell* ceased production, leaving *Hee Haw* still going strong as the only country-variety show on Saturday night. In fact, it was the only country-oriented show on any night.

But several unsettling changes were soon to be made.

# 39

# THE DAY THE CHANTING STOPPED

*"That's all!"—Cathy Baker on* Hee Haw

When Ed Gaylord, Jr., came to Nashville to visit his new acquisition, the capers of our cast of comical characters elicited nary a smile from their dour new owner.

As Frank and I had learned earlier, this was a man who seemed seldom if ever amused. What did capture his fancy were the Opryland TV complex and the real estate surrounding it. By 1983, Gaylord had pretty much bought up everything in sight, including the Opryland Park, the studios housing *Hee Haw* and the Grand Ole Opry, plus the huge colonial Opryland Hotel.

Since the Gaylord Company had devoured the heart of country music and comedy, it was time to divest. Frank and I were the first to go.

In 1984, we were informed that our services would no longer be required. That was actually okay with us. Our visits to Nashville had become less frequent, and we were somewhat demoralized by having to work in a trailer in the parking lot. In fact, we had been mostly fulfilling our writing assignments in L.A. and mailing them in. We hated having lost touch with our once close-knit *Hee Haw* family, and we were saddened by the sudden death of Junior Samples.

Frank had already stopped making trips to Nashville, declaring he'd "had sufficient fun." My own twice-yearly visits were mostly to fulfill my on-going announcing chores, and to supply sardonic comments in the basso voice of Buford the Bloodhound, our fifth and final Wonder Dog—actually, "the stinky dog."

By that time, all the editing and sweetening had been moved from Los Angeles to Opryland. This caused a slight dent in the income of the $17 million post-production facility we had invested in with Nick Vanoff and Saul Pick a couple of years earlier. It was called Complete Post Inc., and luckily was doing great business even without *Hee Haw*.

From that point on, my knowledge of what was going on with the show was limited to what I read in the papers. Sam Lovullo had been retained as producer along with Barry Adelman as head writer, so I picked up the occasional tidbit from them.

I still watched the show on occasion, and it didn't seem to have changed all that much, although Archie was aging rapidly and the absence of Junior left a gaping hole. A local announcer had taken over my old stint opening the show. I had always given my "Welcome to *Hee Haw*!" a cheerful bellow, whereas the new guy sounded like he was introducing a funeral procession. Altogether, the hour had pretty much lost its old zing. Unfortunately, that's not all it was about to lose.

A year later, I read an item that led me to believe the new owners had gone barking

mad. They were dropping Buck Owens from the show! Admittedly, Buck wasn't making
hit records anymore and he was never a laugh riot, but he and Roy together had made a
fine "Pickin' and Grinnin'" team since the very beginning, and I was shocked by the news.
I could only imagine it was a cost-cutting measure, since Don Harron and the Hager twins
were dropped as well.

The *Hee Haw* cast and crew at Opryland Studio, circa 1984. First row, left to right: (seated on floor) Chris Tibbott, Cathy Baker with Buford the Bloodhound; (standing) Buck Owens, Sam Lovullo, John Aylesworth, Roy Clark; (seated on floor) Bob Boatman, Terry Farris, Bix Reichner; second row, left to right: (seated on floor) Charles Barnhart; (kneeling) Oot Sullivan; (seated) unknown, Tom Tichenor; third row, left to right: (kneeling) Paul Resch; (seated) Anita Hostettler, Garry Hood, Lulu Roman, Jackie Phelps, Jimmie Riddle; (standing) Victoria Hallman, Art Brown, Francesca Peppiatt, Ted Wells, unknown, Tom Lutz, Mindy Lutz; (seated) Gordie Tapp, Bud Wingard, Clara Franklin, Ronnie Smith, Danny Wendell; (standing) Faye Sloan; fourth row, left to right: Bob Morrison, Jim Stanley, Truett Smith, Kay Nunnally, Terry Christofferson, Elizabeth Linneman, Gene Moles, Doyle Singer, Archie Campbell, Roni Stoneman, Martin Spencer, George Lindsey, Marcia Minor, Minnie Pearl, Sandy Liles, Junior Samples (profile), Rick Reale, Mackenzie Colt, Rob Noerper,Don Harron, Wendy Suits, Dolores Edgin, Steve Schepman, Kent Green, Bob Britton; fifth row, left to right: Jay Murphy, Leard Davis, Andy York, Buddy Alan, Jim Shaw, Kenny Price, Buck Trent, Linda Thompson, Grandpa Jones, Ann Aylesworth, Misty Rowe, Charlie McCoy, Leon Rhodes, Lisa Todd, Jack McFadden, John Hager, Gunilla Hutton with her son Erik Freeman, Gwen Ankenbauer, Hurshel Wiginton, Martin Clayton, Joe Babcock, Betsy Haney, Jody Karlovic; sixth row, left to right: Tommy Williams, Jerry Whitehurst, Bobby Thompson, Willie Ackerman, Curly Chalker, Skull Schulman, Jim Hager, John Gallagher, Don Wilkins, unknown, Gailard Sartain, Anna Wilkins; seventh row, left to right: Russ Hicks, Peter Alex, unknown, unknown, unknown, Henry Strzelecki, Grady Nutt, Barry Adelman. (Courtesy Gaylord Program Services, Inc.)

**Glen Campbell flanked by the women of *Hee Haw* during a CBS special, *Country Comes Home*, 1984. First row, left to right: Gunilla Hutton, Diana Goodman; second row, left to right: Roni Stoneman, Glen Campbell, Victoria Hallman; third row, left to right: Lisa Todd, Lulu Roman, Linda Thompson; fourth row, left to right: Cathy Baker, Misty Rowe.**

Invitation to *Hee Haw* 20th Anniversary Celebration, March 30, 1988.

Even worse, Lisa Todd would no longer be on the show. This could only spell doom for a show that, I was convinced, owed its long life to her fervent chanting. The writing was on the wall. Lisa Todd would chant no more.

No more chanting, no more show.

Sure enough, the ratings began to plummet as *Hee Haw* limped along for a couple more seasons with Roy Clark joined by a different guest host each week.

In 1987, the show lost another charter member of the cast when that wise old fox, Archie Campbell, passed away. He was soon followed by the demise of dear old Kenny Price. Life in the Cornfield must have become gloomy indeed for the remaining members of the cast.

A year later, Frank and I got a surprise call from Sam Lovullo. Ed Gaylord had decided to have a twentieth anniversary celebration of *Hee Haw* to be taped in the Lazy E Arena at his ranch in Oklahoma City on March 30, 1988.

Frank and I had been asked to write it for a hefty fee, and I would once again be the announcer for that one night only. Buck Owens had been invited to make an appearance for the occasion, after two years in exile, along with George Jones, Loretta Lynn, Barbara Mandrell, Kathy Mattea, Charley Pride, Kenny Rogers, Ricky Skaggs, Ray Stevens, Tanya Tucker, and Conway Twitty.

All that's left of the *Hee Haw* gang in 1989. First row, left to right: Misty Rowe (seated), Roy Clark, Minnie Pearl (seated); second row, left to right: Cathy Baker, Victoria Hallman (Seated), Grandpa Jones, Irlene Mandrell, Lulu Roman; third row, left to right: Hurshel Wiginton, Dolores Edgin, Mike Snider, George Lindsey, Gunilla Hutton, Linda Thompson, Gordie Tapp, Roni Stoneman, Charlie McCoy, Willie Ackerman; fourth row, left to right: Joe Babcock, Wendy Suits, Henry Strzelecki, Russ Hicks, Jeff Smith, Gailard Sartain, Leon Rhodes, Buddy Blackmon, Tommy Williams. (Courtesy Gaylord Program Services, Inc.)

Why celebrate the twentieth anniversary of a show that was slowly dying along with its diminished cast was beyond me, but Frank and I accepted the offer and went to work on a script with Barry Adelman.

A few weeks later, my wife and I got on a plane to fly to Oklahoma City for the big event. Seated across the aisle from us was a decidedly gloomy Buck Owens. He was suffering from a bad cold and laryngitis, no doubt brought on by swallowed pride, but we were glad to see each other. I was particularly happy that Buck and Roy would be reunited, if only for one last bow.

The next day, at the Lazy E Arena, I was warmly greeted by my old friends Lulu Roman,

### Some mighty fine pickin'

I was thrilled by your Cheers for the *Hee Haw Silver Series*—*Hee Haw* the way God intended it ["Cheers 'n' Jeers," May 1]!

As co-creator, with Frank Peppiatt, of *Hee Haw* in its "classic" years, I can only say a heartfelt thank you. After 25 years of sneers, it's great to get cheers.

*John Aylesworth*

**Letter from John Aylesworth to *TV Guide* responding to their "Cheers 'n' Jeers" column finally giving *Hee Haw* cheers, June 1993.**

Minnie Pearl, Misty Rowe, Grandpa Jones, Gordie Tapp, Roni Stoneman, Charlie McCoy with his musicians, the Nashville Edition, and—still crazy after all those years—Gailard Sartain. It was great to see them all again, and we had a fine time reminiscing about "the good old days." Conspicuously missing was our former "chanter-in-chief," Lisa Todd.

The arena itself appeared to be mostly dedicated to horse and cattle shows. A stage had been erected at one end of the rectangular dirt floor of the arena, and planks had been laid for the cameras. Director Bob Boatman was in a remote truck just outside the entrance.

As the cast ran through their various routines, gasoline fumes permeated the arena as the guest stars began arriving in their enormous tour busses, parking in a vast enclosed area behind the stage. This was a far cry from our gala tenth anniversary at the Opry, a first-class production with the entire original *Hee Haw* gang in a state-of-the-art facility.

The Associated Press covered the event in an article that said, "There were no formalities and no tempers lost when taping the anniversary special, despite the complexity of weaving 15 major country music acts into the basic format of hillbilly humor." That was true, although the two-hour special took at least six hours to tape.

The invited audience was both patient and appreciative. The show was broadcast in syndication that spring on most of the *Hee Haw* stations. Although it lacked the zip from the old show that one would have liked, it was a pleasant memento of 20 long years.

In January 1992, *USA Today* made a chilling announcement in a banner headline: "CORNFIELD CLEARED IN 'HEE HAW' OVERHAUL." The article, by David Zimmerman, began, "A pile of bib overalls lies abandoned in a small storeroom just off the 'Hee Haw' set. It's visible evidence that the show you couldn't kill with a stick has updated its look. Gone, too, are the familiar cornfield and ten regular performers who were axed from the show, in its 24th season this month."

Apparently, in a last ditch attempt to keep the show on the air, Misty Rowe, Marianne Rogers, and Gunilla Hutton were purged from the show, along with "Miss Hee Haw" herself, Cathy Baker. Sam Lovullo was quoted as saying the purge was necessary as *Hee Haw*'s demographics had moved into the 50-plus age group and advertising was limited to trucks, beer and Efferdent.

The sets had been updated to a city street and a mall. The only cast members to survive were Roy Clark, Grandpa Jones, Linda Thompson, and Lulu Roman.

Needless to say, the remaining loyal viewers were not pleased. *Hee Haw* wasn't *Hee Haw* anymore, and the last new episode appeared in May 1992. That fall, the Associated Press announced that the show was going into re-runs of its earliest episodes, with Roy Clark doing commentary and introductory remarks. The title was changed to *Hee Haw Silver*, reflecting its 25th year.

In 1993, *TV Guide* printed the following in its "Cheers 'n' Jeers" column:

CHEERS to the "Hee Haw Silver" series—"Hee Haw" the way God intended it. Some things don't need to be updated, upscaled, or upended, and our favorite country show is one of 'em. Now, for a time there, the show's makers forgot that simple truth and put out some newfangled version. Guest stars. Glitz. Wasn't right. So, for the last couple of months, viewers have been treated to 51 of 500-plus old-format episodes—*HH Classic*, if you will. Now the decision has been made to make more of the oldies-but-goodies available for the '93–'94 season. Like a fine Bordeaux, "Hee Haw" just gets better with age.

Amen!

# EPILOGUE:
# SUMMING UP

*"Adios, farewell, goodbye, good luck, so long ... HEE HAW!!!" — Closing song, Buck Owens and Roy Clark*

In 1993, Gaylord pulled *Hee Haw* re-runs out of national syndication and moved the show to their cable outlet as a popular weekly Saturday evening attraction on TNN (The Nashville Network). A few years later, TNN became CMT (Country Music Television) and, for the first time since 1969, *Hee Haw* completely disappeared from the nation's airwaves. For almost a decade, the only place you could see the words *Hee Haw* would be the license plate on my car.

In the meantime, network variety shows, the specialty of Peppiatt and Aylesworth for 40 years, did a similar disappearing act in the mid–1980s. Consequently, we both went into retirement. Frank returned home to Toronto, while I retired in Palm Springs.

In 1987, ABC made an ill-fated attempt to revive the variety format when they made a deal with Dolly Parton for a one-hour weekly show. Since Dolly is a natural talent and a great country performer, the flashy approach taken by the first few shows disappointed her fans, causing the initial high ratings to quickly plummet.

When Nick Vanoff was brought in to shake things up, he asked me to help out with the writing. On my first day in the *Dolly* offices at ABC, I was greeted by a departing Roger Miller. He said he had been brought in to write special material for *Dolly*, which he did, but it was never used so he had spent his last few weeks "just bein' cheerful and tryin' to make everybody feel better" before leaving to join his traveling stage musical, *Big River*.

As for me, it was nice to work with Vanoff again and I did what I could for the show. However, when I was politely asked not to park my car in the lot allocated to the show, presumably since my "Hee Haw" license plate was an embarrassment, I left *Dolly* after an uncomfortable six-week stint.

When the show went off the air at the end of the season, *Dolly* had the distinction of being the last traditional weekly variety show to ever appear on network television. The variety category is now solely represented by award shows, late-night talk shows, and the occasional special.

Frank Peppiatt and I worked as a team one last time in the late 1980s, when we wrote a stage musical based on the life of Jimmy Durante. It had a gala premiere in Toronto before going on the road, where it ended up with rave reviews in Vancouver, B.C., and in San Francisco at the Golden Gate Theater. In the middle of the latter run, the theater was closed by the catastrophic earthquake of 1989. The sets were salvaged, but after a final two-week run at the Shubert in Los Angeles, *Durante—The Musical!* folded and quietly disappeared.

*Hee Haw* was certainly the highlight of our long careers in variety television. Thanks to the release of some of our best shows by Time-Life on DVDs, it will not soon be forgotten. I constantly meet people who see my "Hee Haw" license plate and want to know my connection to the show they grew up hearing on TV in the background of their lives.

As for our original cast that first summer of 1969 at WLAC, only Roy Clark, Lulu Roman, Jeannine Riley, Jennifer Bishop, Cathy Baker, Gordie Tapp, and KORN's Don Harron survive. Minnie Pearl passed away in 1996, Grandpa Jones in 1998 at the age of 84, and Buck Owens in 2006. I hold them all fondly in my memory, along with Stringbean, our "Eefin'" duo Riddle & Phelps, and, of course, Junior Samples.

Of the later arrivals, Grady Nutt, Kenny Price, and John Henry Faulk are now sorely missed. Happily, "Goober" Lindsey, Gunilla Hutton, Misty Rowe, Gailard Sartain, Linda Thompson, and our musical whiz Charlie McCoy are all alive and well as of this writing.

Gene McAvoy, who designed all our original sets, is now happily retired with his wife Kathe in Binghamton, New York, where he is designing sets for local Gilbert & Sullivan productions and having some success as a serious artist.

Nick Vanoff lost interest in the movie business and distinguished himself as co-creator and producer, with George Stevens, Jr., of the Kennedy Center Honors. Vanoff also received a Tony award as producer of the 1990 Larry Gelbart–Cy Coleman Broadway musical *City of Angels*. He passed away the following year of heart failure at the age of 61.

Alan Courtney was 80 when he died in 2000. Bill Harbach, when last I heard, is living in his beloved New York City. Perry Lafferty, my personal mentor for over 40 years and *Hee Haw*'s champion at CBS, died in 2005.

As I write this, Sam Lovullo is still very much with us, as are Bill Davis, Jack Burns, George Yanok, and Barry Adelman. Mike Dann and Fred Silverman are also alive and well. Bernie Brillstein sadly passed away in 2008.

Sadly, Bud Wingard, who made comedy sing on *Hee Haw* with "Gossipy" and "Gloom, Despair and Agony on Me," left us in 2000 at age 67. Bob Boatman died suddenly in the summer of 1989.

I have no idea what became of Bix Reichner. Wherever you are, Bix, thanks a million for "Pffft, You Were Gone."

Frank Peppiatt is now living in Florida with his wife, Caroline. I am still writing in Palm Desert with my wife, Anita.

Yongestreet is still the main street of Toronto. The production company that bore its name no longer exists, nor does Ed Gaylord, Jr., who died at the age of 83, seventeen years shy of his father's century mark.

From a writer-producer's standpoint, *Hee Haw* was the perfect show. It was almost impossible to go wrong. All the characters were likeable, as was the case for all long-running hit comedies from *Cheers* and *The Cosby Show* to *Friends* and *Seinfeld*. The secret is the same as fly fishing: It's all in the casting.

Who wouldn't love Minnie Pearl with that price tag still on her hat? The total innocence of a grinning Junior Samples? The genuine folksiness of Stringbean and Grandpa? The bubbling good humor of Roy Clark? Even Buck Owens earned affection from everyone for trying to loosen up and act goofy.

As for the material, it was foolproof. If a joke wasn't funny, it always got a laugh from a board fence hitting the joke-teller in the butt, or a cartoon skunk holding its nose. If somebody messed up a line, it became an instant blooper to be repeated throughout the show with a bigger reaction each time. It was the kind of show that, if you're lucky, comes once in a lifetime. I'll always be grateful that it came in mine.

Am I glad we sold *Hee Haw* in 1981? Not really. I don't think we would have had we been allowed to stay in our cozy little nest at WLAC where it all began and where my happiest memories of the show still dwell. It was the team spirit of Jimmy Norton, Joe Hostettler, Larry Sullivan, Reed Skinner, Oot, Bear, Charles, and all the rest, whose hustle and hard work without a word of complaint that first summer made the impossible possible.

To everyone involved, I can only say thank you.

# The Creators of *Hee Haw*

## John Aylesworth

John Aylesworth is an award-winning television writer and producer, playwright, author, and personality who has been associated with the entertainment industry since the 1950s. He won the Peabody Award for "Frank Sinatra: A Man and His Music" (1965), co-created the longest running comedy-variety show on American television, *Hee Haw*, and created the longest-running panel-game show on Canadian television, *Front Page Challenge*. Aylesworth is retired, living in Palm Desert, California.

## *Professional Biography*

### Books

| | |
|---|---|
| In process | *A Job Laughing*—In process, a history of variety television and a compilation of anecdotes about the television variety genre, based on humorous encounters with various stars over 40 years |
| 2010 | *The Corn Was Green: The Inside Story of Hee Haw*—McFarland |
| 1998 | *Geezers—Boot Camp for Boomers*—Unpublished |
| 1971 | *Service*—Unpublished; screenplay commissioned by Warner Bros., 1979 |
| 1961 | *Fee-Fi-Fo-Fum*—Paperback, Avon Books, 1961; treatment for 20th Century–Fox, 1964; optioned by Catalina Productions, 1983; optioned by Manhattan Pictures, 1989 |

### Theatrical Credits

| | |
|---|---|
| 1998–1999 | *Palm Springs Confidential* (writer, director). A one-act blackout-skit comedy-variety-musical revue, produced at Palm Canyon Theater, Palm Springs |
| 1997 | *The Comeback of Myrna La Rue* (writer). Professional readings at Palm Canyon Theater, Palm Springs |
| 1989 | *Durante—The Musical* (co-writer). Produced in Toronto, Vancouver, San Francisco, Los Angeles |

### Television

Co-created the longest running musical-variety show on American television, *Hee Haw*, started in 1969 on CBS, later syndicated.

Created the longest running game show on Canadian television, *Front Page Challenge*, started in 1957 on CBC, ran for over 38 years, concept optioned by Dick Clark Productions.

| | |
|---|---|
| 1981–1988 | *Dolly*—Series, ABC, script consultant—Musical-variety show |

*Hee Haw 10th Anniversary Special*—Syndicated, writer, announcer

*New Love American Style*—Series, ABC, script consultant

*The Performers*—6 weeks, BCTV (Canada), interviewer—On-camera interviews with personalities

*The Nashville Palace*—NBC, creator, executive producer, writer—Musical-variety show

*The Grady Nutt Show*—Sitcom pilot, NBC, creator, producer, writer

**1971–1980**    *Hee Haw Honeys*—26 shows, Syndicated, executive producer, writer—Comedy-variety show

*The Stones*—Sitcom pilot, ABC, producer, writer, announcer

*Dorothy Hamill Presents Winners*—Special, ABC, head writer—Variety special

*The Big Show*—13 weeks, NBC, announcer

*Orange Blossom Special*—*Salute to Hank Williams*, producer, writer—Variety special

*The Sonny and Cher Show*—39 weeks, CBS, head writer, announcer—Comedy-variety series

*Shields and Yarnell*—16 weeks, CBS, producer, writer, announcer—Comedy-variety series

*Inside Television*—Special, ABC, producer, writer—Pilot special behind-the-scenes look at the TV industry

*Front-Page Feeney*—Sitcom pilot, Syndication, producer, writer—starred Don Knotts

*Don Knott's Special*—Special, CBS, executive producer, writer—Comedy-variety special

*Hooray for Hollywood*—Special, CBS, executive producer, writer—Comedy-variety special, starring Don Adams and Don Rickles

*Grammy Salutes Oscar*—Special, CBS, producer, writer—Musical special

*Perry Como Christmas Special*—Special, CBS, head writer, announcer—Musical-variety special

*Perry Como Easter Special*—Special, CBS, head writer, announcer—Musical variety special

*Everything Goes*—100 shows, Syndication, creator, executive producer, writer—A 5-a-week talk-variety show, hosted by Norm Crosby

*Keep on Truckin'*—4 weeks, ABC, creator, producer, writer, announcer—Satirical comedy series

*Heck's Angels*—Sitcom pilot, CBS, creator, producer, writer

*Harlem Globetrotters' Popcorn Machine*—CBS, creator, executive producer, writer—Comedy series

*Jackie Gleason Special*—Special, CBS, head writer—Comedy-variety special

*KopyKats*—7 weeks, ABC, head writer—Comedy-variety series, featuring Rich Little, Frank Gorshin, Marilyn Michaels, George Kirby, and guest stars

*The Julie Andrews Show*—26 weeks, ABC, head writer—Musical-variety series

*Hee Haw*—57 weeks, CBS, creator, producer, writer, announcer—Musical-comedy-variety show. After 57 weeks on CBS, it was syndicated in fall 1971 with 26 new shows each year.

**Pre–1971**    *The Jonathan Winters Show*—26 weeks, CBS, producer—Comedy series

*The Brass Is Comin'*—Special, CBS, head writer—Herb Alpert and the Tijuana Brass

*Irving Berlin's 80th Birthday Special*—CBS, head writer—Musical special

*The Kraft Music Hall*—26 weeks, NBC, head writer—Musical-variety series

*The Phyllis Diller Special*—Special, NBC, head writer—Comedy-variety special

*Monaco with Princess Grace*—Special, ABC, producer, writer

*Frank Sinatra—A Man and His Music*—Special, NBC, head writer—Musical special

*Hullabaloo*—52 weeks, NBC, head writer—Musical-variety series

*Wake Me When It's Over*—TV Movie, CBS, writer

*The Judy Garland Show*—15 weeks, CBS, head writer—Musical-variety series

*Dinah Shore Special*—NBC, writer—Musical-variety special

*Perry Como Show*—117 weeks, NBC, writer—Musical-variety series

*Bing Crosby Special*—ABC, head writer—Musical special

*The Andy Williams Show*—13 weeks, CBS, head writer—Musical-variety series

*Your Hit Parade*—39 weeks, CBS, head writer

*After Hours, Big Revue, On Stage*—3 years, CBC (Canada), writer and performer

## Awards

| | |
|---|---|
| 1978 | People's Choice Award |
| | *Hee Haw* |
| 1976 | Emmy Nomination |
| | *The Sonny and Cher Show* |
| 1971 | Emmy Nomination |
| | *The Julie Andrews Show* |
| 1970 | Man of the Year |
| | Academy of Country and Western Music |
| 1965 | Peabody Award and Emmy Nomination |
| | *Frank Sinatra: A Man and His Music* |
| 1956 | Canadian Emmy Award |
| | *Front Page Challenge* |

## *Frank Peppiatt*

Frank's name has been linked with mine for so many years and on so many shows, "Peppiatt and Aylesworth" became a sort of brand in the world of variety television. Therefore, it's only fair to point out that we are two completely different people with individual lives and several separate pursuits.

Frank graduated from the University of Toronto, whereas I was a high school drop out. Frank played college football and has always been very athletic, while I have always been blissfully sedentary competing in nothing more strenuous than Yahtzee and Scrabble. Frank is at least four inches taller than I am, extremely muscular and arguably better looking, while I am somewhat shorter, with a big nose, and forced to scrape by on nothing but dazzling wit and charm.

Professionally, following our years as a Canadian television comedy team, Frank was head writer on Canada's *Jackie Rae Show*, *Here's Duffy*, and *Music Makers*. That was followed by a move to New York where he wrote *The Steve Lawrence and Eydie Gorme Show* and *The Steve Allen Show* in 1958.

From that point on, our resumes were identical as writing and producing partners, until the late 1970s when we once again went our separate ways. Frank became producer of *The Bobby Gentry Show* on CBS, co-produced with Phil Hahn a new Sonny and Cher series for CBS in 1976, and in 1978 returned briefly to his acting roots when he appeared in a recurring role as Admiral Frank Borkman in three episodes of *Operation Petticoat* for ABC.

In the early 1980s, Frank returned to Toronto where he wrote and produced *Check It Out!*, a successful situation comedy starring comedian Don Adams. In 1985, we retired from writing television as a team, after writing *The New Love American Style* for ABC. We then came together and co-wrote a stage musical, *Durante*, which opened in Toronto in 1989 and later toured to Vancouver, San Francisco and Los Angeles. Frank is now retired and lives with his wife Caroline in Florida.

Frank and I have become the Canadian version of "the Sunshine Boys," periodically being invited back to Toronto for various anniversary shows. We were honored with a 1996 tribute special on the Canadian Broadcasting Corporation, *Peppiatt and Aylesworth: Canada's First Television Comedy Team.*

# APPENDIX:
## *HEE HAW* EPISODES

### *1969 Summer Show—CBS Network—Sundays at 9 PM*

1  June 15, 1969: Loretta Lynn, Charley Pride. The perfect pairing for our very first show: the "Queen of Country Music" and country's only African American star.
2  June 22, 1969: Merle Haggard, Jack Burns (cameo).
3  June 29, 1969: Tammy Wynette, George Jones, Faron Young. Tammy and George, together again for the very first time on *Hee Haw*.
4  July 6, 1969: Sonny James, Waylon Jennings, Connie Smith.
5  July 13, 1969: Jerry Lee Lewis, Ferlin Husky.
6  July 27, 1969: Charley Pride, Tammy Wynette, George Jones.
7  August 3, 1969: Merle Haggard, Bonnie Owens, Eddie Fukano.
8  August 10, 1969: Loretta Lynn, Waylon Jennings.
9  August 17, 1969: Jerry Lee Lewis, Conway Twitty. Jerry Lee was worth all the trouble—a wonderful performer.
10  August 24, 1969: Merle Haggard, Bonnie Owens. Bonnie was Buck's ex-wife and then married Merle. An interesting booking.
11  August 31, 1969: Tammy Wynette, Sonny James.
12  September 7, 1969: Loretta Lynn, Jerry Lee Lewis, Charley Pride.

### *1969-70 Season—CBS Network—Wednesdays at 7:30 PM*

13  December 17, 1969: Merle Haggard, Tammy Wynette.
14  December 24, 1969: Loretta Lynn, Dillard & Clark (The Expedition).
15  December 31, 1969: Dottie West, Hank Williams, Jr.
16  January 7, 1970: Henson Cargill, Wanda Jackson.
17  January 14, 1970: Lynn Anderson, Hank Thompson, Buddy Alan.
18  January 21, 1970: Sonny James, Tammy Wynette.
19  January 28, 1970: Loretta Lynn, Merle Haggard.
20  February 4, 1970: Ferlin Husky, Dottie West.
21  February 11, 1970: Lynn Anderson, George Jones.
22  February 18, 1970: Tammy Wynette, Merle Haggard, Henson Cargill.
23  February 25, 1970: Loretta Lynn, Charley Pride.
24  March 4, 1970: Wanda Jackson, Sonny James.
25  March 11, 1970: Dottie West, George Jones.
26  March 18, 1970: Dolly Parton, Faron Young. Who knew that 19 years later, sweet little Dolly would bring about the demise of the television variety show?
27  March 25, 1970: Connie Smith, Stan Hitchcock.
28  April 1, 1970: Merle Haggard, Linda Ronstadt.
29  April 8, 1970: George Jones, Tammy Wynette.

## *1970-71 Season—CBS Network—Tuesdays at 8:30 PM*

30  September 15, 1970: Roy Rogers & Dale Evans, Bobby Bare. God bless Roy and Dale—
they were always there when we needed them.
31  September 22, 1970: Charley Pride, Jeannie C. Riley.
32  September 29, 1970: Ray Charles, Lynn Anderson. Ray Charles' first appearance on *Hee
Haw*—he electrified the studio. What a thrill!
33  October 6, 1970: George Jones, Tammy Wynette.
34  October 13, 1970: Marty Robbins, Connie Eaton.
35  October 20, 1970: Doug Kershaw, Roy Rogers & Dale Evans.
36  October 27, 1970: Sonny James, Peggy Little.
37  November 10, 1970: Jean Shepard, Tom T. Hall. The *Hee Haw* debut of Tom T. Hall, my
all-time favorite musical storyteller.
38  November 17, 1970: Charley Pride, Susan Raye.
39  November 24, 1970: Tammy Wynette, Ed Bruce.
40  December 1, 1970: Ray Charles, Lynda K. Lance.
41  December 8, 1970: Kenny Price, Linda Martell. Kenny's first guest shot. He was soon to
become a beloved part of the *Hee Haw* gang.
42  December 15, 1970: Waylon Jennings, Diana Trask, Johnny Duncan.
43  December 29, 1970: Roy Rogers & Dale Evans.
44  January 5, 1971: Charley Pride, Amanda Blake, Mickey Mantle. Mantle was our first guest
from the world of sports; many more followed.
45  January 12, 1971: Roger Miller, Peggy Little, Bobby Murcer. Roger's first appearance on
*Hee Haw*—direct from the King of the Road hotel.
46  January 19, 1971: Marty Robbins, Connie Smith.
47  January 26, 1971: Tammy Wynette, George Jones, Billy Jo Spears.
48  February 2, 1971: Loretta Lynn, Bill Anderson.
49  February 9, 1971: Roy Rogers & Dale Evans.
50  February 16, 1971: Hank Williams, Jr., Jody Miller.
51  February 23, 1971: Bobby Bare, Connie Eaton, Tom T. Hall.

## *1971-72 Season—Syndication—Saturdays at 7 PM*

52  September 18, 1971: Roy Rogers & Dale Evans. Our first show in syndication. We made it!
53  September 25, 1971: Dale Robertson, Susan Raye.
54  October 2, 1971: Amanda Blake, Buddy Allen.
55  October 9, 1971: George Lindsey, Kenni Huskey. "Goober" George Lindsey's first shot as a
guest before becoming a regular on the show.
56  October 16, 1971: Conway Twitty, Loretta Lynn.
57  October 23, 1971: Sammi Smith, Bakersfield Brass.
58  October 30, 1971: Lynn Anderson, Ray Sanders.
59  November 6, 1971: Roy Rogers & Dale Evans.
60  November 13, 1971: Dale Robertson, Kenni Huskey.
61  November 20, 1971: Conway Twitty, Loretta Lynn.
62  November 27, 1971: Sammi Smith, Buddy Alan, Bakersfield Brass.
63  December 4, 1971: Lynn Anderson, Ray Sanders.
64  December 11, 1971: Susan Raye, Buddy Alan.
65  January 8, 1972: Johnny Duncan, Doug Kershaw, Buddy Alan.
66  January 15, 1972: Sonny James, Jody Miller.
67  January 22, 1972: Tammy Wynette, George Jones.
68  January 29, 1972: Bobby Goldsboro, Susan Raye.
69  February 5, 1972: Jeannie C. Riley, Buddy Alan, Johnny Bench.
70  February 12, 1972: Dolly Parton, Porter Wagoner.
71  February 19, 1972: Brenda Lee, Hank Thompson, George Lindsey.
72  February 27, 1972: Waylon Jennings, Jessi Colter, Johnny Bench.
73  March 4, 1972: Tom T. Hall, Susan Raye.

74    March 11, 1972: Tammy Wynette, George Jones.
75    March 18, 1972: Barbara Mandrell, Ferlin Husky.
76    March 25, 1972: Jody Miller, Buddy Alan.
77    April 1, 1972: Connie Smith, Tommy Ambrose.

## 1972-73 Season—Syndication—Saturdays at 7 PM

78    September 16, 1972: Ray Stevens, Arlene Harden, Dizzy Dean. Ray was hilarious in his *Hee Haw* debut.
79    September 23, 1972: Patti Page, Charlie McCoy.
80    September 30, 1972: Mel Tillis, Sherry Bryce.
81    October 7, 1972: Ray Price, Sandy Posey.
82    October 14, 1972: Johnny Paycheck, Ruby Davis.
83    October 21, 1972: Kenny Price, Penny DeHaven, Dizzy Dean.
84    October 28, 1972: Susan Raye, Tommy Overstreet, Tommy Jones.
85    November 4, 1972: Jud Strunk, Jamey Ryan. Jud was a great new talent. He sang his hit song, "Daisy a Day." Frank and I later did a network special with him before his untimely death in a plane crash.
86    November 11, 1972: Jeannie Seely, Buddy Alan.
87    November 18, 1972: Bobby Bare, Barbara Fairchild.
88    November 25, 1972: Ray Stevens, Donna Fargo.
89    December 2, 1972: Patti Page, Doyle Holly, Charlie McCoy.
90    December 9, 1972: Hank Williams, Jr., Arlene Harden.
91    December 16, 1972: Barbara Mandrell, Paul Richey. Barbara was a real *Hee Haw* favorite.
92    January 6, 1973: George Jones, Tammy Wynette, Buddy Alan.
93    January 13, 1973: Tennessee Ernie Ford, Sammi Smith, Charlie McCoy. At last we get Tennessee Ernie on the show—true country royalty.
94    January 20, 1973: Loretta Lynn, Conway Twitty, Johnny Bench.
95    January 27, 1973: Johnny Paycheck, Sandy Posey, Ruby Davis, George Lindsey.
96    February 3, 1973: Don Gibson, Sue Thompson, Demetris Tapp.
97    February 10, 1973: Frankie Laine, Buddy Alan, Oral Roberts, Richard and Patti Roberts.
98    February 17, 1973: Jody Miller, Tony Booth, Doyle Holly, Joe Stampley.
99    February 24, 1973: Donna Fargo, Tennessee Ernie Ford, Tommy Cash, Charlie Rich.
100   March 3, 1973: Wanda Jackson, Frankie Laine, Tony Booth.
101   March 10, 1973: Tennessee Ernie Ford, Faron Young, Penny DeHaven.
102   March 17, 1973: George Jones, Tammy Wynette, Patsy Sledd.
103   March 24, 1973: Loretta Lynn, Conway Twitty, Ray Griff.

## 1973-74 Season—Syndication—Saturdays at 7 PM

104   September 17, 1973: Jerry Reed, LaWanda Lindsey.
105   September 22, 1973: Johnny Rodriguez, Conny Van Dyke, Catherine McKinnon.
106   September 29, 1973: Charlie Rich, Susan Raye.
107   October 6, 1973: Sonny James, Charlie McCoy.
108   October 13, 1973: Tanya Tucker, George Lindse, Buddy Allen. Tanya was a real handful in those days, but what a great performer.
109   October 20, 1973: Dottie West, Billy Craddock.
110   October 27, 1973: Roy Acuff, Diana Trask. Roy Acuff, a country legend, would soon become a regular on *Hee Haw.*
111   November 3, 1973: Tammy Wynette, George Jones, Johnny Bush.
112   November 10, 1973: Brenda Lee, Buddy Allen.
113   November 17, 1973: Donna Fargo, O.B. McClinton.
114   November 24, 1973: Jerry Reed, Conny Van Dyke, Susan Raye.
115   December 1, 1973: Hank Snow, Diana Trask.
116   December 8, 1973: Jeanne Pruett, Joe Stampley.

117   December 15, 1973: Charley Pride, Susan Raye, Ronnie Milsap.
118   January 5, 1974: Roy Acuff, Jim Ed Brown, Marcie & Margie Cates.
119   January 12, 1974: Tex Ritter, Catherine McKinnon, Bruce Bradley, Don Rich. Tex was actor
      John Ritter's dad. He died not long after appearing on this show.
120   January 19, 1974: Loretta Lynn, Kenny Starr, Stoney Edwards, Jerry Clower.
121   January 26, 1974: Tennessee Ernie Ford, Jody Miller, Tommy Overstreet, Larry Scott.
122   February 2, 1974: Tom T. Hall, Sunday Sharpe, Charlie McCoy, Johnny Bench.
123   February 9, 1974: Charley Pride, Barbara Fairchild, Tony Booth, Craig Scott.
124   February 16, 1974: Johnny Cash, Jean Shepard, George Lindsey. Johnny Cash finally
      appears on the *Hee Haw*—what a thrill!
125   February 23, 1974: Pat Boone, Skeeter Davis, Ronnie Milsap, Bill Taylor.
126   March 2, 1974: Loretta Lynn, Conway Twitty, David Houston, Jerry Clower.
127   March 9, 1974: Tennessee Ernie Ford, LaWanda Lindsey, Red Shipley.
128   March 16, 1974: Johnny Rodriguez, Susan Raye, Oak Ridge Boys.
129   March 23, 1974: Lester Flatt, Hugh Hefner, Buddy Alan. Lester Flatt and Hugh Hefner—
      what a combination!

## 1974-75 Season—Syndication—Saturdays at 7 PM

130   September 14, 1974: Ernest Borgnine, George Lindsey. Borgnine was a pal of George
      "Goober" Lindsey. This was a nutty booking, but great fun.
131   September 21, 1974: Loretta Lynn, Kenny Price, Buddy Allen.
132   September 28, 1974: Freddie Hart, Leona Williams, Barbi Benton.
133   October 5, 1974: Danny Davis & The Nashville Brass, Susan Raye.
134   October 12, 1974: Jody Miller, Pee Wee King, Redd Stewart.
135   October 19, 1974: Ernest Borgnine, Loretta Lynn, Kenny Starr.
136   October 26, 1974: Bobby Bare, Conny Van Dyke.
137   November 2, 1974: Faron Young, LaWanda Lindsey, Charlie McCoy.
138   November 9, 1974: Boots Randolph, Hugh Hefner, Barbi Benton. "Yackety Sax" meets
      *Playboy*. Go figure.
139   November 16, 1974: Bill Anderson, Susan Raye, Nashville Edition.
140   November 23, 1974: Barbara Mandrell, Buddy Allen, Tony Booth.
141   November 30, 1974: Sonny James, Johnny Carver, Crystal Gayle.
142   December 7, 1974: Chet Atkins, Jan Howard.
143   December 14, 1974: George Jones, Tammy Wynette.
144   December 21, 1974: Donna Fargo, George Lindsey, Tony Lovello.
145   December 28, 1974: Red Steagall, Susan Raye, LaWanda Lindsey, Gov. Winfield Dunn.
146   January 4, 1975: Mac Wiseman, Tony Booth.
147   January 11, 1975: Molly Bee, Charlie McCoy, Buddy Alan.
148   January 18, 1975: Bob Luman, Boots Randolph, Barbi Benton.
149   January 25, 1975: Johnny Russell, LaWanda Lindsey.
150   February 1, 1975: Brenda Lee, Chet Atkins, Johnny Carver.
151   February 8, 1975: George Jones, Tammy Wynette, Mickey Gilley.
152   February 15, 1975: Dolly Parton, Kenny Price, Terry McMillan, Barbi Benton.
153   February 22, 1975: Kitty Wells, Freddie Weller.
154   March 1, 1975: Connie Smith, Don Williams, Buddy Alan.
155   March 8, 1975: Tommy Overstreet, Susan Raye, LaWanda Lindsey.

## 1975-76 Season—Syndication—Saturdays at 7 PM

156   September 13, 1975: Johnny Cash, John Carter Cash.
157   September 20, 1975: Loretta Lynn, Kenny Starr, Jana Jae.
158   September 27, 1975: George Gobel, Jack Ruth, Barbi Benton.
159   October 4, 1975: Tammy Wynette, Billy Walker, George Lindsey.
160   October 11, 1975: Ray Stevens, Susan Raye.
161   October 18, 1975: Barbara Mandrell, Doyle Holly, Buck Trent.
162   October 25, 1975: Freddy Fender, Melba Montgomery, Kenny Price.

163 November 1, 1975: Jody Miller, Little Jimmy Dickens.
164 November 8, 1975: Mel Tillis, Sammy Jo.
165 November 15, 1975: Mickey Gilley, LaWanda Lindsey, Nashville Edition.
166 November 22, 1975: Barbara Fairchild, Joe Stampley.
167 November 29, 1975: Ronnie Milsap, Buddy Alan, Tony Lovello.
168 December 6, 1975: Conway Twitty, Susan Raye.
169 December 13, 1975: Johnny Cash, La Costa.
170 December 20, 1975: George Gobel, Tommy Ambrose.
171 January 3, 1976: Don Gibson, Sue Thompson.
172 January 10, 1976: Loretta Lynn, Conway Twitty.
173 January 17, 1976: Roy Acuff, Tammy Wynette.
174 January 24, 1976: Cal Smith, Statler Brothers, LaWanda Lindsey.
175 January 31, 1976: Dottie West, Charles Ginnsberg, Garner Ted Armstrong.
176 February 7, 1976: George Jones, Sunday Sharpe.
177 February 14, 1976: Tom T. Hall, Susan Raye.
178 February 21, 1976: Faron Young, Crystal Gayle.
179 February 28, 1976: Sonny James, David Wills, LaWanda Lindsey.
180 March 6, 1976: Kenny Rogers, Mel Street. The beginning of a whole new career for Kenny.
181 March 13, 1976: Merle Travis, Brush Arbor.

## *1976-77 Season—Syndicated—Saturdays at 7 PM*

182 September 18, 1976: Tammy Wynette, Will Geer, Kenny Price.
183 September 25, 1976: George Gobel, Billie Jo Spears.
184 October 2, 1976: Donna Fargo, Red Sovine.
185 October 9, 1976: Jimmy Dean, Buddy Alan, Buck Trent, Jana Jae. With Jimmy Dean on the show, it was like going back to 1963 in New York City.
186 October 16, 1976: Bobby Goldsboro, Barbi Benton.
187 October 23, 1976: Ray Stevens, Susan Raye, Jackie Phelps.
188 October 30, 1976: C.W. McCall, Crystal Gayle, Brush Arbor.
189 November 6, 1976: Charley Pride, Dave & Sugar.
190 November 13, 1976: Terry Bradshaw, Barbi Benton.
191 November 20, 1976: Jimmy Dean, George Gobel, Susan Raye.
192 November 27, 1976: Johnny Paycheck, Mel Street.
193 December 4, 1976: Sonny James, Narvel Felts.
194 December 11, 1976: Larry Gatlin, Statler Brothers. Larry used to work in our prop room—a real success story.
195 December 18, 1976: Jimmy Dean, Margo Smith.
196 January 8, 1977: Roy Rogers & Dale Evans.
197 January 15, 1977: Tennessee Ernie Ford, Brenda Lee, Merle Travis, Jimmy Henley.
198 January 22, 1977: Jim Ed Brown, Helen Cornelius.
199 January 29, 1977: Mel Tillis, Susan Raye.
200 February 5, 1977: Loretta Lynn, Conway Twitty, Lorne Greene. Lorne was an old friend of mine back in my Canadian days.
201 February 12, 1977: Barbara Mandrell, Hoyt Axton.
202 February 19, 1977: George Jones, Tammy Wynette.
203 February 26, 1977: Ernest Tubbs, Jody Miller.
204 March 5, 1977: Bill Anderson, Mary Lou Turner, Gerald Smith.
205 March 12, 1977: Mickey Gilley, Susan Raye, Jimmy Henley.
206 March 19, 1977: Barbara Mandrell, Faron Young.
207 March 26, 1977: Tennessee Ernie Ford, Connie Smith, Merle Travis.

## *1977-78 Season—Syndication—Saturdays at 7 PM*

208 September 17, 1977: Mel Tillis, Susan Raye, Thompson Brothers, Duke of Paducah. The Duke finally got his shot!

209    September 24, 1977: Roy Rogers & Dale Evans, Sons of the Pioneers, Harper Twins, Duke
       of Paducah.
210    October 1, 1977: Kenny Rogers, Jana Jae, Cathy Barton.
211    October 8, 1977: Jerry Reed, Sammi Smith, Jimmy Henley, East Virginia Toadsuckers.
212    October 15, 1977: Freddy Fender, Dottie West.
213    October 22, 1977: Larry Gatlin, Phelps & Riddle, Jimmy Henley.
214    October 29, 1977: Charley Pride, David Huddleston, Hank Thompson.
215    November 5, 1977: Loretta Lynn, Sons of the Pioneers, Ernest Rey, Russell Knight.
216    November 12, 1977: Dennis Weaver, Eddie Rabbitt, Jana Jae.
217    November 19, 1977: Sonny James, Oak Ridge Boys, Kenny Price, Bob Montgomery.
218    November 26, 1977: Tom T. Hall, Sons of the Pioneers, Harper Twins, Kenny & William
       Price.
219    December 3, 1977: Don Williams, Dave & Sugar, Jimmy Henley.
220    December 10, 1977: Floyd Cramer, Kenny Roberts, Thompson Brothers.
221    December 17, 1977: Dennis Weaver, Susan Raye, Jimmy Henley.
222    January 7, 1978: Larry Gatlin, Susan Raye, Vernon Presley. Vernon was Elvis Presley's dad.
223    January 14, 1978: Barbara Mandrell, Larry Mahan, Billy Carter, Jimmy Henley.
224    January 21, 1978: Jeannie C. Riley, Johnny Bench, Tommy Lasorda, D.J. Peterson.
225    January 28, 1978: Roy Rogers & Dale Evans, Alan King, Jimmy Henley.
226    February 4, 1978: Patti Page, Brush Arbor, D.J. Sarginson, Buddy Alan.
227    February 11, 1978: Kenny Rogers, Joe Higgins, The Kendalls.
228    February 18, 1978: Johnny Rodriguez, Susan Raye, Jimmy Henley, C.B. Slane, Sheriff
       Katherine Crumbley, Duke of Paducah.
229    February 25, 1978: Ruth Buzzi, David Houston.
230    March 4, 1978: Little Jimmy Dickens, George Savalas, Dottsy, Harper Twins, Mel Jass.
231    March 11, 1978: Billy Carter, Stuart Hamblen, Randy Gurley. Billy was President Carter's
       embarrassing brother. Remember "Billy Beer"?
232    March 18, 1978: Patti Page, Danny Davis & The Nashville Brass, Jerry Clower, Johnny
       Jobe.
233    March 25, 1978: Statler Brothers, Linda Hargrove, Jimmy Henley.

## *1978-79 Season—Syndication—Saturdays at 7 PM*

234    September 16, 1978: Bill Anderson, Mary Lou Turner, Lonzo & Oscar, Jana Jae.
235    September 23, 1978: Tennessee Ernie Ford, Barbara Fairchild.
236    September 30, 1978: John Hartford, Moe Bandy.
237    October 7, 1978: Oak Ridge Boys, Bobby Goldsboro, John Ritter.
238    October 14, 1978: Hank Williams, Jr., Connie Smith.
239    October 21, 1978: Sons of the Pioneers, Rex Allen, Jr., Billy Carter, Doc Randall, Doctor
       Paul Braun.
*Special* October 22, 2978: 10th Anniversary Celebration.
240    October 28, 1978: Larry Gatlin, Ava Barber, Joe Higgins.
241    November 4, 1978: Tom T. Hall, Don Gibson, Jimmy Henley.
242    November 11, 1978: Barbara Mandrell, John Hartford, Roy Acuff.
243    November 18, 1978: Mel Tillis, Roy Head, Gerald Smith.
244    November 25, 1978: Don Williams, Tennessee Ernie Ford, The Kendalls.
245    December 2, 1978: Ronnie Milsap, Stoney Mountain Cloggers, Margo Smith.
246    December 9, 1978: Sonny James, Jim Stafford, Jana Jae.
247    December 16, 1978: Tennessee Ernie Ford, Jody Miller, Nashville Edition.
248    January 6, 1979: John Hartford, Jimmy Henley.
249    January 13, 1979: Charley Pride, T.G. Sheppard, Jimmy Henley.
250    January 20, 1979: Mickey Gilley, Faron Young.
251    January 27, 1979: Jim Stafford, Charlie McCoy, Touch of Country.
252    February 3, 1979: Johnny Duncan, Janie Fricke, Johnny Gimble, Jana Jae.
253    February 10, 1979: Ray Price, Bill Anderson, Roy Acuff.
254    February 17, 1979: Conway Twitty, Dave & Sugar.
255    February 24, 1979: Charlie Rich, Mary K. Miller.

256    March 3, 1979: Tennessee Ernie Ford, Stella Parton.
257    March 10, 1979: Johnny Paycheck, Dickey Lee.
258    March 17, 1979: George Jones, Eddie Rabbitt, Stoney Mountain Cloggers.
259    March 24, 1979: Jim Stafford, Zella Lehr, Eddie Low.

## 1979-80 Season—Syndication—Saturdays at 7 PM

260    September 15, 1979: Senator Robert Byrd, Hoyt Axton, Con Hunley, Riddle & Phelps. The
          Senator was one heck of a fiddle player!
261    September 22, 1979: Joe Stampley, Clarence "Gatemouth" Brown, Moe Bandy.
262    September 29, 1979: Tennessee Ernie Ford, Jimmie Rodgers, Bobby Butler, the Rev. Dr.
          Billy Graham. The Reverend dropped by to remind us that God has a sense of humor.
263    October 6, 1979: John Conlee, Susie Allanson, Jana Jae.
264    October 13, 1979: Gene Autry, Statler Brothers, Randy Barlow, Joe Frazier.
265    October 20, 1979: Jim Ed Brown, Helen Cornelius.
266    October 27, 1979: Tennessee Ernie Ford, Cristy Lane, Jones Family, Curly & Lil Kimbler,
          Riddle & Phelps.
267    November 3, 1979: Larry Gatlin, Foster Brooks, Becky Hobbs.
268    November 10, 1979: Senator Robert Byrd, Dave & Sugar, Donna Darlene, Mike Edwards.
269    November 17, 1979: Don Williams, Billy Parker, Gerald Smith, Riddle & Phelps.
270    November 24, 1979: Tennessee Ernie Ford, Tammy Wynette, Karel Gott, James Family.
271    December 1, 1979: Dennis Weaver, Clarence "Gatemouth" Brown, Alan Wayne.
272    December 8, 1979: Freddy Fender, Mission Mountain Wood Band, Stoneman Family.
273    December 15, 1979: Conway Twitty, Ronnie Prophet.
274    January 5, 1980: Ed McMahon, Faron Young, Barbi Benton, Kathy Kitchen.
275    January 12, 1980: Hank Thompson, Janie Fricke, Wally Lattimer.
276    January 19, 1980: T.G. Sheppard, Gene Watson, Jed Allan, Stoneman Family.
277    January 26, 1980: Dottie West, Pat Buttram, Jimmy C. Newman, Lonnie Brooks.
278    February 2, 1980: Oak Ridge Boys, Charly McClain, Marty Sullivan.
279    February 9, 1980: Billy "Crash" Craddock, Louise Mandrell, Tommy Cash.
280    February16, 1980: Ray Stevens, Ava Barber, Boxcar Willie.
281    February 23, 1980: Hank Snow, Margo Smith, Rodney Lay.
282    March 1, 1980: Barbara Mandrell, Sonny James, Jethro Burns.
283    March 8, 1980: Dennis Weaver, Randy Boone, Dottsy, Jana Jae, Woody Woodbury.
284    March 15, 1980: Tammy Wynette, Jimmie Rodgers, Big Al Downing, Barbi Benton.
285    March 22, 1980: Blackwood Brothers, Wendy Holcombe, Ralph Sloan.

## 1980-81 Season—Syndication—Saturdays at 7 PM

286    September 13, 1980: Kenny Rogers, Ethel Merman, Million Dollar Band. Ethel Merman
          was one of the weirdest bookings we ever had, but somehow it worked.
287    September 20, 1980: Merle Haggard, Tennessee Moonshine Cloggers, Leona Williams.
288    September 271080: Janie Fricke, Norm Crosby, Buck White.
289    October 4, 1980: The Kendalls, Million Dollar Band, Razzy Bailey.
290    October 11, 1980: Ray Stevens, Sylvia, Susan Guttmann.
291    October 18, 1980: Ed McMahon, Bellamy Brothers, Jimmy Henley, Marty Stuart.
292    October 25, 1980: Hoyt Axton, Joe & Rose Lee Maphis, Million Dollar Band.
293    November 1, 1980: Tom T. Hall, Jeanne Pruett, Henny Youngman. Henny was an even
          weirder booking, but very funny! Somehow, we always lucked out.
294    November 8, 1980: Statler Brothers, Jimmi Cannon, Ralph Case Dancers.
295    November 15, 1980: Loretta Lynn, Million Dollar Band, Rodney Lay, Jimmy Henley.
296    November 22, 1980: Barbara Mandrell, Roger Maris, Sonny Curtis.
297    November 29, 1980: George Jones, John Anderson, Marty Stuart, Susan Raye.
298    December 6, 1980: Dennis Weaver, Buddy Alan, Million Dollar Band.
299    December 13, 1980: Porter Wagoner, Lacy J. Dalton, Joe Maphis.

300	January 3, 1981: Merle Haggard, Slim Pickens, John Conlee.
301	January 10, 1981: Bill Anderson, Curly Putman, Buddy Alan, Wayne Massey & Mary Gordon Murray.
302	January 17, 1981: Mickey Gilley, Johnny Lee, Million Dollar Band.
303	January 24, 1981: Bruce Jenner, Reba McEntire, T.G. Sheppard, Rodney Lay.
304	January 31, 1981: Paul Anka, Sylvia, Chubby Wise, Gene Swindell.
305	February 7, 1981: Brenda Lee, Thrasher Brothers, Million Dollar Band.
306	February 14, 1981: Helen Cornelius, Billy Grammer, Jack Worley, John D. Loudermilk.
307	February 21, 1981: Dennis Weaver, Tom T. Hall, Tommy Hunger.
308	February 28, 1981: Rex Allen, Sr., Rex Allen, Jr., Eddy Raven, Margo Smith, Million Dollar Band.
309	March 7, 1981: Ray Price, Boxcar Willie, Kentucky Chimes Dancers.
310	March 14, 1981: Ray Charles, Slim Whitman.
311	March 21, 1981: Slim Pickens, Don Gibson, Jacky Ward, Million Dollar Band.

## *1981-82 Season—Syndication—Saturdays at 7 PM*

312	September 12, 1981: Ed Bruce, Gail Davies, Wendy Holcombe.
313	September 19, 1981: Loretta Lynn, Conway Twitty, Dian Hart, Million Dollar Band.
314	September 26, 1981: Jeannie C. Riley, Big Al Downing.
315	October 3, 1981: Audrey Landers, Earl Thomas Conley, Willis, Carlan & Quinn.
316	October 10, 1981: Alabama, Harlan Howard, Mackenzie Colt, Million Dollar Band, Carolina Kids Cloggers.
317	October 17, 1981: Hank Williams, Jr., Janie Fricke, The Niningers.
318	October 24, 1981: Big Bird, Sonny James, Billy "Crash" Craddock.
319	October 31, 1981: Joe Stampley, Terri Gibbs, Boxcar Willie, Million Dollar Band.
320	November 7, 1981: Kitty Wells, Doc Severinsen, Thrasher Brothers, Governor Lamar Alexander. The incredible variety of guests who appeared on *Hee Haw* over the years continues to amaze me.
321	November 14, 1981: Faron Young, Sylvia, Chubby Wise.
322	November 21, 1981: Loretta Lynn, Conway Twitty, Glaser Brothers.
323	November 28, 1981: Johnny Rodriguez, Helen Cornelius, Hank Cochran.
324	December 5, 1981: Ernest Tubb, Billie Jo Spears, Cheryl Handy.
325	December 12, 1981: David Frizzell & Shelly West, Oscar the Grouch, Million Dollar Band, The Shoppe.
326	January 2, 1982: Jeannie Seely, Ronnie McDowell, Sheb Wooley, Jerry Pate.
327	January 9, 1982: Razzy Bailey, Leslie Nielsen, The Kendalls, Little General Cloggers.
328	January 16, 1982: Charly McClain, Ed McMahon, Sonny Shroyer, Charlie McCoy & Laney Smallwood.
329	January 23, 1982: Bill Monroe, Doc Severinson, Rex Allen, Jr., Dianne Sherrill, Million Dollar Band.
330	January 30, 1982: Bobby Bare, Stoneman Family, Glaser Brothers, Kippi Brannon.
331	February 6, 1982: Mickey Gilley, John Hartford, Carl Smith, Jimmy Henley.
332	February 13, 1982: Roy Acuff, Brenda Lee, Jimmy C. Newman, Mac Wiseman.
333	February 20, 1982: Jimmy Dean, Wilburn Brothers, Cotton Ivy, Charlie Lamb.
334	February 27, 1982: Ernest Tubb, B.J. Thomas, Merle Travis, Stan Kann.
335	March 6, 1982: Don Williams, John Hartford, Connie Smith, Danny Flowers.
336	March 13, 1982: Roy Acuff, Margo Smith, Steve Wariner, Cotton Ivy.
337	March 20, 1982: Jacky Ward, Reba McEntire, Jimmy Henley, Terri Merryman.

## *1982-83 Season—Syndication—Saturdays at 7 PM*

338	September 11, 1982: Donna Fargo, Lee Greenwood, Real Hillbilly Band, Moonshine Cloggers.
339	September 18, 1982: Ray Stevens, "Scatman" Crothers, Million Dollar Band.

340  September 25, 1982: Louise Mandrell, R.C. Bannon, Charlie Walker, Ben Peters.
341  October 2, 1982: Mickey Gilley, Johnny Lee, Terry Gregory, Connie B. Gay, Buckwheat
       Cloggers.
342  October 9, 1982: Jim Stafford, Gail Davies, Cripple Creek Band.
343  October 16, 1982: Sammy Davis, Jr., Eddy Raven, James Bacon, Georgia Peaches.
344  October 23, 1982: Ed Bruce, John Schneider, Al Downing, Felice & Boudleaux Bryant.
345  October 30, 1982: Mickey Gilley, Johnny Lee, Sylvia, Sammy Jackson.
346  November 6, 1982: Paul Williams, Charly McClain, Chuck Morgan, Buckwheat Cloggers.
347  November 13, 1982: David Frizzell, Shelly West, Phil Harris, Kim & Karman Reid.
348  November 20, 1982: Loretta Lynn, Wright Bros., Dew Drops, Million Dollar Band.
349  November 27, 1982: T.G. Sheppard, Billy Barty, Bill Caswell, Cumberland Boys.
350  December 4, 1982: Boxcar Willie, Ronnie Prophet, Penny DeHaven, Cotton Ivy.
351  December 11, 1982: Mel Tillis, Charlie Walker, Darrell Waltrip, Custer's Last Band.
352  December 18, 1982: Jim Stafford, Earl Thomas Conley, Merle Travis, Million Dollar Band.
353  January 8, 1983: Oak Ridge Boys, Jim Ed Brown, Jerry Chestnut, Moonshine Cloggers.
354  January 15, 1983: Sammy Davis, Jr., Dub Taylor, Barbi Benton, Red Steagall.
355  January 22, 1983: Charley Pride, Family Brown, Butch Baker, Gerald Smith, Million Dollar
       Band.
356  January 29, 1983: Ricky Skaggs, Sonny James, Cindy Hurt, John Hartford & Real Hillbilly
       Band.
357  February 5, 1983: Dottie West, John Schneider, Burrito Brothers, Cotton Ivy, Little General
       Cloggers.
358  February 12, 1983: Conway Twitty, John Anderson, Jerry Clower, Wright Brothers, Rodney
       Lay.
359  February 19, 1983: Janie Fricke, Osmond Brothers, Dub Taylor, Cliffie Stone, Beverly Cot-
       ton.
360  February 26, 1983: Hoyt Axton, Gene Watson, Irlene Mandrell, Jack Kaenel, Kentucky
       Hoedowners.
361  March 5, 1983: B.J. Thomas, Helen Cornelius, Bill Carlisle, Dayne Puckett.
362  March 12, 1983: Paul Williams, Steve Wariner, Willard Scott, Million Dollar Band.
363  March 19, 1983: Faron Young, Leon Everette, Dub Taylor, Bobby Braddock.

## *1983-84 Season—Syndication—Saturdays at 7 PM*

364  September 17, 1983: Charley Pride, Razzy Bailey, Jan Howard, Darrell Adams, Gerald
       Smith.
365  September 24, 1983: Tanya Tucker, Carl Perkins, Million Dollar Band, Rip Taylor, Moon-
       shine Cloggers & Dewdrops.
366  October 1, 1983: Alabama, Skiles & Henderson, Big Al Downing, Dub Taylor, Onie
       Wheeler.
367  October 8, 1983: Louise Mandrell, Irlene Mandrell, Boxcar Willie, Buddy Killen, Ted Gay.
368  October 1, 1983: Ricky Skaggs, The Whites, Dub Taylor, Vern Gosden, Carroll Baker.
369  October 22. 1983: Reba McEntire, Tom Wopat, Don Crawley, Del Wood, John Garrett.
370  October 29, 1983: Tennessee Ernie Ford, David Frizzell, Shelly West, Skip Stephenson.
371  November 5, 1983: Loretta Lynn, Johnny Rodriguez, Cedar Creek, Johnson Sisters, Steve
       "Shotgun Red" Hall.
372  November 12, 1983: Statler Brothers, George Strait, Aldridge Sisters, Stoney Mountain
       Cloggers.
373  November 19, 1983: Barbara Mandrell, Chris Golden, Jimmy Henley, Ben & Butch McCain,
       Lee Arnold.
374  November 26, 1983: John Anderson, Charly McClain, Dub Taylor, Million Dollar Band,
       Grant Turner.
375  December 3, 1983: Tennessee Ernie Ford, Chet Atkins, Earl Klugh, Michael Murphy, Ger-
       ald Goodwin.
376  December 10, 1983: Ricky Skaggs, Lee Greenwood, The Whites, Billy Edd Wheeler.
377  December 17, 1983: Lynn Anderson, Johnny Lee, Buster Wilson, Dub Taylor, Moonshine
       Cloggers & Dewdrops.

378    December 31, 1983: Charley Pride, Jack Greene, Susan Raye, Buster Wilson, Steve "Shotgun Red" Hall.
379    January 7, 1984: Mickey Gilley, Charly McClain, Tom T. Hall, Mel McDaniel, Tari Hensley, David Holt, Million Dollar Band.
380    January 14, 1984: T.G. Sheppard, Gene Watson, Vic Willis Trio, Trilly Cole, Leroy Troy Boswell.
381    January 21, 1984: Bobby Bare, Jeannie C. Riley, Skiles & Henderson, Steve "Shotgun Red" Hall.
382    January 28, 1984: Ed Bruce, James Galway, Karen Taylor-Good, Sonny Throckmorton.
383    February 4, 1984: Glen Campbell, Mel Tillis, Mac Wiseman, Jerry Pate, Kentucky Hoedowners.
384    February 11, 1984: Barbara Mandrell, Chet Atkins, Earl Klugh, Johnny Tillotson, Little Jimmy Dickens. What a lineup of talent!
385    February 18, 1984: Larry Gatlin, Atlanta, Pinkard & Bowden, The Kendalls, Onie Wheeler.
386    February 25, 1984: Tennessee Ernie Ford, Janie Fricke, Vaughn Horton, Benny Wilson, High Country Cloggers, Million Dollar Band, Steve "Shotgun Red" Hall.
387    March 3, 1984: Roger Miller, Tom T. Hall, Gary Morris, Seidina Reed.
388    March 10, 1984: Vic Damone, Tommy LaSorda, Moe Bandy, Gus Hardin. How much fun is it to get to put together a guest list like this?
389    March 17, 1984: Glen Campbell, Mel Tillis, Bill Monroe, Steve Wariner, Zeke Sheppard, Red O'Donnell.


## *1984-85 Season—Syndication—Saturdays at 7 PM*

390    September 22, 1984: Louise Mandrell, Ronny Robbins, Million Dollar Band.
391    September 29, 1984: George Jones, Brenda Lee, Moonshine Cloggers & Dewdrops.
392    October 6, 1984: Lee Greenwood, The Judds, Keith Whitley, Roy Acuff.
393    October 13, 1984: Loretta Lynn, Ronnie McDowell, Sawyer Brown.
394    October 20, 1984: David Frizzell, Shelly West, Cliffie Stone, Dale Christenson.
395    October 27, 1984: Porter Wagoner, Amy Grant, Million Dollar Band, Twin River Cloggers.
396    November 3, 1984: Alabama, Lorrie Morgan, Gary Wolf, Bob Murphey, Len Ellis.
397    November 10, 1984: Dottie West, Hoyt Axton, Cotton Ivy & Noopey, Joe Maphis.
398    November 17, 1984: Osmond Brothers, Stan Freese, Charlene Gordon, Marijane Vandivier.
399    November 24, 1984: John Conlee, Gary Morris, Donna Douglas.
400    December 1, 1984: Sylvia, Boxcar Willie, Dennis Weaver, Ronnie Porter.
401    December 8, 1984: Louise Mandrell, Con Hunley, Million Dollar Band, The Cannons, Buddy & Kay Baines.
402    December 15, 1984: George Jones, Kathy Mattea, Lionel Cartwright.
403    December 22, 1984: Charley Pride, Riders in the Sky, Victoria Shaw, Million Dollar Band.
404    December 29, 1984: Bill Anderson, Tom & Mary Grant, Babcock Family, Sonja Shepard & Keith Brady, Million Dollar Band.
405    January 5, 1985: Loretta Lynn, Vern Gosdin, David Holt, Lloyd Lindroth.
406    January 12, 1985: Joe Stampley, Lorrie Morgan, Keith Stegall, Jed Allan.
407    January 19, 1985: Statler Brothers, The Whites, Bobby Vinton, Rise & Shine Cloggers.
408    January 26, 1985: Reba McEntire, Billy Walker, Dan Seals, Kerry Gilbert.
409    February 2, 1985: Willie Nelson, Kris Kirstofferson, Roy Acuff, Anita Bryant.
410    February 9, 1985: Ricky Skaggs, Bill Monroe, Dobie Gray, Million Dollar Band.
411    February 16, 1985: Oak Ridge Boys, Herve Villechaize, Eddy Raven, Darlene Austin.
412    February 23, 1985: Earl Thomas Conley, Exile, Bill Baker, Kimberly Chapman & Chip Woodall.
413    March 2, 1985: Tom T. Hall, Jim Glaser, Million Dollar Band.
414    March 9, 1985: Willie Nelson, Faron Young, Jim Stafford, Buddy Alan, Palmetto State Cloggers.
415    March 16, 1985: Statler Brothers, Kieran Kane, Stan Musial, Victoria Hallman.

## 1985-86 Season—Syndication—Saturdays at 7 PM

416 September 21, 1985: Exile, Hank Thompson, Stan Freese, The Girlstown Band.
417 September 28, 1985: Reba McEntire, Osmond Brothers, Moonshine Cloggers, John Hartford.
418 October 5, 1985: Louise Mandrell, Steve Wariner, Bobby Vinton.
419 October 12, 1985: Jerry Lee Lewis, Bill Medley, Million Dollar Band.
420 October 19, 1985: Janie Fricke, Bobby Bare, Ralph Emery, Benny Wilson.
421 October 26, 1985: Charlie Daniels, Eugene Fodor, Minnesota Fats.
422 November 2, 1985: Mel Tillis, George Strait, Stan Freese, Million Dollar Band.
423 November 9, 1985: Willie Nelson, Kris Kristofferson, McCain Brothers, J.T. Jackson, John Hartford.
424 November 16, 1985: Gary Morris, Sonny James, Don Cherry, Melvin Sloan Cloggers.
425 November 23, 1985: Loretta Lynn, Mel McDaniels, Patricia McKinnon, John Hartford.
426 November 30, 1985: Marie Osmond, Burl Ives, Dan Seals, Williams & Ree.
427 December 7, 1985: Ray Stevens, Shelly West, Ernest Borgnine.
428 December 14, 1985: Jerry Lee Lewis, Sawyer Brown, Jim Stafford.
429 December 21, 1985: Louise Mandrell, Del Reeves, Danny Darst.
430 December 28, 1985: Lee Greenwood, Roger Miller, Rockin' Sidney, Blue Grass Express Cloggers, Jane Robelot.
431 January 4, 1986: Loretta Lynn, Johnny Rodriguez, Boxcar Willie, Million Dollar Band, John Hartford.
432 January 11, 1986: Charley Pride, Becky Hobbs, Jim Varney, Stonewall Jackson.
433 January 18, 1986: Loretta Lynn, Helen Cornelius, Nitty Gritty Dirt Band, Tennessee River Boys, John Hartford.
434 January 25, 1986: Ricky Skaggs, Connie Smith, Tommy Hunter, Misty Lord & Jay Ledford Cloggers.
435 February 1, 1986: Hank Williams, Jr., Sylvia, Michael Johnson, Charlie Walker, David Holt.
436 February 8, 1986: Eddie Rabbitt, Ray Stevens, Forester Sisters, Mac Wiseman, Grant Turner.
437 February 15, 1986: George Jones, Loretta Lynn, Johnny Russell, Million Dollar Band, John Hartford, Gov. Lamar Alexander.
438 February 22, 1986: Roger Miller, The Judds, Hank Thompson, Jim Varney, Steele Family Cloggers.
439 March 1, 1986: Oak Ridge Boys, Faron Young, David Holt, Billy Parker.
440 March 8, 1986: Hank Williams, Jr., Keith Whitley, Merle Kilgore, Rattlesnake Annie.
441 March 16, 1986: Loretta Lynn, Riders in the Sky, Holly Gilreath & Jon Hasler Cloggers, John Hartford, Million Dollar Band.

## 1986-87 Season—Syndication—Saturdays at 7 PM

442 September 20, 1986: Loretta Lynn (cohost), Exile, Girls Next Door, Jake Leg and the Rum Dummies.
443 September 27, 1986: Johnny Cash & June Carter Cash (cohosts), Gatlin Brothers, Kathy Mattea, Moonshine Cloggers & Dewdrops.
444 October 4, 1986: Reba McEntire (cohost), Bellamy Brothers, Forester Sisters.
445 October 11, 1986: Mel Tillis (cohost), Randy Travis, Judy Rodman, Danny White, Willful Stumble.
446 October 18, 1986: Jerry Reed, Barbara Fairchild, Pake McEntire, David Holt.
447 October 25, 1986: Loretta Lynn (cohost), Mickey Gilley, The Whites, George Hamilton IV, Steele Family Cloggers, John Hartford.
448 November 1, 1986: Johnny Cash & June Carter Cash (cohosts), Dwight Yoakam, Billy Grammer, The Cannons.
449 November 8, 1986: Reba McEntire (cohost), Tanya Tucker, Tommy Hunter, Kyle Petty, Paul Brown, Rick Hines.
450 November 15, 1986: Mel Tillis (cohost), Louise Mandrell, George Lindsey, John Anderson, John Hartford.

451 November 22, 1986: Johnny Cash & June Carter Cash (cohosts), Gatlin Brothers, Kentucky Country.

452 November 29, 1986: Loretta Lynn (cohost), T. Graham Brown, Florence Henderson, Leather & Lace Cloggers.

453 December 6, 1986: Jerry Reed (cohost), Dottie West, Ray Pillow, David Holt, Dr. Sam Faulk.

454 December 13, 1986: Reba McEntire (cohost), Loretta Lynn, Pat Boone, Keith Stegall, Clyde Roley Cummins.

455 January 3, 1987: George Jones (cohost), Kenny Rogers, Vince Gill, Holly Dunn, Million Dollar Band, Roy Acuff.

456 January 10, 1987: Oak Ridge Boys (cohosts), Loretta Lynn, k.d. lang, Dobie Gray, Mike Snider.

457 January 17, 1987: Glen Campbell (cohost), Johnny Cash, June Carter Cash, Keith Whitley, Mel Tillis, John Campbell, Rodney Lay.

458 January 24, 1987: John Schneider (cohost), Louise Mandrell, New Grass Revival, Million Dollar Band.

459 January 31, 1987: Marie Osmond (cohost), Eddie Rabbitt, Ralph Stanley & Bill Monroe, Paul Davis.

460 February 7, 1987: Hank Williams, Jr. (cohost), Sawyer Brown, Sweethearts of the Rodeo, Loretta Lynn.

461 February 14, 1987: Glen Campbell (cohost), George Jones, Judy Rodman, Mel Tillis, Sonja Shepard & Bobby Revis.

462 February 21, 1987: John Schneider (cohost), Loretta Lynn, Gary Morris, Riders in the Sky, Mike Snider, Shirley Gilbert.

463 February 28, 1987: Oak Ridge Boys (cohosts), Janie Fricke, Bill Monroe, Mike Williams & Michael Liter, Million Dollar Band.

464 March 7, 1987: Ray Stevens (cohost), Loretta Lynn & Ernest Lynn, Mel McDaniel, Southern Lawmen.

465 March 14, 1987: Marie Osmond (cohost), Gene Watson, Nicolette Larson & Steve Wariner, Stan Freese.

466 March 21, 1987: Hank Williams, Jr. (cohost), Marty Stuart, k.d. lang, Merle Kilgore, David Holt.

467 March 28, 1987: Ray Stevens (cohost), Loretta Lynn, Lyle Lovett, Steve Wariner, Million Dollar Band.

## 1987-88 Season—Syndication—Saturdays at 7 PM

468 September 19, 1987: John Schneider (cohost), Freddy Fender, Sweethearts of the Rodeo.
469 September 26, 1987: Ralph Emery (cohost), Ray Stevens, Johnny Lee, Hillbilly Jim.
470 October 3, 1987: Mel Tillis (cohost), Ronnie McDowell, Desert Rose, John Hartford, Mike Snider.
471 October 10, 1987: Roger Miller (cohost), Keith Whitley, Johnny Russell & David Wilkins, Million Dollar Band.
472 October 17, 1987: Charley Pride (cohost), Osborne Brothers, Patty Loveless.
473 October 24, 1987: Loretta Lynn (cohost), T.G. Sheppard, Williams & Ree, Sherry Glass & Bobby Revis, Jr.
474 October 31, 1987: Tanya Tucker (cohost), Randy Travis, Roy Acuff, Whitfield Ward, Paul Davis, Paul Overstreet.
475 November 7, 1987: John Schneider (cohost), Forester Sisters, Charlie Walker, Million Dollar Band.
476 November 14, 1987: Ricky Skaggs (cohost), Ricky Van Shelton, Roy Acuff, Famous San Diego Chicken.
477 November 21, 1987: Loretta Lynn (cohost), B.J. Thomas, David Wills, Hawkins County Hoedown Cloggers, Jack Roper.
478 November 28, 1987: Brenda Lee (cohost), Sawyer Brown, Charlie Louvin, Million Dollar Band.
479 December 5, 1987: Mel Tillis (cohost), Del Reeves, Judy Rodman, Michael Johnson.

480  December 12, 1987: Roger Miller (cohost), Sylvia, Jack Greene, Million Dollar Band.

481  January 9, 1988: Louise Mandrell (cohost), Glen Campbell, Steve Wariner, Billy "Crash" Craddock, Steele Family Cloggers.

482  January 16, 1988: Hoyt Axton (cohost), Larry Gatlin & Gatlin Brothers, K.T. Oslin, Jim DePaiva, David Holt.

483  January 23, 1988: Lee Greenwood (cohost), Kathy Mattea, Million Dollar Band, Highway 101, Famous San Diego Chicken.

484  January 30, 1988: Roy Acuff and Minnie Pearl (cohosts), Glen Campbell, Stella Parton, Bill Anderson.

485  February 6, 1988: Barbara Mandrell (cohost), Exile, Dan Seals, Hillbilly Jim.

486  February 13, 1988: Randy Travis (cohost), Mel McDaniel, Girls Next Door, Million Dollar Band.

487  February 20, 1988: Ricky Skaggs (cohost), The Whites, Famous San Diego Chicken, Joe Edwards.

488  February 27, 1988: Statler Brothers (cohosts), John Conlee, k.d. lang, Sherry Glass, Burton Edwards.

*Special* Live to tape March 30, 1988 (various airings): 20th Anniversary Show.

489  April 23, 1988: Jim Stafford (cohost), Mickey Gilley, Lorrie Morgan, David Holt, Cliff Dumas, Vicki Rae Von.

490  April 30, 1988: Janie Fricke (cohost), George Jones, Vince Gill, Hillbilly Jim.

491  May 7, 1988: Barbara Mandrell (cohost), Larry Gatlin & Gatlin Brothers, T. Graham Brown, Jim De Paiva.

492  May 14, 1988: Tammy Wynette (cohost), Porter Wagoner, Lyle Lovett, Famous San Diego Chicken.

493  May 21, 1988: Statler Brothers (cohosts), Jeannie C. Riley, Eddy Raven.

## *1988-89 Season—Syndication—Saturdays at 7 PM*

494  October 1, 1988: Johnny Cash and June Carter Cash (cohosts), Judy Rodman, Famous San Diego Chicken.

495  October 8, 1988: Tennessee Ernie Ford (cohost), Oak Ridge Boys, McCarter Sisters, John Hartford.

496  October 15, 1988: Porter Wagoner (cohost), George Jones, Little Jimmy Dickens, Patty Loveless, Grant Turner.

497  October 22, 1988: Brenda Lee (cohost), Bellamy Brothers, Wolfman Jack, Buckles & Bows.

498  October 29, 1988: Crook and Chast (cohosts), Highway 101, Keith Whitley.

499  November 5, 1988: Charlie Daniels (cohost), Janie Fricke, John Anderson, Million Dollar Band.

500  November 12, 1988: Tanya Tucker (cohost), Michael Martin Murphey, Johnny Russell.

501  November 19, 1988: Ricky Skaggs (cohost), The Whites, Hillbilly Jim.

502  November 26, 1988: Johnny Cash & June Carter Cash (cohosts), Holly Dunn, Million Dollar Band.

503  December 3, 1988: Garry Morris (cohost), Asleep at the Wheel, Becky Hobbs, Million Dollar Band.

504  December 10, 1988: Jimmy Dean (cohost), Marie Osmond, Billy Joe Royal, David Holt.

505  December 17, 1988: Mel Tillis (cohost), Sweethearts of the Rodeo, Jerry Jeff Walker, Dude Mowrey.

506  January 7, 1989: Ray Stevens (cohost), Forester Sisters, Jennifer Powers, Grant Pettingill, John Hartford.

507  January 14, 1989: Brenda Lee (cohost), Ricky Van Shelton, Mel Tillis, Steele Family, Million Dollar Band.

508  January 21, 1989: Charley Pride (cohost), Sawyer Brown, Mary Chapin Carpenter, Jerry Jeff Walker, Hoyt Axton, Bobby Rose.

509  January 28, 1989: Roger Miller (cohost), Glen Campbell, Kathy Mattea, Ricky Skaggs and Sharon White, Big Al Downing.

510  February 4, 1989: Waylon Jennings (cohost), Louise Mandrell, Mac Wiseman, Ralph Emery, David Holt.

511    February 11, 1989: Reba McEntire (cohost), Gene Watson, Canyon, Susie Luchsinger.
512    February 18, 1989: Merle Haggard (cohost), Randy Travis, Cale Yarborough, The
       McCarters.
513    February 25, 1989: Loretta Lynn (cohost), John Denver, Telia Summy, Misty Carter, Brent
       Montgomery, Mike Snider & Gerald Smith.
514    April 29, 1989: Waylon Jennings (cohost), Tammy Wynette, T. Graham Brown, Richard
       Petty, Kyle Petty, Million Dollar Band.
515    May 6, 1989: Reba McEntire (cohost), Kitty Wells, Lyle Lovett, Louis Nye.
516    May 13, 1989: Glen Campbell (cohost), Alabama, Burch Sisters, Ace Cannon.
517    May 20, 1989: Loretta Lynn (cohost), Vern Gosdin, Jo-El Sonnier, Ken Kercheval, Billy
       Holt, Million Dollar Band.

## 1989-90 Season—Syndication—Saturdays at 7 PM

518    September 16, 1989: Barbara Mandrell (cohost), Larry Gatlin and Gatlin Brothers, Williams
       & Ree, Jim DePaiva.
519    September 23, 1989: Jimmy Dean (cohost), Lorrie Morgan, Skip Ewing.
520    September 30, 1989: Steve Wariner (cohost), Forester Sisters, Big Al Downing, John Hart-
       ford.
521    October 7, 1989: Holly Dunn (cohost), Kenny Rogers, Carl Perkins, Drema Hinton, Chuck
       Gifford.
522    October 14, 1989: Roy Rogers & Dale Evans (cohosts), Riders in the Sky, Big Al Downing.
523    October 21, 1989: George Jones (cohost), Patty Loveless, Leather & Lace.
524    October 28, 1989: Robin Leach (cohost), Don Williams, Highway 101, David Holt.
525    November 4, 1989: Barbara Mandrell (cohost), Baillie & the Boys, Sherry Glass and Bobby
       Revis, Lloyd Wells & Ernie Ford.
526    November 11, 1989: Kathy Mattea (cohost), Clint Black, Restless Heart, Williams & Ree,
       John Hartford.
527    November 18, 1989: Ray Stevens (cohost), Lacy J. Dalton.
528    November 25, 1989: George Jones (cohost), Nitty Gritty Dirt Band, Steele Family Cloggers,
       Tommy Lasorda.
529    December 2, 1989: Regis Philbin and Kathie Lee Gifford (cohosts), The Judds, Shenan-
       doah.
530    December 9, 1989: Roger Miller (cohost), Foster & Lloyd, Suzy Bogguss.
531    January 13, 1990: Tanya Tucker (cohost), Garth Brooks, LaCosta, Vicki Bird.
532    January 20, 1990: Orville Redenbacher (cohost), Charley Pride, Daniele Alexander, Stan
       Freese.
533    January 27, 1990: Crystal Gayle (cohost), David Ball.
534    February 3, 1990: Waylon Jennings, Connie Smith, David Holt.
535    February 10, 1990: Ricky Van Shelton (cohost), Desert Rose Band.
536    February 17, 1990: Charlie Daniels (cohost), John Hiatt, Vicki Bird.
537    February 24, 1990: Oak Ridge Boys (cohosts), Moe Bandy.
538    March 3, 1990: Lionel Cartwright (cohost), Janie Fricke, David Holt.
539    March 10, 1990: Waylon Jennings (cohost), Sawyer Brown, Jessi Colter.
540    March 17, 1990: T. Graham Brown (cohost), Jennifer McCarter & The McCarter Sisters.
541    March 24, 1990: Hank Thompson (cohost), Glen Campbell.

## 1990-91 Season—Syndication—Saturdays at 7 PM

542    September 15, 1990: Garth Brooks, Suzy Bogguss.
543    September 22, 1990: Glen Campbell, Alan Jackson, David Holt.
544    September 29, 1990: Barbara Mandrell, Jo-El Sonnier, Magnum Cloggers.
545    October 6, 1990: Vern Gosdin, Baillie & the Boys.
546    October 13, 1990: Eddie Rabbitt, Jann Browne.
547    October 20, 1990: Hoyt Axton, Holly Dunn, Kentucky Country.
548    October 27, 1990: Lee Greenwood, Wild Rose.

549  November 3, 1990: Conway Twitty, Sweethearts of the Rodeo, Jim DePaiva.
550  November 10, 1990: Tanya Tucker, Paul Overstreet.
551  November 17, 1990: Patty Loveless, Mark Collie, David Holt.
552  November 24, 1990: Ricky Skaggs, The Whites, Merlin Olsen.
553  December 1, 1990: Lorrie Morgan, Travis Tritt, Moonshine Cloggers.
554  December 8, 1990: Loretta Lynn, Jim & Jesse, Henry Cannon.
555  December 15, 1990: Louise Mandrell, Canyon, Charlie Nagatani.
556  January 15, 1991: Ray Stevens, Forester Sisters, David Holt.
557  January 12, 1991: Marie Osmond, Asleep at the Wheel, Mac Wiseman.
558  January 19, 1991: Glen Campbell, T. Graham Brown, Ramona and Alisa Jones.
559  January 26, 1991: Lionel Cartwright, Shelby Lynne, David Holt.
560  February 2, 1991: Tony Orlando, Charley Pride.
561  February 9, 1991: Reba McEntire, Aaron Tippin, Mac Wiseman.
562  February 16, 1991: Oak Ridge Boys, Alison Krauss and Union Station.
563  February 23, 1991: Tammy Wynette, Steve Wariner.

## *1991-92 Season—Syndication—Saturdays at 7 PM*

564  January 4, 1992: Barbara Mandrell, Vern Gosdin, Joe Diffie.
565  January 11, 1992: Merle Haggard, Alison Krauss and Union Station, Les Taylor.
566  January 18, 1992: Garth Brooks, Trisha Yearwood, Diamond Rio.
567  January 25, 1992: Lorrie Morgan, Desert Rose Band.
568  February 1, 1992: Ronnie Milsap, Highway 101, Aaron Tippin.
569  February 8, 1992: Alabama, Pam Tillis, Brooks & Dunn.
570  February 15, 1992: Patty Loveless, Doug Stone, The Dillards.
571  February 22, 1992: Garth Brooks, Louise Mandrell, Billy Dean.
572  February 29, 1992: Alan Jackson, Kathie Baillie & The Boys, Matraca Berg.
573  March 7, 1992: Barbara Mandrell, Sawyer Brown, B.B. Watson.
574  March 14, 1992: Oak Ridge Boys, T. Graham Brown, Robin Lee.
575  March 21, 1992: Forester Sisters, Mark Collie.
576  March 28, 1992: Ricky Skaggs, Jim & Jesse, Clinton Gregory.
577  April 4, 1992: Holly Dunn, Mark Chesnutt, Gold City.
578  April 11, 1992: Lionel Cartwright, Marty Stuart, The Remingtons.
579  April 18, 1992: Marie Osmond, Ronnie Milsap, Eddie London.
580  April 25, 1992: Lee Greenwood, Linda Davis, Marty Brown.
581  May 2, 1992: Brenda Lee, Exile, Jim & Jesse.
582  May 9, 1992: Merle Haggard, Steve Wariner, Donna Ulisse.
583  May 16, 1992: Asleep at the Wheel, Shelby Lynne, Dude Mowrey.
584  May 23, 1992: Eddie Rabbitt, Suzy Bogguss, Rob Crosby.
585  May 30, 1992: Gary Morris, Sweethearts of the Rodeo, Hal Ketchum.

# SOURCES

"Also on the Fall Schedule: The Not So Bold Ones." *Time*, Sept. 23, 1972.

Amory, Cleveland. Foreword to *Worst TV Shows Ever—Those TV Turkeys We Will Never Forget ... (No Matter How Hard We Try)*, by Bart Andrews with Brad Dunning. New York: E.P. Dutton, 1980.

"Archie Campbell." *http://en.wikipedia.org/wiki/Archie_Campbell*.

Aylesworth, John. "A Break for John Henry Faulk." *Newsweek*, Dec. 1, 1975, "Letters," p.18.

Blackledge, Brett J. "'Hee Haw' Laughing All The Way to the Bank." *Associated Press*, n.d. (Article regarding the 20-year success of *Hee Haw*, noting the show "outlasted every other variety show in television history ... with more than 1 billion viewers in two decades.")

Blim, Julie, and Scott Ross. "Lulu Roman: Hee-Hawing Through Life." *The 700 Club*. http://www.cbn.com/700club/ScottRoss/Interviews/Lulu_Roman.aspx.

Brooks, Tim, and Earl Marsh. *The Complete Directory to Prime Time Network Shows, 1946–Present*. New York: Ballantine, 1985.

Brown, Les. *Television—The Business Behind the Box*. New York: Harcourt Brace Jovanovich, 1971.

Causey, Warren B. *The Stringbean Murders*. Nashville: J&C Enterprises, 1975.

"Cheers to the Hee Haw Silver Series—Hee Haw the Way God Intended It." *TV Guide*, "Cheers 'n' Jeers," May 1–7, 1993.

*Congressional Record*. Vol. 124, no. 142, Sept. 13, 1978. Text of speech by Sen. Sasser honoring *Hee Haw* on its 10th anniversary.

Early Museum of Tape Editing. "EECO Tape Editing." *http://www.sssm.com/editing/museum/eeco/eeco.html*.

Edwards, Joe. "After 25 Years, Last Laughs for 'Hee Haw.'" Associated Press, April 21, 1993.

"Gailard Sartain." *http://www.mazeppa.com/about_the_show.html*.

Goolrick, Chester. "Television Critics Scoff, but 'Hee Haw' Has the Last Laugh." *Wall Street Journal*, July 22, 1981, p.1.

Hay, Graham D., Vice President, Director Network Relations, Compton Advertising, Inc., 625 Madison Avenue, New York NY 10022. Memo dated November 5, 1971.

Hee Haw episodes: tv.com, *http://www.tv.com/hee-haw/show/ 1784/episode.html?om_act=convert& om_clk=tabssh&tag=tabs;episodes*; tv iv, *http://tviv.org/Category:Hee_Haw/Episodes*; and Lovullo and Elliot.

Hickey, Neil. "Who's Laughing Now?" *TV Guide*, March 7, 1970.

"Junior Samples." *http://en.wikipedia.org/wiki/Junior_Samples*.

Kaufman, Dave. "Vanoff, Partners Establish $17 Mil Post-Prod'n Firm." *Daily Variety*, vol. 195, no. 47, May 11, 1982.

Lawson, Richard. "Executives Marketing 'Opry,' 'Hee Haw' in Wave of Nostalgia." *The Tennessean*, February 27, 2002.

Lovullo, Sam, and Marc Elliot. *Life in the Kornfield*. New York: Boulevard, 1996.

MacMinn, Aleene. "A Front-Porch Philosopher Gets in the Swing Again." *Los Angeles Times*, Sunday, November 9, 1975, p. 30.

"'Mannix' Finally Atop Nat'l Nielsen." *Daily Variety*, vol. 150, no. 25, Jan. 13, 1971.

Metz, Robert. *CBS—Reflections in a Bloodshot Eye*. Chicago: Playboy Press, 1975.

Nutt, Grady. *So Good, So Far ...* Nashville: Impact, 1979.

"Returning Syndicated Shows." *Daily Variety*, Oct. 1, 1975, Radio-Television section, p. 92.

Rosenberg, Howard. "A Turkey in the Straw Celebrates." *Los Angeles Times*, Oct. 20, 1978, Part IV, p. 38.

Ryan, John Fergus. "Press a Button and Out Comes 'Hee Haw.'" *Country Music Magazine*, Sept. 1973.

"Stringbean." *http://en.wikipedia.org/wiki/Stringbean*.

"A 10th Birthday Party Confirms That Those Who Hee Haw Last, Hee Haw Best." *People*, Oct. 16, 1978.

"Who Wins Season Rests on Pair of CBS Shifts in Dec." *Daily Variety*, Dec. 24, 1969, Radio-Television section, p. 26; Television Reviews, p. 30.

"Youngstreet Prods., 'Hee Haw' Library Sold to Gaylord." *Daily Variety*, vol. 193, no. 52, Nov. 17, 1981.

Zimmerman, David. "Cornfield Cleared in 'Hee Haw' Overhaul." *USA Today*, Jan. 30, 1992, p. 3D.

# INDEX

Numbers in **bold italics** indicate pages with photographs.